Gilles Villemure's Tales from the Ranger Locker Room

By
Gilles Villemure
and
Mike Shalin

Sports Publishing L.L.C.
www.sportspublishingllc.com

Director of production: Susan M. Moyer
Project manager: Tracy Gaudreau
Developmental editor: Noah Amstadter
Copy editors: Ashley Burum and Cindy McNew
Dust jacket design: Kerri Baker

ISBN:1-58261-308-7

Printed in the United States of America

Sports Publishing L.L.C.
www.sportspublishingllc.com

For my mom and dad who supported and followed me from the first day I played hockey, and to my wife and children—I love you all!

—G.V.

For my sons, Joshua, Taylor and Mackenzie— I love you guys!

—M.S.

For all the heroes of September 11— we will NEVER forget!

Contents

Foreword

by Ed Giacomin

Gilles Villemure is probably the most honest individual I've ever been associated with.

The man's word was his bond. I've valued that quite a bit because we've had very many different dealings, and he's always come through a hundred percent. I knew him a long time before we actually played in the National Hockey League together. He's just one fine individual.

Hockey was his love. Horse racing was his passion—but when he got to the game he was all business.

It took Gilles a long time to make it to the NHL, but like myself, coming from Canada and living hockey your whole life, you didn't want to be a failure. He wanted to be a very successful story, and by sticking it out, eventually it paid off for him just like it paid off for me.

The hardest thing for both myself and for Gilles when we got to the Rangers is that both of us wanted to play. But I was more open and more critical about it because I always said that I should be playing. That's me, and if I didn't say that I have no business being in sports. Gilles was the type of a person who *wanted* to play but could accept not playing, which I found was a little bit different. When he did play, he gave you 100 percent and he always performed very, very well. I admired him so much because I found it very hard thinking: how can he play like that and play so well while not playing as much?

He was a unique character, and that's why we became such a good team. He probably resented the fact that I played so much, but he was able to accept it, and the greatest thing is when we won the Vezina Trophy together.

I never asked him if he wanted to go somewhere where he could play every day. That never crossed our minds. I know it never crossed my mind. I just felt that he accepted that role and he was able to perform so well in it. He had a passion for horses, so that was kind of an out for him—so if he knew I was playing Wednesday night, he could go out Tuesday night and go to the track. That was unique. It was different, and if anything should have happened to me, he was always ready.

You have to be a special person to be able to take on that kind of a role and not be bitter about it—he always had an open mind, he was always flamboyant, and he was always very happy. Whatever the team did, he was always 100 percent for it.

—Ed Giacomin, June 2002

Introduction

by Gilles Villemure

The date was June 14, 1994—a special spot on the calendar every Ranger fan should have etched into his or her brain. On that very special night, the New York Rangers ended the curse and tasted the thrill of winning the Stanley Cup for the first time since 1940, ending the questions and the horrible chants of "nine-teen, for-ty, nine-teen, for-ty."

I didn't play for the Rangers that night—when Mark Messier, Brian Leetch, Mike Richter & Co. finally brought it home—I had retired from hockey in 1977, 17 years earlier, and had left the Rangers two years prior to that. But I was there with those guys on that special night, and it's a night I'll never forget.

Remember the words from that song in *West Side Story?* "When you're a Jet, you're a Jet all the way, from your first cigarette 'til your last dying day." That's the way it is when you're a Ranger—you're a Ranger til your last dying day. Special team. Special place.

If you've forgotten—and if you're reading this book, the chances are there's no way you'll ever forget—the Rangers, who had survived the New Jersey Devils after Messier's incredible guarantee and personal follow-through in Game 6 and Stephane Matteau's wraparound goal in Game 7, won three of the first four games against the Vancouver Canucks in the finals. The Cup was finally going to be ours. But the

Canucks won Games 5 and 6, and a Game 7 was necessary —at the Garden.

The Rangers set up a special alumni area for that game, down near the glass. I was there. So was Rod Gilbert. And Steve Vickers. And Walter Tkaczuk—four teammates who had come so close to winning the Cup with the Rangers, reaching the finals in 1972 and losing to the Bruins. We were all there, in special seats right near the home penalty box on the 31st Street side of the Garden.

Later, I would read that Gilbert, perhaps the greatest Ranger of them all, said, "I hurt my hands thumping on the glass ... and I lost my voice in English and French."

Marv Albert, the longtime Ranger announcer, said that night, "The Rangers win the Stanley Cup: words that a lot of people never thought they would hear in their lifetime." One fan held up a now-famous sign that read: "Now I can die in peace."

That's the way it is being a Ranger—or a Ranger fan. That's why I still get recognized on Long Island and at the Garden 25 years after I finished playing. I grew up close to Montreal, in the town of Trois Rivieres (Three Rivers), Quebec, and people up there are crazy for the Canadiens. But Canadian loyalty to a hockey team is one thing—that's where the game was born. In New York, you're fighting with the other sports, but Ranger fans are a special breed. And on that night in 1994, they finally got their wish.

The Rangers have struggled since. They haven't made the playoffs for five straight seasons. They came up short even with The Great One, Wayne Gretzky, wearing his No. 99 on Broadway, reunited with old Edmonton pal Messier. But Ranger fans are there every night, and they're as rabid as they were before the Cup.

It's all part of being a Ranger, which I was for so much of my life.

About that life. I started skating at age five—and was able to live the dream of almost every Canadian boy—to grow up to be a real professional hockey player. I played 17 years of pro hockey, seven full years and parts of three others in the National Hockey League. I played five full seasons with the New York Rangers, two with the Chicago Blackhawks. I am 61 years old now. I retired at age 37.

It took a lot of hard work, dedication and commitment, along with a lot of hard knocks, to make it to the top, even sharing a Vezina Trophy with Eddie Giacomin in my first full year in the NHL. But along with the game I loved so much, I got to meet and know many great people and start friendships I hope I'll never forget or lose.

In the coming pages, I hope to share with you some of the things that happened to me in my hockey career, with a heavy emphasis on those five special years inside the Ranger locker room. I played with and against many great players and characters, and I will share some of that with you in these pages.

My coauthor, Mike Shalin, was a season ticket holder back when I came up, and like most Ranger fans, he can remember more than the players on some of these things. His insights will be intertwined and he will make all this make some sense, because ... well, I stopped hockey pucks for a living and did a lot of it without wearing a mask. But I got more help on this book—you will read chapters throughout the book under the title, "With a Little Help From My Friends," and then read the words of some of my teammates and of our leader, the great Emile Francis. I think that all of this will take you back to a special time.

The Beginning

I belonged to the Rangers when I was 16, when I signed a "C" Form that tied me to them. Years ago, there were no draft choices. It was just sign a "C" Form and you belonged to that team. I was playing hockey in my hometown and the Rangers had a scout, Yvan Prud'homme, come to see me for a few games. He liked what he saw and asked me to sign the form. That was it—my long career with the New York Rangers organization was underway. I was 16 then and stayed with the Rangers until I was 35, when I was traded to the Chicago Blackhawks for the last two years of my career.

What a thrill! They gave me $100 to sign that form and a $500 bonus when I made the pros, which I did with the Vancouver Canucks (they were a minor-league team then) in 1962. Imagine that—a hundred bucks to sign and five hundred when I turned pro—we're talking hundreds here, not thousands or millions. You think the game has changed at all today?

I got that money and thought they were really giving me something. But the money aside, they gave me the chance to do what I loved—play hockey. I arrived as a pro when there were only six teams in the NHL, and I needed expansion and the faith of Emile Francis to finally make it to the league on a full-time basis in 1970. It was a long haul, but I wouldn't trade it for anything, because being a hockey player is what I always wanted, and to be able to play in the National Hockey League? Wow! And I was able to step into a lineup that was on the verge of greatness, a team that would come so close to winning the Stanley Cup that would elude the franchise for two more decades before that great night in 1994.

Introduction

by Mike Shalin

Through much of his time with the New York Rangers, Gilles Villemure may have heard a voice from above calling down to him at Madison Square Garden. That voice, which came from Section 440, Row A, Seat 10 in the mezzanine, now has the great pleasure of working with the former Ranger goaltender on this book.

As a former Ranger season ticket holder who went on to become a sports writer and now lives in Boston and works for the *Boston Herald*, I saw Villemure join Ed Giacomin and form the best one-two goaltending punch in the National Hockey League. I saw Villemure not only lighten the load on Giacomin but also get more than one person saying the newcomer was the actual No. 1. Now, all these years later, it's with great pleasure that I get to help Villemure share his and, yes, even some of my own *Tales from the Ranger Locker Room*.

A book like this is a labor of love for someone like me, someone who once attended 110 straight games at the Garden, a streak broken only by my brother's wedding—March 1, 1970, a 3-1 Ranger loss to the Chicago Blackhawks, much of which I heard from the parking lot outside the reception because I just couldn't stay completely away. A crazy fan who once had a rubber chicken in a noose with Derek Sanderson's number on the back, attended road games, waited for autographs, did all those kinds of things. I used to run a goal-scoring pool in my section, and I kept a detailed scrapbook on the yearly doings of this team (some of it is illustrated in these pages). Later, after Villemure left for Chicago and then for retirement, I wound up covering the team for both United Press International and the *New York Post* before moving to Boston in 1983. Most of my years since have been spent away from covering the sport I love so much, but the close ties never go away. Now, getting to do this book with one of *my* Rangers brings me back home— to New York and the team I love.

As a fan, I met the Ranger PR team of John and Janet Halligan, always friendly and helpful to us as we passed through the press box after games as fans, giving us extra sets of what we considered to be precious press notes and stats that detailed everything we needed to know. Both were helpful when I jumped the line from fan to writer, making press credentials available for young journalists whenever possible. John, who always seemed to feel "one hundred percent" and is now working for the league, has been extremely helpful on this project, which now makes me grateful to him for over 30 years.

There are others to thank on a long road that leads to a book like this. Norman MacLean, one of the true characters of the hockey world, was always there at the beginning, always helping me get my foot in the door. There was Jill Knee out on Long Island, opening the Islander press box to young guys like myself and future Ranger and Islander broadcaster Howie Rose, another rabid nut in those days. And Stan Fischler, "The Maven," who helped get me started. There was Marv Albert, who was always helpful to young folks trying to make it in the business. Later, working with people like Sam Rosen, now one of the great voices of hockey, and Frank Brown, the former outstanding hockey writer with the Associated Press and the New York *Daily News* who is now working as the NHL's head PR guy. On and on the list runs.

This hockey fan, who had the great pleasure of covering the miracle of Lake Placid hockey gold in 1980, became primarily a baseball and college sports writer as his career went on, but the love of hockey never left, which is what made it so easy to be a dad to three hockey-playing sons.

Finally, I'd like to thank the Rangers of my youth and teen years—one of them whose words you'll read in these pages. The Rangers didn't win the Stanley Cup back then, but they provided plenty of entertainment for so many of us. And here's hoping these pages provide even more. Enjoy!

Testing Your Ranger Knowledge

Throughout these pages, at the ends of the first 10 chapters, you will find questions—10 of them—that will truly test your knowledge of the New York Rangers. If you can get six or seven of these without looking, you know your Ranger stuff. If you get more than that, you're a Ranger genius.

"I was in hockey 50 years, from the day I started to the day I quit—and that group of people that I had from about '70 through '76, they were the best bunch of players that I've ever seen in my life, that I ever played with or ever handled.

"The thing about them is there was nobody jealous of one another. They were a team through and through. There was no one player concerned about what the other guy was making. Nobody was jealous because one guy was getting more ice time than the other guy. They knew what their jobs were—if I was killing penalties, if I was on the power play ... they were really a group that got along well together, and that's what made them as good as they were. In order to win the Stanley Cup, you gotta be good and you gotta be lucky, and we sure as hell weren't lucky."

—Emile Francis on his teams during the first half of the seventies, perhaps the best team ever that never won a Stanley Cup

1

Getting Started

A Little About Me

I started playing in goal when I was 14. One goaltender got hurt—we had outside rinks in Three Rivers, 20 below, 30 below every day—and I used to be a forward, a good forward. I used to win the scoring championship. But the goaltender got hurt, I went in, and that was it. I stayed in goal for the next 23 years.

But I remember that I froze. You're not moving around and I didn't get that many shots, so I stood still a lot. When it's 20 degrees below zero and you're not moving ... I'll never forget, I was cold! But I played. I lived through it.

Monarch, École St-Paul
1952

Here I am (second from the right) at age 12—before
I started playing goal. (Gilles Villemure)

I was good and they came after me. But my dad had to find out if I was good enough. They sent me to Troy, Ohio, when I was 17. I couldn't speak English. They sent me there for three or four weeks, I played three or four games in the Eastern Pro League—I guess they called it that—and I went back home and did my Junior "B" when I was 18 and my Junior "A" when I was 19, with Guelph, Ontario. Then I went on.

Years ago, we had no education. The kids now can go to college and then go on to the National Hockey League. We didn't even think about college when I played as a kid—nobody went to college—nobody. There was no college then. People are always asking why it took so long—until this year —for Canada to win a gold medal. Well, for so many of those years, college kids represented the country, and in most cases the reason they were in college was that they weren't good enough to go on and play in the NHL. There's one major change between those days and now.

Who Else Could I Root For?

Growing up in Quebec and being a French-Canadian, there was really only one hockey team I could root for—the beloved Montreal Canadiens.

No real choice here—the Habs—Maurice Richard, Jean Beliveau, Boom Boom Geoffrion, Bert Olmstead, Jacques Plante ... we didn't have television then; I was a young kid, and I would just listen to the the radio every night. I was a Montreal Canadiens fan 100 percent.

My first memory of that team and those players was how good they were. They were something else. What a team they had. They used to say, "Boomer's taking a slap shot from the point and it goes right through the goaltender." I'll never forget them. I was 10 or 11 years old, and I was 70 miles from Montreal, but I never got there as a kid. In Trois Rivieres (Three Rivers), I used to go watch the juniors or the seniors play— that was pro then. I used to watch the games at home.

But we couldn't afford to go to Montreal when I was a kid. I'm the oldest of three brothers, and it was tough—my father worked his butt off, but he wasn't making much money. That's why when the Rangers came in with the "C" Form and gave me a hundred dollars, I jumped. I said, "Give it to me now." A hundred dollars is *big* money. That was huge—I had never seen a hundred dollars in my life and I was 15 or 16 years old.

I quit school when I was 17 years old, but my dad had to ask everyone around if I had a chance to make it. "Is he good enough to make it?" I guess the answer to that turned out to be "yes."

Junior Hockey

I played junior hockey in Guelph, Ontario for a farm team of the New York Rangers. I was there for one year, 1958.

Two of my teammates there were Rod Gilbert and Jean Ratelle. Since I could not speak a word of English, Rod and Jean, who were also French-Canadian, were able to help me through that year. They had been there two years before I got there.

From junior league, they went to the National Hockey League, and I went to the Long Island Rovers in the Eastern League. We were reunited a few times over the next several years, and for good as teammates for the Rangers in 1970. We played five more years together.

Traveling Man

In the 1960-61 season, I played in the Eastern Hockey League for the New York Rovers. What an experience that was.

We used to travel by bus from Commack, Long Island, to Nashville, Knoxville, Charlotte, Johnstown (Pennsylvania), etc. We would play seven games in eight nights, travel hundreds of miles between games, and travel all day to play a game at seven o'clock that night. Many times, we got to the game late, and when we got there our equipment was always damp because we only had one set and had no time to dry it because of the bus trips.

The Long Island Arena in Commack was our home rink. It was sold out for every game. The fans were great. Remember, there were only six teams in the National Hockey League at the time, so if you wanted to be a hockey fan, you had to take it anywhere you could get it—and these people came to the arena every night for our games.

Instead of glass behind the goal, the Long Island Arena had chicken wire, and the side boards had nothing to protect the fans. People would be sitting behind the boards and they used to grab the opposition's players to slow them down. The players would get so mad they would jump into the stands and fight with the fans. It was crazy.

The rink was dark, the ice was not as bright as it is today, and the ice wasn't painted. The players would make snow with their skates in front of my net, which would enable me to see the puck a little better. It wasn't that long of a ride into Manhattan, but this place was light years away from Madison Square Garden (it was the old Garden back then, the one on 8th Ave. and 50th Street).

I was the only goaltender on our team and had no backup. In 1960, I wasn't wearing a mask. One night, I broke my nose during a game. They took me to the dressing room, where the doctor sat me down, put my head against a wall, and with his two big hands pushed my nose back into place. Then, without batting an eyelash, he said to me, "You're ready to go back on the ice." I went back on the ice and finished the game.

Those were the days.

The Old Garden

I played my first games for the Rangers in 1963—at the old Garden on 8th Ave. and 49th-50th Streets. It was an old rink that was on its way out, and we actually had to practice upstairs.

First, we had to get dressed on the main floor in our regular locker room, and then we had to walk to the second floor to the practice rink. We would have our skate guards on for the walk to the second floor.

To go on the ice, we had to jump the boards. But on one particular day, I forgot to take my skate guards off—something every kid in youth hockey has done once or twice in his or her life—and I took a dive and almost broke my back. The guys got a kick out of that one.

The boards in this rink were aluminum, and every time a shot hit them it sounded like an explosion. Practice was an hour and a half long and you'd leave the ice with a headache every day. Think the players were happy when they built the new place a few years later?

Fred Shero

Obviously, Emile Francis was the coach who had the greatest impact on my hockey career and my life. But the second guy, right behind him, would be Freddie Shero.

Shero coached me in the American Hockey League in Buffalo when we won a championship—The Calder Cup. He was great—and he went to Philadelphia after that and won two Stanley Cups.

He had hockey sense. I don't know if the guy knew how to write, but he had hockey sense. He knew everything. Even little, minor things. He would put an extra guy out on the ice at the end of a game, put six guys out, seven guys out. Seven? I know that sounds crazy, but he did it. We scored. Seven guys—oh, yeah—eight guys sometimes. He got away with it. I don't know how, but he did.

He'd take somebody else's stick on the other team and throw it on the ice, the other team would get a penalty for having an extra stick on the ice. That's right, just grab one of their sticks from next to the bench and throw it on the ice. They'd get a penalty.

*Here I am during the 1967-68 season, when I played for
Fred Shero at Buffalo in the American Hockey League.
(Gilles Villemure)*

*Here's the mask I started wearing in 1966
(left) next to the kind they wear today. Pretty
different, huh? (Gilles Villemure)*

He had more tricks than you could ever imagine. The
the stuff he used to do was unbelievable.

People ask me if Freddie was strange. Strange? No, he
wasn't. Not strange. He was funny. In the American Hockey
League, we used to go by bus all the time—we never took a
plane, never. We'd have a four-hour trip, a three-and-a-half-
hour trip, amd he'd be sitting in the front. After half an hour,
everybody would be up in the front listening to him. I'm talking about stories here, not jokes, but stories. Everybody would
listen to him. He was unreal.

We had a great team in Buffalo. We didn't have a lot of
guys who played in the NHL, but in 1969-70, we won everything. I think we lost about 10 games, and I had eight shutouts and a 2.52 goals-against average to lead the league. I also
had a 2.13 in the playoffs, which was the best in the AHL. We
just had a great year.

And Freddie was right there at the front, teaching us
things, tricking the opposition and the referees—and helping
us win. It was no surprise to anyone that he went on to become such a great coach in the National Hockey League.

Putting On the Mask

I didn't wear a mask until I was 26 years old. In the mask you sweat a lot, and the sweat gets in your eyes and everything, and you can't breathe. It's a pain. But it has its obvious benefits, which is why I finally went to one in 1966.

Jacques Plante was the first goalie to put one on in an NHL game, and they didn't want him to wear it. But as the shots kept getting harder, one by one the goalies fell. I think Gump Worsley and Joe Daley were the last two holdouts.

Before the mask, I got hurt pretty bad a couple of times. I was in training camp without the mask on and I fell down. Jimmy Neilson got the puck and he fell on my head, and all my teeth went down my throat. I asked, "Where's my teeth?" I went to the bench and Frank Paice, the longtime Ranger trainer, was there. I said, "Frank, where's my teeth?" He pushed them all back in and I went back and played. They aren't my real teeth, but they were in the back of my throat—and Frank on the bench just snapped them back on and I went back in the net.

The other time, I broke my nose when I was with the Long Island Ducks. I heard a snap and I said, "Geez." My nose was over to the side. I had gotten hit with a stick and didn't have a mask. I remember a big doctor in the locker room said, "Come here, Gilly, put your head against the wall." I'll never forget that. He said, "Don't move." He pushed my nose right back in and said, "OK, you're ready."

I was with the Rangers in camp in 1966. I wound up playing 70 games in Baltimore that year. I didn't make the Rangers, but I decided to go to the mask because everyone else was starting to wear them. I had to put one on. And mine was different than just about any other. I opened up the eyes on my mask and opened up my mouth, because I couldn't breathe. When you're not used to a mask, you can't breathe and can't see, so I opened up my eyes and my mouth, like a smile.

But masks were different then. We only had masks over our faces—we had nothing over the top of our heads. I remember that during one game in Montreal, I put my head down, and the puck hit me on top of my head and I got 20 stitches. That's part of the game, though.

Stitches? Before the mask? Forget about it. I got hit many times. After I started wearing the mask, I got hit many, many times in the face and the mask protected me. The shots were getting harder, there were a lot of screen shots—you needed the protection. If you remember, Bruins goalie Gerry Cheevers used to draw stitches on his mask to show how many different cuts he would have had without his mask protecting his face.

Sure, I got hit before I went to the mask, but there was nothing major. There was nothing to my eyes—nothing serious—and I'm grateful for that. Bernie Parent lost an eye—that's serious. But we didn't know any better. We just played goal, and if you got hurt, you got hurt. I never thought even once that I would have to quit because I got hit. Never. That's the way we grew up—we grew up without the mask and people thought we were crazy. But we just wanted to play hockey.

Plante put his mask on during a game after he'd gotten hit, and I think his coach, the great Toe Blake, told him to take it off. But he started something—and now, with the equipment they have, kids are lucky. Can you imagine standing in front of an Al MacInnis slapshot with nothing covering your face? Think about that. We had Bobby Hull to worry about. Everyone seems to shoot the puck hard now. The shots are harder, those shots are *coming,* and even with the mask, Mike Richter suffered a fractured skull this year. Those kids can shoot these days. The game got bigger and the ice remained the same size. These guys are huge!

 **Rangers Trivia**

 # 1

*Who holds the Ranger record for power-play
goals in a season?*

2

A Little Help From My Friends:

Emile Francis

"Everywhere Gilles Villemure went, he played well. The only thing was—it wasn't until the late fifties that you started using two goalkeepers. To me, I didn't want him there unless he was going to play. Having been a goalkeeper myself, I wanted to play. It would only stymie his development if you brought him up and he played 10 games here. That's why I'd bring in Simmons, Sawchuk—because I knew Giacomin was going to play 60 games. But then the time came when you were going to bring in Villemure and you wanted him to play and if not alternate, have him play his share. Guys come in today, 18, 19 years old, and they figure they should step right in the league. But when he came in, he was prepared to play.

"It was a funny thing. I don't think we were trying to hold him back. But I don't think people really realized how good he was because a couple of times, in deals that could

Emile Francis always thought I was "a real good goalkeeper." (New York Rangers)

have been, as far as I was concerned, key deals, I'd say, 'You need goalkeeping, and if we can make this guy move, I've got a goalkeeper who can play in the National League.' They'd say, 'Who?' I'd say, 'Villemure.' And you could never sell somebody in the idea that he was a National League goalkeeper. It was the darndest thing I'd ever seen—and to me, he was. I thought he was a real good goalkeeper.

"He is one of the best guys you could ever want to have on your hockey club. Wherever he played, he was the best goalkeeper in the league—and they loved having him when he played there. He just had to wait for his time to come in the National League, and he took advantage of it when it did."

On Bobby Orr's effect on the 1974 finals:

"If you remember, Boston got us down against Giacomin, and I put [Villemure] in there. He went in and he beat Boston right in Boston, and they came back, and the only reason they beat us is it was a nothing-nothing game and Boston had a power play. Bruce MacGregor, who was one of our best penalty killers, couldn't get it by Orr. Orr gave him that deke to the inside, stepped around the outside, and fired it into the net. There's only one guy who could make a move like that, and it was Orr."

On Villemure's Style:

"Villemure was a stand-up goalkeeper. He played his angles. He never beat himself. If you're gonna beat Gilles Villemure, you had to beat him; he didn't beat himself. He was an old-time goalkeeper. He was a goalkeeper along the lines of a Johnny Bower—he played the angles, he stood up and if you're gonna beat him, beat him, go ahead."

On the Giacomin-Villemure team:

"One guy caught with his left hand, Giacomin, and the other guy caught with his right hand. Honest to God, sometimes I don't think shooters paid attention to it because it was unorthodox to see a goalkeeper who caught with his right hand. I think that fooled a lot of players. Villemure and Giacomin to us were like the old Boston Braves, when they Spahn and Sain and then the rain. One was a lefty, one was a righty and that's what we had."

On that duo winning the Vezina Trophy:

"Obviously, it would have been great to win the Stanley Cup. But I was so proud when he and Giacomin won the Vezina Trophy. No matter what happened, they can't take that away from him. Gilles didn't have an easy time getting there, and to do something like this in his first full year in the league is a credit to both our goalkeepers and the team in front of them."

On coming so close to winning the Stanley Cup:

"We had a knack on that team of getting the wrong guy hurt at the wrong time. The year before Rolfe hit Ratelle, we were playing the Vancouver Canucks and beating them easily. The game meant nothing. This was in March—it always happened in March. The Saturday night before, they had a track meet at Madison Square Garden. They had to put on the stuff that they ran on, but it seeped through to the ice. Now, when we started that night there was a hole right to the left of Eddie Giacomin, right in the faceoff circle. They sprayed it three or four times. So here we are, late in the third period, the puck's shot in our end, Brad Park's going back to pick it up and steps right in the hole that they'd been filling all night. He lost his balance, went into the boards, and tore up his knee. All these goofy things happened."

On being second-class citizens at the Garden:

"Ned Irish, who started the New York Knicks, would never agree to put the floor down on the ice, so the Knicks would play Saturday night, and then they'd try to make that ice up fast. We always seemed to be on every other Sunday afternoon at one o'clock. The basketball game would be over at 11 at night and they had until one o'clock to have it ready for us to play. We were always away on Saturday and getting home at three in the morning. We'd get to the Garden at 10:30 a.m. and, Christ, I saw guys skate by with sparks flying (from the concrete) because there wouldn't be more than like an eighth of an inch of ice on there because they didn't have time to make it again.

"He wouldn't leave the ice in because he said it would be too cool on the basketball fans' asses, that's what it amounted to. We were being treated like second-class citizens, really. I was so teed off after the night Dale Rolfe got hurt, I was talking to the press, and I told them, 'You know, I've seen better ice on the roads of Saskatchewan, where I come from, than here at Madison Square Garden.' Irving Felt, who was chairman of the board, saw it in all the papers and he said, 'You know, as chairman of the board of Madison Square Garden, I'm insulted about what you said about the ice at Madison Square Garden.' I said, 'Well, I've been here at Madison Square Garden long before you. The ice was horseshit when I came, it's horseshit now, and it will be as long as we continue to do what we're doing.' I said, 'You go back to Saskatchewan, like I said, and you'll find out that the ice is better on the highways than what we have.'

On trading younger players for veterans because they were close to winning:

"The thing then was that you had your protected list. We had a very good farm system, and I knew that if we didn't protect some of these guys we were going to lose them, that we had a chance to lose them for nothing. You would deal a guy that would bring you a guy that would maybe put you over the top in that particular year. That protected list is why you had to make some of those deals, because you end up with nothing, except $30,000, which is nothing. I dealt Syl Apps for Glen Sather, and what we were lacking at that time was a little aggressiveness, another guy to put on the checking line, and the guy was a good penalty killer. If we had kept Apps, Apps wasn't going to make the team, and when we go in to put our protected list that summer, we would have lost them."

On the highlight of all his years with the Rangers:

"First of all, I think it was the teams I had there in the seventies. That five-year span. When I took over the team they'd missed the playoffs nine out of 10 years, and I remember the worst thing that happened to the Rangers before I got there was nobody wanted to play there. They dealt Bill Gadsby and Billy McNeill to Detroit for Red Kelly. Gadsby and McNeill took right off. They couldn't wait to go to Detroit. In the meantime, Red Kelly wouldn't come to New York, so a short time later, there's no deal. So the Rangers said, 'Hey, we want our guys back,' and they sent them back. Gadsby and McNeil had to go there, Kelly sat on his ass, and Toronto made a deal for Kelly. Toronto went on to win four Stanley Cups in five years. So, when I took over the Rangers, I started dealing left and right. I had two or three guys who said, 'Oh, no, we won't come to New York.' I said, 'Fine, sit on your ass, and after you miss a few paychecks, maybe you'll decide to come then.' They all came. The minute you build a competitive club, everybody wants to come, but you had to build a competitive team.

"I remember when I came to New York, [hearing] comments from players who said, 'We don't like playing in New York because nobody recognizes us.' I remember saying, 'I'll tell you what—if I missed the playoffs nine out of 10 years, I wouldn't want anybody to recognize me.' But I said, 'They'll recognize us, they'll recognize us when we win!' And it's amazing when you build a competitive team how the people respond. Those, to me, were the best years of my life because it was worthwhile work. I never took a vacation, I worked and worked because it was for the sake of the team, but more for the sake of the fans because of the way they responded and supported you. So, the highlight to me is building a team and watching the way fans support the team."

On hearing that Ace Bailey wasn't even supposed to be on the ice when he scored the winning goal in game one of the 1972 finals:

"I didn't know that. We were on the way to one of the greatest comebacks in playoff history. We were down 5-1, and we tied that thing up with about five minutes to go. We were controlling the play. We had beaten Chicago four in a row, and they were playing St. Louis, and we had to wait around a week for that series. You try everything, you give them a couple of days easy and then you work like hell, but that time of year, if you get that time off, you know you're going to have a tough time. We had to go open in Boston, and, Christ, they had us down 5-1. We came back and tied it, and then Bailey broke our backs with that goal. That, to me, if I looked at that whole series—and Bobby Orr's goal in the sixth game was a great goal—that goal there was a back breaker. First game of the series, having come back from four goals back, and then to lose it like that ... that was a tough loss."

On the Rangers finally winning the Stanley Cup:

"When the Rangers finally won against Vancouver, they went down to that seventh game. The faceoff was in the Ranger end, to the right of the net, and I think there were about 18 seconds left. I was doing the color for them on TV. I was standing down there in the runway, and I was looking up in the stands just to see the expressions on people's faces. Some of them were crying. The one guy had a sign that said everything: 'Now I Can Die In Peace.' That says it all right there."

On demanding the Rangers never lose a home playoff date to the circus:

"In 1950, the Rangers were in the finals against Detroit, and in those days, they got thrown out of the Garden because of the circus. They upset the Canadiens playing the last two games in Montreal, and the next series, against Detroit—five games in Detroit and two in Toronto. That's the Rangers' two home games. The last four were in Detroit, and the Rangers lost Game Seven in double overtime. Then, when I was getting the opportunity to take over the Rangers, I said under one condition. I remember Bill Jennings asked, 'What's that?' I said, 'Well, first of all, there's no more loyal fans than Ranger fans, and I'll never forget what happened in 1950— that's not fair to the fans, and it's sure as hell not fair to the players. I will have nothing to do with the New York Rangers unless you guarantee me we get in the playoffs, which we will, that we're going to get every home game that we're entitled to.' So, he says, 'I'll have to look into that before I can guarantee that," and he talked to the circus. The circus is a big thing in April and May, and he said, 'The only problem is that they still want their three performances. If we're to do that, you'd have to play at 8:30.' And I said, 'I don't give a damn if we play at midnight, we want to play at home, in our building, and with our fans there.' And from that day on they've never lost a home game that they're entitled to."

On sharing the Garden with the circus—and the smell:

"Wasn't that beautiful? And I can remember my office was right under the fifth floor, and those animals are there for two months. One day I came into my office and guess what was coming right through the ceiling? Elephant piss. Right through the floor and the ceiling. My office smelled like a barn. After two months, it seeped right through the elevators, into the offices, the whole building."

On Villemure's other career:

"I go to Roosevelt Raceway one night, and who the hell do you think is racing? Villemure. People were telling me to bet on him. I said, 'No way, he's a goalkeeper, he's not a driver.' Guess what—he won the race."

 **Rangers Trivia**
#2

Emile Francis holds the Ranger records for games coached (654) and winning percentage (.602). He's third in losses. Name Nos. 1 and 2?

3

Glory Days

My Greatest Moment

It would be easy to look at my career and point to the Vezina Trophy, or getting to the Stanley Cup finals, as the highlights of my career. But I don't know about that. There are two or three things that I did that I'm proud of.

Individually, I won the Most Valuable Player in the American Hockey League two straight years, 1969 and 1970, before I came up and stayed with the Rangers. That was big. Then, we won the Calder Cup in the American Hockey League as a team and that was special. And then the Vezina Trophy— those three are pretty close together. Maybe the Most Valuable Player in the league two years in a row might be the top.

Remember, that was a time when I thought that might be as high as I would go. I was 30 years old. I thought I was finished. Do you know how many guys there are who stay in the American Hockey League that never make it to the NHL but were good enough to make it to the NHL? There were only so many teams.

I was happy when they expanded. But I was 30 years old by 1970. I never thought I was going to make the NHL. I knew I had great years the last two years I played in the American Hockey League. MVP in the league two years in a row—you can't go any higher than that. But I was making $15,000 a year in 1969 and didn't know it would ever get better than that. I was living on that—I had no choice.

But Emile Francis gave me a chance. I took that chance, and I played seven years after that in the NHL because of Emile. If it wasn't for Emile Francis, I might never have made it. Who else is going to pick me up at 30 years old? Nowadays, 30 years old is old. But I made it from 30 to 37 years old, and he's the one who gave me the break. Maybe I deserved it because of the two years I had, but still, I needed somebody to give me the break, and Emile did it.

He followed me closely the last year I was in the minors. He was in Buffalo all the time. Imagine that.

Cat's Team

Because it was so hard for Emile Francis to be both coach and general manager, he tried to give up coaching—three times.

First, it was Bernie "Boom Boom" Geoffrion. Then, Larry Popein. Finally, Ron Stewart, the only one of the three who didn't wind up giving the job back to The Cat, who got fired when John Ferguson took over.

When the change was made from Popein during the 1973-74 season, it was clear to everyone we just played better under Emile. We turned things around.

Here I am talking with two of the greats. That's me on the left, with Maurice "The Rocket" Richard (center) and Emile Francis. (Gilles Villemure)

"This can be a turning point for us," Bruce MacGregor said back then. "This is Emile's team; he's good for us. It's a much easier situation for all of us now that he's back."

This was always Emile's team.

Emile Francis

When people ask me about Emile Francis, the main thing I say is he was a man who was just *living* hockey.

I'll never forget the way the man used to work. He was our coach and general manager, and we used to take charter flights out of town, and he was in front of the plane, always working. He was always writing something down—I don't know what he was writing, but he was always writing.

I remember once that after flying into a city, when we got to our hotel, our rooms weren't ready. Emile got so mad. He said, "Let's get out of here. We're going somewhere else." That was it, we went somewhere else. Everything has to be ready. Everything has to be on time—if you're not on time, you miss the bus, take a cab. You had to be there.

Everything had to be just right—that's just the way he ran things—and he ran the whole show.

He lived hockey, he knew his hockey, knew who we were playing against. He had a system that was unbelievable— and the best thing is that everybody was following that system. And we had the greatest years the Rangers ever had.

Emile was great—he would cover up everything for everybody. If a guy got in trouble on the road—there were a lot of single guys on our team and sometimes things happen—he would say, "I'll take care of it," and he did.

He used to call the referees all kinds of things. "You hot dogs," that was his favorite thing. "You hot dog, you."

Emile Francis deserved the Stanley Cup, and I know every player on those teams would say the same thing. He's the best I've seen. And now, when we get together with him, we're always talking to him about all the things we did on and off the ice, and he can't believe the stories. When he was a coach, he wasn't looking for anything, "Do your job on the ice, then there's no problem, and if you get in trouble off the ice, I'll take care of it." How many guys will do that for you? It's incredible, what he did for a couple of guys that got in trouble, got in big trouble, and he took care of it. That's the kind of guy he was.

He hated losing. I remember the year we lost against the Islanders, our last year together as a group, he was very upset. We came back from a 3-0 deficit, and we tied them up. He was upset, not about the players, but that fluky goal—the puck went over somebody's stick to J. P. Parise, blind, and it went in.

I started that game. The night before, I played against the Islanders, and we beat them out on the Island, 8-3, and I hurt my knee. It wasn't too bad. I started the game. We were down 3-0, The Cat took me out, which was the right thing to do, we tied up the game and a fluky goal beat us. He was upset. He was down.

I'll never forget—I saw his face coming into the locker room, and the man was out. He worked so hard all year, and all of a sudden a fluky goal beats you and that's it. And, as it turned out, those would be our last playoffs together because they started breaking the team up the next year.

The guy deserved a Stanley Cup. He did everything possible; he had a lot of good years.

Now, when we talk to him about the team, he doesn't shut up. He just loves to talk about it with us. I remember I was at a golf outing; Brad Park was standing with us, Steve Vickers, Rod Gilbert, and Vic Hadfield. We were talking about those years, the good times, off-the-ice stuff, he was listening and taking it all in. The thing is how hard we worked for him. And you know what? He was shaken—he knew the guys worked hard for him, but the way we were talking, he appreciated that.

His players were his players. They respected him; they worked very hard for him. That's just the way it was. What a man!

Money Talks

In 1972, we were in Oakland on a long road trip and Emile Francis called me into his hotel room. It was around 11:30 a.m. Boy, did I get scared. I thought he was going to give me bad news, like being traded.

Much to my surprise and elation, Emile had a new contract offer for me and he was waiting in his room for me to tract offer for me and he was waiting in his room for me to sign it. This was back in the days when not too many guys had agents to help them with their contract and you dealt with your club directly.

I was making $45,000 a year when I walked into that Oakland hotel room, and it took me a long time in hockey to get to that level. The new contract offer was for $90,000 a year for three years. That was a $270,000 deal. This was the time the WHA was threatening the NHL, and hockey players started getting a bit more—but double? Wow! What a surprise! I didn't even know what to say to Emile. I told him I'd be back in an hour with my answer. I think I must have been in shock.

Half an hour later, I went back to see him, and I don't know why, but I said, "I want 95." I wanted him to make it $95,000 a year for three years. I don't know why I asked for the extra $5,000, because I knew I was happy with $90,000 (I was doubling my salary for Gods sake), but Emile just said, "No problem—sign the damn thing and I'll change it." I guess I did it because $95,000 was MY choice.

Thank you, Emile.

I really was stunned to get that kind of money. My paycheck more than doubled in one morning—and it was retroactive back to the start of the season. This was in November, I think.

That was *big* money.

But the money was there, and the salaries had been so low. You had agents coming into the game at the time and that drove Emile crazy. He hated agents and thought they were killing the league. We didn't have agents before that and the salaries were low, but that was all changing for the better.

I didn't have an agent, but to get that kind of money I guess I didn't need an agent. I was thrilled.

I have heard that all the big contracts our players were signing back then made us a fat-cat team. But we still played well for a year or so. Then, I don't know what happened after that—just before they traded everybody, we went flat! The team went flat. For what reason, I don't know. I never found out why, but it happened, and we just weren't the same.

Eddie Giacomin

Eddie Giacomin and I shared the goaltending duties for the Rangers for five years, and we were dealt out of New York the same week in 1975.

At first, I felt Eddie was a little uncomfortable. He was used to playing all the time and here I was ready to share his time. But as time went on, he got used to sharing it with me. Eddie played 55 percent of the game and I played 45 percent. When time came for the playoffs, Eddie was ready.

"It's no fun sitting on the bench; you want to be out there all the time," Eddie said after we settled into the new system and did so well. "But if it helps the team, then I'm all for it. That's what means the most to me."

And it did help the team—we won the Vezina Trophy our first year together, the Rangers' first Vezina since Davey Kerr won it in 1939.

"I knew in training camp that Eddie and Gilles could be the best one-two goaltending punch in hockey," Emile said. "The league has gone from six to 14 teams, and the schedule from 70 games to 80 games. You travel coast to coast, more than 80,000 miles a year, and play as many as seven games in 12 nights. You can't expect one man to handle all your goalkeeping anymore."

Eddie didn't want to give up playing time, but once he started to get to know me, after a while, he was perfect with me. He agreed with the system; it gave him a chance to rest

*Eddie Giacomin and I teamed up in goal for the Rangers
and won the Vezina trophy in 1970-71. (Gilles Villemure)*

for the playoffs and it didn't hurt him—he played very well and won the Vezina for fewest goals-against in the league.

I think it made him last a couple of more years in the league, and we were the best of friends.

At the beginning, it was tough because I knew he didn't want me around because he played all those years by himself. He thought I was trying to get his job, which was a hundred percent wrong. But after a while, we were roommates, we used to go out all the time for dinner and things like that on the road, and we got along very well.

The quotes you read above came from an article Hugh Delano wrote in the Ranger program back then. He started that story by recalling a bus ride we had taken.

"Who's making all that noise up front?" asked Brad Park. "The goalies are at it again," said Rod Gilbert. Added Vic Hadfield: "Just a couple of old ladies who can't stop talking."

Said Emile: "Goalkeepers are like that. Always talking to each other. Comparing notes about different forwards and teams around the league and how they played, or think they should have played, a certain shot.

"Eddie and Gilles are always talking shop. Just like business partners."

And we were business partners who had paid off huge dividends for the business. In that same story, Emile said, "There's no doubt in my mind that the play of Eddie and Gilles was the biggest factor in our success." The other players used to call us "The Goaltenders' Union."

Eddie said: "I guess Emile knew what he was doing. Right? Not playing every game and getting the occasional rest helped me. I felt much stronger physically and mentally when we went into the playoffs. I felt sharper, more relaxed, and I found it easier to concentrate."

When it was my turn in net, Eddie would always cheer for me. He was there to help me with the players and their moves because he knew them all. That helped me a great deal.

"I guess we know better than anyone how much pressure there is for a goaltender. So we pull for each other," Eddie said. "When I'm on the bench and Gilles is in trouble, I wish I could go out there and help him make a save."

When I was asked about our situation and people's comments that we didn't get along, I answered, "Eddie and I are teammates, not rivals. I ask Eddie a lot about shooters around the league since he knows them so well. He's a big help to me. We always try to perk each other up before games, regardless of who's playing."

In five years together, we never had an argument. We were close right after we got over that stuff at the beginning.

And we won that trophy. That year, I played in 34 games and Eddie in 46. We had a well-disciplined team. My goals-against average that year was 2.29. But I almost blew the damn thing.

There were two games left in the regular season (the awards are for regular season games), and we had a 10-goal advantage on Montreal for best average. The next to last game of the season was in Montreal and we lost, 7-2, with me in goal. This made me feel terrible, because our lead was down to five goals. But Eddie played our last game of the regular season and we won, 6-0. What a relief! Eddie and the guys came through. We won the Vezina—at the top of our profession.

Eddie, who had played all 70 games in each of the two previous seasons, had a 2.16 goals-against and eight shutouts. I had four shutouts, and the 12 by us combined was the most by a Ranger since a guy named John Roach had 13 in 1928-29 (heck, even I wasn't born then).

Another thing about Misters Giacomin and Villemure as a team: we were named to the All-Star team in both 1971 and 1973—the only goaltending pair from the same team ever to make the All-Star Game. And we did it twice. That makes me as proud as anything.

I was traded to Chicago on Oct. 28, 1975. Eddie went to Detroit on waivers three days later. I saw recently where Rod Gilbert, talking on a chat on the Rangers' web site, said, "It was a very sad moment. I think it was telling us that anyone could be traded, and it made me realize that hockey was a business."

As luck would have it, Eddie's first game with Detroit was back at the Garden. It was a very emotional night. Eddie was welcomed back like a returning hero. He beat the Rangers, and Wayne Dillon even said he was sorry when he scored on Eddie.

There was no reason to feel sorry for Ed Giacomin. He's a Hall of Famer. He and Rod Gilbert have the only retired Ranger numbers. Eddie had 54 shutouts in the National Hockey League and was as responsible as anyone for making the Rangers a viable franchise on the ice. He'll always have his place in Ranger history and in my heart. I loved my time with Ed Giacomin.

When he got traded, it was clear that they were breaking up the old gang, and Eddie went along with it. Things weren't going well and upper management decided it was time for a change, the big deal with the Bruins coming just a week or so later.

One of the strangest things that happened after the trade was a game I played against Eddie in Chicago. He was with the Red Wings and I was playing for the Blackhawks. He was at one end of the rink and I was at the other. He was looking at me, I was looking at him. We didn't know how to act. We're making signs at each other on the ice like, "How ya doin'?" That was fun.

I can't remember who won. They probably did because they had a good team then, but I don't remember the final score. But it was fun—he was looking at me and I was waving at him. It was a very strange night for both of us and made it sink home even more that those glory days with the Rangers were actually behind us.

Coming Close

I'd like to talk about our Ranger team between 1970 and 1975, a great group of guys, and a great leader who came very close to winning the Stanley Cup and who may have had the greatest Ranger team of all time.

Eddie Giacomin and I shared the goaltending, and we were a strong duo. Eddie played most of the playoff games. In front of us, we had a great bunch of guys.

We had a terrific power play with Brad Park, Rod Gilbert, Jean Ratelle, Vic Hadfield, and Bobby Rousseau, etc. We had a couple of penalty killing units—Walter Tkaczuk and Billy Fairbairn were the best in the business at that, and we had Peter Stemkowski and Bruce MacGregor also killing up front. Rod Seiling, Jim Neilson, and Dale Rolfe were also among those joining Park on the blueline. We always had strong defensemen and we had a great coach in Emile Francis.

Eddie and I played our game, but the players in front of us and Emile made our job so much easier. The system was so good that we had strong punch as well as defensive skill. And we had guys who cared about what they did. We used to have an optional skate at 11 a.m. the day of the game, and everybody would show up. Later on, when things started going downhill and after many of our players had signed big contracts that kept them from going to the new World Hockey Association, people called us "The Cat's Fat Cats," but other things kept us from winning the Stanley Cup. In my humble opinion, the effort was always there.

The most frustrating part about not winning the Stanley Cup was not winning it for head coach Emile Francis, who gave us his all. (New York Rangers)

We were a family. Every time we went on the road, the whole team would stick together. We'd stop for a few beers and some food and spend all our time together. It was truly a special group.

Why didn't we win?

We had two years in a row there when we had the best, but guys got hurt. Dale Rolfe got hurt and Jean Ratelle got hurt. Goaltender Bernie Parent beat us in one series—he was unbelievable; he just stood on his head when we had a heck of a team. I think we had the best team the Rangers ever had, but we didn't win it because of injuries and goaltending that beat us. It was not because Eddie didn't play well. Eddie was outstanding, but Parent, he had 40-something shots in the seventh game I think. What can I tell you?

Triple OT

On April 29, 1971, the New York Rangers played one of the greatest games in the history of the franchise. I'd have to say it was the greatest game ever that I *didn't* play in.

I was on the bench that night. It was the sixth game of the series and one that could have put us into the Stanley Cup finals. We had beaten the Toronto Maple Leafs in six games in the opening round and were engaged in a truly classic series with the Chicago Blackhawks—Bobby Hull, Stan Mikita, Tony Esposito, etc.

We won the first game of the series in Chicago when Peter Stemkowski scored at 1:37 of overtime. It see-sawed through four games before Hull's OT goal gave them a 3-2 lead. Then came Game Six—which I think will forever be known as "Game Six" in the hearts of Ranger fans.

They were beating us, 2-0, but Rod Gilbert scored in the second period, and Jean Ratelle in the third, and we tied the game. What happened next was not to be believed.

We played through the first overtime and into the second. In the second overtime, Stan Mikita, a Hall of Famer and one of the greatest ever to play the game, had an open net—an open, open net. Bill White's shot from the point beat Eddie Giacomin and hit the post and came right out to Mikita. He had the puck on his stick, he shot and hit the goal post. It could have and should have been over right there. Instead, there was Stan, my future teammate and friend, draped over the top of the net after the whistle blew. He couldn't believe what happened to him. I couldn't either. "I should have just slid it in," said Mikita, who scored exactly 600 times in his long and proud NHL career. It should have been 601.

No one in the building could believe it. It was like the play happened in slow motion. We were supposed to be dead and then, suddenly, we weren't. And we would live to play another game.

We were alive, and Stemmer scored in the third overtime. We had just killed a penalty, and Tim Horton dumped the puck into the Chicago end. Teddy Irvine shot it from a bad angle, and Stemmer pushed home a rebound from just in front of Esposito at 1:29 of the third OT. The place went nuts. On the radio, Bill Chadwick, the Hall of Fame referee who was one of our announcers, yelled, "This team is gonna be tough to beat in Chicago on Sunday."

Well, we lost in Chicago on Sunday on a fluky goal that I think hit Cliff Koroll in the seat of the pants and dropped in. The final was 4-2, and the Blackhawks went on to lose to Montreal in seven games in the finals. Our Vezina Trophy season had ended, but not before the Rangers won the longest game the franchise had played in 33 years and at least avoided being eliminated on home ice. The fans went home happy. We were sleepy—it was midnight—but happy.

The G-A-G Line

The name, supplied by Rangers statistician Art Friedman, stood for Goal A Game—which is what the line of Jean Ratelle, Rod Gilbert, and Vic Hadfield produced at the very least.

The line, which I think was the best in the National Hockey League at the time and maybe ever, really exploded during my first two years in New York. Ratty and Rod were responsible for the finesse, and Hadfield was one of the toughest guys in the league, one of the best at digging the puck out of corners. He also had a great shot. The line, sometimes also called the T-A-G (for two goals a game), was also the cornerstone of our strong power play, which had Brad Park and Bobby Rousseau at the points.

Rod Gilbert is still the Rangers' all-time leading scorer. You can also still make the argument that he's the greatest Ranger of all time.

Think about it—there are only two guys with their numbers retired in the rafters of Madison Square Garden: Eddie Giacomin's No. 1 and Rod Gilbert's No. 7.

Rod was very, very good. He had a good centerman, Jean Ratelle. I played junior with them. Oh, the passes were unbelievable. Jean used to set up plays and Rod would put it in. That was easy. You never saw the left wing—the left wing had to hang back. He would still score 20 goals, but those guys would work the offensive magic; they had the puck all the time, and that's why they played so well in the NHL for 15 years—they knew each other so well.

Rod had an incredible shot, but he needed Jean. Jean was the passer and set him up.

Off the ice, they were a little bit different. Jean was very quiet, but Rod used to go with the boys, have a beer, have something to eat. But Jean, after one or two, that was it for him and then he was gone. We had a good bunch of guys that liked to stay out. We didn't make a lot of money, but we had fun.

Anyway, I said the left wing skating with them just had to hang back and worry about defense. But in the 1971-72 season, Vic Hadfield, their left wing, became the first Ranger ever to score 50 goals in a season. He finished that off with two goals in the final regular season game, and that feat ranked right up there for us as a team with the Vezina Trophy I had shared with Eddie the previous year.

Any time someone from some group of guys does something, it's a team honor. We all felt a part of what Vic and the line were able to do. Eddie and myself were also happy we didn't have to face them—except in practice, where it only counted when we played shootout games after practice had ended.

Check the Ranger record books. Rod Gilbert is No. 1 in points, with 1,021, the only Ranger ever to score 1,000 points in a Ranger uniform. Jean Ratelle is third with 817, while Vic Hadfield is ninth at 572. Gilbert is first in goals, second in assists and games; Ratelle is second in goals and third in assists; and Hadfield is fifth in goals and 10th in assists.

No. 7, No. 19 and No. 11. The GAG line. I never played with one any better.

The 1972 Finals

In 1972, we went to the Stanley Cup finals and faced the Boston Bruins—two outstanding teams against each other, both featuring outstanding players. The days when these two old franchises were at the bottom of the National Hockey League were long gone. The Bruins had won the Cup a few years earlier, and the Rangers were clearly ready—heck, it had been since 1940, so there was no time like the present. But, if you're reading this, chances are you know we didn't win the series.

Outstanding players? Boston had Bobby Orr, the greatest player ever to play the game, in my humble opinion. The Bruins had Esposito, Bucyk, Hodge, and Cheevers in goal. We had Gilbert, Park, Vickers, Hadfield, Seiling, Neilson, and Eddie Giacomin in goal, along with that Villemure guy. But we came into the series without Jean Ratelle, who would make it back for the finals but certainly wasn't the player who dominated for so much of the season.

We lost the finals, four games to two.

Eddie played the first four games. In the fifth game, he started, but he got hurt in the second period. The score was 2-2. Emile Francis put me in for the third period. I hadn't played for awhile, but, boy, I was ready to go. We won the

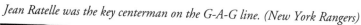

Jean Ratelle was the key centerman on the G-A-G line. (New York Rangers)

game, 3-2, in the Boston Garden. I stopped 18 shots in that third period. Bobby Rousseau, who had taken Ratelle's place after Ratty got hurt, scored the winning goal. The world was expecting us to go away quietly in that game, but we won and forced a Game Six back at our place.

I guess because I played well in that last period, Emile put me back in goal for Game Six, at home. We lost, 3-0. I didn't play poorly, but Gerry Cheevers was better. We couldn't beat him. He stopped everything, and Orr was his usual magical self, clearly the star of the game as they avoided a trip back to Boston for Game Seven (with us having won five and six and captured the momentum). Mr. Orr beat us—he's just like a quarterback, that guy. And Cheevers was just too good.

Let me tell you, it wasn't easy sitting in the locker room while the Boston Bruins skated around the Madison Square Garden ice—*our* ice—with the Stanley Cup, knowing we had come so close after a very special season. I never had that experience before—to play the last game of the year. It was something. It was an experience.

We lost in six, but you can go back to Game One to see how the Bruins took control of the series. What a wild game that was. We had a layoff and came out flat and saw them take a 5-1 lead. Our wakeup call arrived in time and we stormed back to tie it, 5-5, in the third period. Then, Ace Bailey, never known for his scoring, broke around Brad Park and beat Eddie for the winning goal.

It was one of the two playoff goals Bailey scored in 10 years in the league.

Ace Bailey died in the September 11 tragedy. He was remembered in Boston and throughout the hockey world. I read an article in the Boston Globe that revealed Bailey wasn't even supposed to be on the ice when he scored that goal—again, bad luck beating the Rangers in a big game.

"I had told Ace specifically not to go on the ice, because I didn't think he was checking that well," Tom Johnson, his coach that day, said in the article. "Then somebody came off and nobody went on—there was a little miscommunication. So Ace jumps on, goes around Park, and scores the winning goal. I told him later, 'This is a secret between you and me.'"

Funny, years later, the Bruins lost a playoff series to Montreal when they had too many men on the ice. Here they may have won the Stanley Cup because they didn't have enough. Strange how things work sometimes.

Anyway, Phil Esposito said in that story: "I remember that goal like it was yesterday [so do we, Phil]. I can still see it, see Ace going around Brad Park. That goal turned the series around, and I told him that."

There was always something to keep us from getting to the promised land.

Bobby Orr

Rod Gilbert was doing an online chat on the Ranger web site recently and was talking about our trip to the Stanley Cup finals in 1972.

"I think that the two teams were equally balanced, except for possibly the one player that made the difference ... what's his name ... No. 4 for Boston? Oh, the great Bobby Orr. He made the difference out there."

Bobby Orr made the difference in every hockey game he ever played in. I have never seen a player control a game the way he did, which is why I think he's the best ever to play the game.

Years ago, in the 1950s and 1960s, a defenseman was strictly defensively minded. They never carried the puck. They passed it all the time, and they couldn't pinch inside the other team's blue line. Bobby Orr changed all that.

Here I am shaking hands with Bobby Orr, who was the difference in the 1972 Stanley Cup Finals. (Gilles Villemure)

He carried the puck all over the ice. He pinched all the time, carried it deep, had the speed to get back, had a terrific shot, and won scoring titles. He made his teammates better hockey players by passing them the puck at the right time, right place. Just be in position; you'll get the puck. Just let him go where he wants to go, because he was all over the ice with it, and just get ready. Phil Esposito, in one game against me, with Bobby Orr on the point, had 15 shots. He was in the slot and Bobby just passed him the puck—he didn't have to do anything. He had Ken Hodge in the corners and Johnny Bucyk in the corners, but Bobby was controlling the whole game. And as soon as he went up the ice, he was back.

He was the greatest ever—because of all the things he could do on the ice. It's just too bad he got hurt and had bad knees. But he was the best. He won the scoring title with 50 goals, 70, 80, 90 assists, Stanley Cup winner, Most Valuable Player in the league, great guy.

I remember one time I was playing against him in Boston, he fell on top of me. He says, "Gilly, are you all right, are you all right?" He was worried I was hurt, for Pete's sake. I said I was OK and went back to his defensive position. Imagine that, how nice he was—usually a guy will punch you down again to keep you down.

Comparing Orr to some of the other greats I saw, Bobby Hull only had one dimension: shoot the puck. It was shot hard and went in, but Orr had 20 dimensions; he used to do everything from defensive skill to offensive skill. I wish I could name you a quarterback that would be outstanding, that would run the whole game, not only passing, but killing the clock and things like that, because quarterbacks could do that. He was the same way.

Lemieux and Gretzky only have one dimension, too—offensive skill. These guys were outstanding, you have to give them credit. And Gordie Howe was a tough guy, with a good shot, but Bobby had more. He was doing everything else, killing penalties—if you would give him the puck when you were a man short, he would kill the two minutes all by himself.

I once played an All-Star Game with Bobby Orr at the Boston Garden, his home rink. The other team shot the puck into our zone and I stopped it. Instead of giving the puck to Orr, I shot it around the boards. Well, the Boston fans got on me. Bobby was their man and they were 100 percent right! He was the best and I should have just given him the puck.

I played with Bobby in Chicago, and I had the chance to talk to him. He was as fine a gentleman as he was a hockey player. I was by myself in Chicago, and we used to go for lunch after practice, and he was there every day with the boys, one of us. I can't say enough about this guy. If he reads this book, he'll know who I am, because I had a good time with him.

Bobby's career numbers? How about 915 points in 657 regular season games and another 92 in 74 playoff contests? Think about that, a defenseman! Also think about what would have happened if he had two good knees. There's only one Bobby Orr.

Rangers Trivia
#3

Which of the "original six" has never been a Ranger foe in the Stanley Cup finals?

4

A Little Help From My Friends:

Eddie Giacomin

"First of all, when I was 26 years old, stepping on Madison Square Garden ice, to me, that was an accomplishment in itself because that was my dream I'd always looked forward to. But then to go on and be fortunate enough to win the Vezina Trophy with Gilles Villemure, that became a reality, and here I am. Now, we've won something, and now my name is inscribed in that, and they can't take that away. And then, for me later on, to be inducted into the Hall of Fame, it shows you don't have to be a Stanley Cup winner in order to make that, and I do remember when I accepted the Hall of Fame that I accepted on behalf of all my teammates who are not going to be as fortunate as I am.

"But the thing that hurts me the most is seeing that Stanley Cup when Boston beat us that sixth game at Madison Square Garden, 3-0, and seeing that Cup being paraded

Emile Francis took a chance with a young goalie named Eddie Giacomin, and came up big. (New York Rangers)

around. I had visions of wanting to charge and grab that Cup and take off. It was so frustrating because you've played all those years and that's as close as you're ever going to come to it. Not being able to manhandle that thing was very, very frustrating, not only for me but for many players. You don't get that opportunity, and there are tons of teams that never get the opportunity and we did have the opportunity. We weren't fortunate enough to win it.

"We never seemed to go into the finals, or any of the playoffs, at one hundred percent. We were always struggling. I always maintain, even today, that the healthiest team will end up winning. We never want to use that as an excuse for why we didn't win, but we know how bad the individual is— I mean, I can remember Brad Park, he could barely lace his skates on, but once you get out there, it's a whole different ballgame."

On the Giacomin-Villemure team:

"We complemented each other so well because I caught with my left hand and he caught with his right hand. Any time there was a game involved, and Gilles was playing, it took the opposing team quite a while to catch on, and then if I was playing the next night, it was vice versa."

On the closeness of this team:

"Because our time together spanned seven or eight years, there was always good continuity amongst everybody. You always have a few little cliques where three or four would go one way, but in the course of a year, we were always together somewhere along the line. Today in sports you don't see that and that was neat for us.

"When I first started with the Rangers, Harry Howell had carte blanche to go to Great Neck Country Club, and this guy, Jerry Wolk, told Harry, 'Whenever you want to bring the team here, be my guest.' He was the president of the club at the time. That's when we were practicing at Skateland in New Hyde Park, and we would go, I would say between 16 and 18 strong, over to Great Neck Country Club and they'd just love it when we came there. Bagels and lox, pitcher of beer, you name it, anything we wanted to order. Harry Howell would just sign the check, and all we had to do was compensate Jerry Wolk with some free tickets to Ranger games, no big deal. And here we are, in a strictly Jewish club, and everybody's drinking this beer—they hardly even drink that stuff, and here we are drinking by the gallon. It was always great, whenever we wanted to have a team meeting.

"This team was always together. Even when I was living in Manhattan and most of the guys lived in Long Beach, we were always together. Sometimes, it led to some long nights, but I've always said that's sports, that's cameraderie. I'd go home and have to pay the price, but I always looked at it as part of the game, and I always enjoyed that. That's changed now."

On Emile Francis:

"Watching the NBA Finals, and seeing how Shaq played for Phil Jackson, I kinda feel the same way about all the years I played for Emile. First of all, Emile gave me the opportunity. He brought me to New York, put his neck out, and traded all those players for me. Then, a couple of things didn't go well, but he still stuck up for me. After that, I always referred to him as my father. I would go through a pane of glass for that man.

"He had a vision. And in order for him to go to Providence, R.I. and give up five players for me—especially me coming in at 26 years old—he didn't know what he was getting involved with, but he had this vision he had to start from the goal out and prioritize his hockey team. He had a philosophy that if you had a good goaltender and strong center icemen then you'll end up with a pretty good team, and he did that. He ended up getting good centers and myself, and a couple of years later bringing in Gilles Villemure, and we became the dynamic duo playing in goal.

"He made the New York Rangers in the 10 years I was there. He tried so many times to bring in other coaches, but it never worked out and he always ended up going back to the bench. He was the only one who could coach that team.

"Emile knew how to handle Rod Gilbert. He knew how to handle Ed Giacomin. He knew how to handle Bruce MacGregor. He handled everybody basically the same. He treated us with kid gloves and once we became part of him, we were like sons to him. He puts us up there on a special echelon—we were special people to him, and he was very, very special to us.

"He was a special man. I give him so much credit. He got us out of trouble; he was always fighting for us at Madison Square Garden because we only had 40 dates on the big Garden calendar. He fought corporations on behalf of this hockey team. He tried to get us an extra half-hour on the ice —whatever it took for his guys."

On coming back to play against the Rangers after going to Detroit:

"I go on record saying it's because of that game, and it's because of how the fans responded, that kind of really, really set the standard to the Board of Governors for my selection to the Hall of Fame. I didn't win the Stanley Cup. The majority of people that make it have won the Stanley Cup. I didn't, but it showed how popular I was and how the fans reacted to you, and I credit the fans an awful lot as one of the reasons I'm in the Hall of Fame."

On what he said to Derek Sanderson to trigger a huge playoff brawl at the Garden:

"All I said to him was, 'We're gonna get you.' That's it. Those were the only words. It was a stupid thing because it was a commercial, nothing going on, and he was standing at that faceoff circle, and I just decided I would skate right up to him. And, of course, Derek being Derek, he just played that to the hilt and said we had a bounty and everything like that. Jennings came out and said, 'If we're going to pay anybody to

Eddie Giacomin's No. 1 is one of only two numbers the Rangers have retired. (New York Rangers)

get someone, it's going to be Bobby Orr, it's not going to be Derek Sanderson.' But all I said was 'We're gonna get you," and that was it. As soon as we dropped the puck, and they went into the corner, that's when all helter skelter broke out. But none of the players knew what I said. Nobody. Those were the only words I said, and it worked."

On his final playoff game with the Rangers:

"We were playing the Islanders and we were down 3-0 after two periods. Emile Francis yanks out Villemure and puts me in for the start of third period. First of all, I was pissed off because I wasn't playing and now I would be going into the third period with no warmup. Who comes down but Garry Howatt? I chase him all the way up to the blue line, and I wanted to fight with him. But he wouldn't have anything to do with it. I'm skating up and I'm swinging at him and everything. He wouldn't drop his gloves or anything. Later on, we tied up the game, 3-3, but then we lost in overtime right off the first shot—bang, in the net, game over, and that's when the Islanders started their regime."

On Bill White and Stan Mikita both hitting the post in the second overtime in 1971:

"[Mikita] had a couple of chances to end that game. I've always said the goalposts are part of the goaltender's equipment."

On facing Bobby Hull:

"The theory always goes that Gilles Villemure would get to play against Chicago the majority of the time when we were together, because, believe me, who the heck in their right mind would want to play against Bobby Hull, anyway? But then when playoffs came, I had no choice, I had to play— or at least that's the way it seemed like it went."

Rangers Trivia
4

When Eddie Giacomin and I won the Vezina Trophy in the 1971-72 season, it marked the second of the three times the Rangers have captured that honor. Dave Kerr won it in 1939. Who won it after us and in what year?

5

Teammates

Brad Park

Brad Park was one of the top five defensemen in the National Hockey League. He was always being compared to Bobby Orr, the greatest ever, and Denis Potvin of the rival Islanders.

Brad always had the green light from Emile Francis to move up on the play and be an offensive force, much the way Brian Leetch has been for the Rangers since he got there.

Brad was up in the play all the time. He was good at it. He used to keep the puck in the other end all the time. He was just as good as Brian Leetch, and Brian Leetch is good at it—keep the puck in the zone and keep the pressure on. Outstanding. Brad kept the puck in there all the time—and he only needed a foot or two to move the puck and do some-

Brad Park was one of the top five defensemen in the National Hockey League when he played. (New York Rangers)

thing with it. That's all Brad needed. That's how good he was with the stick.

Naturally, any time you have a defenseman taking chances on the offensive end, you face your share of two-on-ones against the goaltender. But we had Dale Rolfe and Jimmy Neilson—and sometimes Rod Seiling—on the left side, and they were always there to take care of things when Brad got trapped. Any one of those three guys knew how to play the odd-man rush perfectly. Whenever Eddie or myself was in goal, the defense would stay in the middle of the ice and play the pass. The only thing the goalie would have to worry about was a shot from a bad angle.

But Brad Park didn't get caught that much. And he was just a tremendous offensive player—and as tough as they came, too. He made our power play go, shifting over to the left side with Bobby Rousseau on the right.

Injuries hurt Brad during his days with the Rangers, days that ended with that shocking trade to Boston in 1975. But as soon as Park arrived in New York, he was a fan favorite. He had this face like a little boy, but he played like a lion. I remember one big story on him—I think it was in *The Sporting News*—and the headline read: "Ranger Rookie Amazes, Amuses Garden Fans." This kid was special. We played together in Buffalo, but he wasn't there long—17 games. He was quickly on his way to Manhattan, where he should have played his whole career.

As well as Emile Francis got along with his players, and he was always fair to us, Brad was a contract holdout in 1970 and missed the opening game. With the WHA looming, The Cat wound up giving Brad the biggest contract in the league at that time. He was our captain when he was traded to Boston.

For his career, which ended in Detroit, Brad Park scored just over 1,000 points, counting playoffs. He's fourth on the Rangers' all-time defensemen scoring list, even though he scored more points after he left New York than he did with the Rangers.

Brad Park in a Boston uniform never really looked right or made sense, but he was able to continue his Hall of Fame career there and make all of us regret the day he was traded away. It's also a shame Brad never got to win that Stanley Cup, even playing for some very good Boston teams after leaving us. But that can't do anything to diminish a brilliant NHL career for a great guy.

Bob Nevin

Bob Nevin was captain of the New York Rangers when I got to the National Hockey League on a full-time basis.

The fans didn't always appreciate Bobby and they booed him a lot. But what a hockey player. He had hockey sense.

Nevin never said anything, but I appreciated him. Every time I had the puck, I used to shoot the puck around the boards. I had two good guys for me—Billy Fairbairn and Bob Nevin. I didn't have to look; they were there. I've got the puck, guys are coming in, I shoot the puck around the boards to my right, and both those wingers would be there for me every time! On that side, I was covered. I didn't have to worry about anything. Ever.

Nevin was a good hockey player. I remember a goal he scored to eliminate Toronto in a playoff series in 1971, his last year with the Rangers. In Game Six at 9:07 of the first overtime, the captain scored, the goal giving us the first playoff series win for the franchise in 21 years. I remember the shot because it stuck in the Toronto net and just stayed there. The series was over and Nevvy had left the winning goal stuck in the twines. Then we went on to that great seven-game series against Chicago where Pete Stemkowski scored two OT goals.

Nevin could score—he had 31 goals in a season twice in the NHL, once in Los Angeles after he got traded away, first to Minnesota for Bobby Rousseau and then on to L.A. (on waivers). He scored 307 goals in the National Hockey League, but he didn't have a big shot. He had skill.

The Rangers got him from Toronto in that big trade in 1964—the one that sent Andy Bathgate and Don McKenney to the Leafs and brought Nevin, Arnie Brown, and Rod Seiling to New York. You have to wonder if New York fans resented Nevin for replacing a popular guy like Bathgate, but Bob Nevin had a good career in New York and never let the fans bother him.

Slats

Dave Schultz and Glen Sather were both tough guys in the National Hockey League at the same time. Schultz, one of the proud leaders of the Philadelphia Flyers, the Broad Street Bullies, was bigger than Sather, the man we called "Slats," who would eventually wind up running the Rangers. I don't care about Schultz's size, though; no one was tougher than Slats and no one had a bigger heart.

So, the size thing didn't matter when these two guys hooked up. One night at the Garden, we were playing the Flyers, and it was always a night of action when those guys were in town. Good hockey, good goaltending, and there were a lot of superstars on both sides. And there was plenty of rough stuff and the Garden crowd was always into it in a big way. It was special when the Flyers and Rangers played at the Garden in those days.

On this one night, I happened to be near Schultz and Sather when a whistle blew, and they started to push each other. I hear Schultz say to Slats, "I have to prove myself in this league." He wasn't talking about scoring goals here; Schultz would score 79 goals in his NHL career. He was talking about fighting. Glen looks at him and says, "Well, let's go."

They dropped their gloves and went at it. It was one of the best fights I'd ever seen. Glen never backed off because Schultz was bigger. Glen earned my respect and the respect of his teammates right there. Tough guy, Glen Sather.

Sather, who went on to have all that success in Edmonton before moving back to New York, scored 80 goals (one more than Schultz) in an NHL career that saw him play in Boston, Pittsburgh, New York, St. Louis, Montreal, and Minnesota. But he has a small place in history for a goal he scored that doesn't count in any record book—he scored the first goal ever at the Nassau Coliseum when we played the Islanders in their first exhibition game there.

Walter Tkaczuk

Phil Esposito scored 778 goals in the National Hockey League, including playoffs. During the 1971-72 season, he had 66 goals in the regular season and nine more in the playoffs, leading the league in both.

But when we played the Boston Bruins in the Stanley Cup finals, Espo was held scoreless. Six games, no goals, with Walter Tkaczuk the primary man checking the Bruins' big gun. No ordinary task, but Walter was no ordinary hockey player.

The following year, we knocked the Bruins out of the playoffs, and Walter was brilliant again. When that series was over, Derek Sanderson said, "He's New York's best center, better than Ratelle. You've got to put him right up there behind

*Walter Tkaczuk held Phil Esposito scoreless in the
1971-72 Stanley Cup finals. (New York Rangers)*

Phil Esposito. He's a superstar, but he just doesn't know it. He may be the best two-way player in hockey."

To which Emile Francis added: "He's what two-way hockey is all about."

Walter Tkaczuk—what a hockey player. He was strong and impossible to knock off his feet, and he had a career that was a great one with the Rangers and would have been better had it not been for injuries; the last, an eye problem that forced his retirement.

He was the most honest player on the ice. He could do everything. You couldn't hit him, couldn't put him down. I remember one time when he had his head down and somebody hit him. If it would have been somebody else, he would have been out. He just stood there and shook it off and kept on going.

He was a good defensive player, mostly a defensive player, and he and Billy Fairbairn were so great at killing penalties for us. They were unbelievable. Walter was a strong man. He didn't score too many goals, but he had so many skills and his line—the Bulldog Line, with Fairbairn on the right and first Dave Balon and then Steve Vickers on the left—was a perfect No. 2 line for us.

Walter suffered a broken jaw one year, was out two weeks with the jaw wired shut, lost a lot of weight, came back, and scored two goals in his first game. That night, The Cat said, "He's quite a guy. He's out for two weeks, can't eat or breathe properly, has a busted jaw, and comes back and pops two goals." Bep Guidolin, who was coaching the Bruins that night, said, "He's a remarkable hockey player."

He was. Said Walter after that game: "My pregame meal was two glasses of tomato juice, chicken soup and a milk shake."

Tkaczuk scored 246 goals, counting playoffs, in a 14-year career all spent with the Rangers. Through the end of the 2001-02 season, he was still fifth on the team's all-time scoring list, fifth in assists and games, and ninth in goals. No. 18 is truly one of the Ranger greats.

Bill Fairbairn

When people talk about Billy Fairbairn, they always say the same thing about him—he was a very hard worker who was willing to do anything to make his team win.

He was quiet, hard-nosed guy, and I always knew where Billy was in the defensive zone. If I had the puck and I had to shoot it at somebody, and he was on my right side, which was my forehand because I was a left-handed goalie, I just had to shoot it around the boards and he was there. One hundred percent of the time I could depend on him.

He and Walter Tkaczuk were great penalty killers. They were tireless. Billy didn't have the talent of a Rod Gilbert or anyone like that, but he was a defensive player and he did his job. And could he ever take a hit along the boards to make a play.

And he could score. Billy scored 175 goals in the NHL counting playoffs, so we can remember him as more than just a checker. No. 10 was a complete hockey player in my book.

Jim Neilson

"He stops shots. He clears the puck. What else can you ask of a defenseman?"

The words were spoken nearly 30 years ago. It was *me* talking about Jim Neilson, "The Chief" and a great defenseman.

As a defensemen, Jim Neilson was a goaltender's best friend. (New York Rangers)

In those days, Brad Park was one of the best defensemen in the game, but he was an offensive defenseman, and we had guys, Jim Neilson, Rod Seiling and Dale Rolfe, there to back him up. Jimmy Neilson was a goaltender's best friend. I knew exactly what Jimmy would do in front of me, and he always knew what I was going to do.

He used to block shots and he didn't care if he got hurt. And he was a hell of a guy—he was quiet, did his job. He was kind of a joker, too, a hell of a guy. He wasn't flashy at all, a defensive defenseman. He was like my buddy back there.

Jimmy Neilson played almost 1,100 games in the National Hockey League, finishing his career in Calgary and Cleveland. He scored 70 goals, one in the playoffs. This guy was true defenseman and a real teammate.

Steve Vickers

Steve Vickers is one of my friends you're hearing from in this book. And he was one of the toughest hockey players I ever played with.

Tough? Dave Schultz would have no part of him—no part. Steve asked him many times to go. They were both left wings. They would meet and Steve would say, "Any time you want, I'm here, man." Steve was tough.

If somebody did something to Walter, or Billy, or anyone on the ice, Steve was right there.

He could also score. Vickers replaced Dave Balon on the left side of the Bulldog Line with Walter Tkaczuk and Billy Fairbairn and eventually replaced Vic Hadfield on the GAG Line.

It was hard to move Steve away from his "office" in front of the net, and those guys were so good finding him there, and he was great putting away rebounds. I read once that

*Steve Vickers, part of the Bulldog Line, put in
270 goals in his career. (New York Rangers)*

Steve said, "Any dummy can stand by the post. It's getting the puck to go in that can be tough. Sometimes it does, sometimes it doesn't."

For Vickers, it went in 270 times in a career that lasted until 1981-82, and it was all with the Rangers. He joined us the year after we went to the finals but got to go with the team when they lost to the Canadiens in 1979.

The Captain

In the 1971-72 season, Vic Hadfield became the first New York Ranger to score 50 goals in one season. And he did it in style, scoring his 49th and 50th goals on the final day of the regular season.

The game itself didn't mean anything. But we knew what the day was all about—Vic. It was on national television against the Montreal Canadiens, the team we would beat in the first round of the playoffs. We lost, 6-5, to extend our season-ending winless streak to six games. But Vic got his goals, and the place went crazy.

Vic was more than just a goal scorer. He was our captain after Bob Nevin left. He was a hard-nosed hockey player, and any time the game would get rough, he would take over. Vic would drop his gloves against anyone. He never scored more than 31 goals in any other NHL season, and never more than 28 in any other year with the Rangers, but everything worked for him as the left wing on the GAG line that one year.

They were the best line in the league, and Vic was the protector of the other two. The Rangers weren't known for being that tough in those days, but no one was tougher than Vic Hadfield.

For his career with the Rangers and Pittsburgh Penguins, Vic, No. 11, scored 323 goals and had 389 assists. He also had 1,154 penalty minutes in 1,002 games, scored 27 goals, and had 117 penalty minutes in 73 career playoff games.

Quite a guy, Vic Hadfield.

Stemmer

Pete Stemkowski was probably the funniest guy I ever played with.

We called him "The Stemmer," and he became known for scoring that triple-overtime goal against Chicago in 1971. We knew him as much more than that.

During practice, Stemmer would shoot the puck at my head. He thought this was a riot. I would skate back after him and try to shoot the puck back at him. Emile Francis would be in shock. He didn't know what to think watching this little goalie skating after one of his centers. The bottom line was that Stemmer never hit me and everything was in fun.

He was also one of the greatest joke tellers. Before games, we would come in from the warmups and the guys would be all keyed up for the game. Everything would be quiet in the dressing room, and then along came Stemmer. He had a way of making the guys relax and taking the pressure off by telling jokes or firing one-liners. He kept everybody alive. You were down in the dressing room, we lost a couple of games in a row, and Stemmer would stand up and tell a few jokes before the game, after the game, *during* the game—he was that kind of guy. Wide open all the time. Never down. He was funny.

I remember in Boston during the fifth game of the 1972 Stanley Cup finals, that after the second period, the score was tied, 2-2. If we lost, we would go home and the Bruins would win the Cup. Eddie had gotten hurt and I was going to play the third period. The dressing room at the Garden was quiet, and then along comes this one voice—Stemmer. He said,

Pete Stemkowski was probably the funniest guy I ever played with.
(New York Rangers)

"Guys, if we lose, we're playing golf tomorrow." Well, we went out for the third period and won the game, 3-2.

Stemmer didn't have enough magic words for the next game, though—the Bruins beat us 3-0 and skated around the Madison Square Garden ice with the Stanley Cup.

We got Stemmer from Detroit for Larry Brown on Halloween, 1970, my first full year with the Rangers. I knew what kind of hockey player he was, a big, strong guy, good on faceoffs, and a great defensive player who turned us into an even better defensive hockey club, but I didn't know what kind of guy he was in the locker room.

You need somebody like him in the locker room to loosen everybody up because there can be a lot of pressure all the time. They talk about trades and things like that, and you've got a guy like him to perk everybody up. You need that, and he was it.

Stemmer finished his NHL career in 1978 after playing one year for the Los Angeles Kings following his release by John Ferguson (he also played 24 games for Springfield of the AHL in '78-79). He played in 887 regular season games, scoring 193 goals—never more than 25 in a season—and adding 331 assists. In the playoffs, he had 53 points in 81 games, including TWO overtime winners in that series against Chicago. Stemmer now teams in Ranger history with Don Raleigh (the 1950 finals against Detroit) and Stephane Matteau (the '94 semis against the New Jersey Devils) as the only three Rangers to score two overtime goals in the same playoff series.

One more thing about Stemmer that people tend to forget about—he came up with Toronto and was part of one of the biggest trades in the history of the NHL. On March 3, 1968, the Maple Leafs traded Frank Mahovlich, Garry Unger, Stemmer, and the rights to Carl Brewer to the Detroit Red Wings for Norm Ullman, Paul Henderson, and Floyd Smith. Pretty big names right there.

Mahovlich and Ullman are in the Hall of Fame. Henderson scored that famous goal for Team Canada against the Russians in 1972. And Unger became the iron-man cornerstone of the St. Louis Blues for all those years.

If you're going to make a trade, you might as well make it a big one, like the one Emile Francis and Harry Sinden shocked the world with in 1975.

Tim Horton

My first full year in the NHL was also Tim Horton's only full season with the Rangers. The future Hall of Famer came up in 1951 with the Maple Leafs, and the Rangers got him from Toronto for the stretch run of the 1969-70 season. Look at his record—the guy had 10 seasons in which he played all 70 games for the Leafs and one where he played 74.

He fit in well with our team—he was a monster. He was the greatest—I roomed with him. A big guy, he used to wrestle with you. Forget about it—he'd put you down in a second, that's how strong he was. What a great guy he was! He would do anything for you.

When he died in a car accident, you had that surprised feeling because you thought he was too strong for anything like that to kill him. And he was doing very well—he had Tim Horton's Doughnuts back home and he was doing very well for himself. They have those in some places in the States now, but in Canada it's huge. He was a great guy.

Terry Sawchuk

Before I finally joined the Rangers for good, Emile Francis had problems finding the right backup to Eddie Giacomin. The Cat knew Eddie was playing too much but just couldn't come up with the right answer for the backup. The last one before me was future Hall of Famer Terry Sawchuk, who was there for the 1969-70 (I was at Buffalo again that year) but only played in six games. One of those saw him record the 103rd shutout of his distinguished career.

I roomed with him. He was at the end of his playing days. Great guy. He was teaching me how to play because I thought he was one of the greatest ever: Sawchuk and Johnny Bower. I learned a lot from him.

Sawchuk was 3-1-2 with a 2.91 goals-against average in eight regular season games for the Rangers and lost his only playoff decision. He died during the off season after an incident with another teammate, Ron Stewart, who later became my last Ranger coach. I don't know what happened, but it was ruled an accident. But knowing Sawchuk for the time I did helped me a lot in my hockey career.

The All-Time Leader

Rod Gilbert made an interesting comment the night he passed Andy Bathgate and became the Rangers' all-time leading scorer with 730 points.

"Johnny and Vic will probably score 1,000 before me," he said that night. "They're much stronger guys than me."

At the time, Johnny and Jean Ratelle, had 685 points. Vic Hadfield had 730. Neither got to 1,000 before Gilbert, who still stands as the only Ranger ever to score 1,000 points in his Ranger career.

All three have their place in Ranger history. What a line! But Gilbert was the big-name guy, the guy made for New York City. He's still there and is still working for the Rangers.

Ron Greschner

One of the greatest Rangers ever is a guy you don't always hear a lot about: Ron Greschner.

Think about it—Gresch played 982 games in the National Hockey League, all with the New York Rangers. That's third on the team's all-time list. He is sixth on the Rangers' all-time scoring list and is also second in points, goals and assists by Ranger defensemen, second to Brian Leetch in all three. He played forward later in his career.

Gresch, the picture of smoothness and stickhandling, came up to the Rangers for the 1974-75 season, as a 19-year-old kid, and it was clear right away that he was something special—just the way he carried himself on the ice.

One of the important factors in any team's defensive system is communication between the goaltender and his defense. Ronnie was always willing to listen and learn. Whatever I said, he did. He lasted 16 years in the National Hockey League, so I guess I didn't hurt him.

*Rod Gilbert still stands as the only Ranger ever to score
1,000 points in his Ranger career. (New York Rangers)*

Only Harry Howell and Rod Gilbert played more seasons with the Rangers.

Gresch, who hailed from the great town of Goodsoil, Saskatchewan, battled through terrible back problems and became one of the great Rangers. He was a great guy.

I read quotes in the Rangers Encyclopedia produced by this company a few years back that showed what Gresch had to say about the great city of New York—interesting comments for a kid from a small town in western Canada. Late in his career, Gresch, who married supermodel Carol Ault, said, "I think anybody who says something negative about New York doesn't deserve to play here. It's a fascinating city; there's always something going on."

Ron Greschner scored 179 goals and 610 points in 982 regular season games, and another 17 goals and 49 points in 84 playoff games. All of his numbers would have been greater had it not been for the back trouble that limited an outstanding career.

Ron Harris

Ron Harris was a tough defenseman on our team who scored only 24 goals in over 500 National Hockey League games, counting playoffs, in a career that also included stops in Detroit, Oakland and Atlanta. But three of those goals came in the same playoff year, 1974, and one of those was a crucial overtime winner in Montreal.

The series was tied, 2-2, and the fifth game was up there. We were down, 2-1, late in the game and pulled Eddie Giacomin for a sixth skater in the final minute. Bruce MacGregor, who scored our first goal, tied it with 16 seconds left in regulation. In the overtime, Peter Stemkowski won a faceoff from Peter Mahovlich in the Montreal zone and got

Ron Greschner played 982 games in the NHL—all with the New York Rangers. (New York Rangers)

faceoff from Peter Mahovlich in the Montreal zone and got the puck to Harry, who was playing right wing in the game. He one-timed the puck past Bunny Larocque; we won the game and went on to win the series, and they were the defending Stanley Cup champions. We then lost to Philadelphia in seven games, and they went on to win the Cup.

Anyway, here's the thing about the Harris goal. "I told my wife if there was an overtime, I was going to score the winning goal," Harry said after the game. Imagine that, a guy who never scored. She must have thought he was crazy. Turns out he wasn't that crazy.

In another playoff, Harry took Phil Esposito out with a clean hip check and knocked him out of the series with a knee injury. Espo knew it—if you cross the blue line, and you've got your head down, Ronnie's going to get you. It was a clean check, which is what he usually threw.

Years ago, there used to be hip checks at the blue line all the time. There was Ronnie, and Bobby Baun, from Toronto, and Leo Boivin. Brad Park was good at it, too. You used to go right over the boards if you weren't careful. Ron Harris was good at it and very strong. He didn't play dirty. Strong man!

I know one time, in Philadelphia, he was on the ice, on his back, and one of the big guys on the Flyers, Dave Schultz or Gary Dornhoefer, was on top of him and fighting him, and Ron was on his back and beat the heck out of the guy, on his back! Very strong.

One more thing about the Espo hit by Harris—Phil wound up in the hospital with knee surgery, and his teammates wound up kidnapping him from the hospital in his bed and taking him down Causeway Street in the bed to the team's season-ending party. I guess that's just the way hockey players are.

Rick Middleton

I couldn't believe it when the Rangers traded Rick Middleton to the Boston Bruins for Kenny Hodge on May 26, 1976.

Middleton scored 22 goals his first year, 24 his second, and was on his way to a great National Hockey League career that would see him finish with almost 500 goals, counting playoffs.

He proved how good he was with Boston, and they called him "Nifty," but I always liked him. He could do so many things, was a good skater, had good hands and great talent. This was one of the first deals the Rangers made after Emile Francis was fired and replaced by John Ferguson. Fergy figured Hodge, who was Phil Esposito's right wing in Boston, would help Espo adjust to New York. The trade was a disaster for the Rangers.

You could tell Middleton was going to be a good hockey player. His hands were unbelievable. He wasn't a big guy, but could he play!

Some people say he got traded out of New York because of the night life, and that may well be true. But once he got to Boston, just like Brad Park, his career took off. He had 38 goals his second year with the Bruins, and it was already clear by that time the Rangers had made a big mistake.

Career numbers? He had 448 goals (as many as 51 in a season) and 988 points (a high of 105) in 1,005 regular season games and added 45 goals and 100 points in 114 playoff games. Any time you average almost a point a game in your National Hockey League career, you are a great player. He's also third on the Bruins' all-time goal-scoring list, fourth in points, and sixth in assists.

Hodge scored 21 goals for the Rangers in 1976-77 and two in 1977-78, and his career was over. Middleton played until 1988. Nice trade, guys.

Ted Irvine

On Feb. 28, 1970, Emile Francis traded Juha Widing and Real Lemiuex to the Los Angeles Kings for Ted Irvine, a tough left winger who had gone to the Kings from the Bruins in the expansion draft. Irvine would become a solid player for the Rangers before moving on to St. Louis in the 1975 trade that brought John Davidson to the Rangers.

After getting Irvine, The Cat said, "We need some muscle. I saw him in the playoffs [when he scored five goals in 11 games] when he got into a dragout brawl with Bob Plager. That Plager's a pretty tough guy in a fight. Teddy more than held his own. That sold me on him. Right then and there I knew I wanted him."

Irvine scored 20 goals in his first full year with the Rangers (also my first full year) and later had 26 in a season. He had 170 goals, counting playoffs, in an 11-year NHL career.

 **Rangers Trivia**

 # 5

Who holds the Ranger record for playoff games played?

6

A Little Help From My Friends:

Rod Gilbert

———————————

"Gilles comes from Three Rivers, and I come from Montreal. We met, actually, in Guelph, Ontario—three little French Canadians out of the water, basically trying to learn how to speak English. There was not that much of it where we came from—Ratelle, Gilles and myself.

"We had this really, really tough coach named Eddie Bush. He was really something. His job was to try to discourage the kids to see if they had enough guts to survive all his nonsense. His teachings were very different from anybody else's. He used to beat up on guys; he used to fight in the locker room with some of the players, wrestle them down, and call them gutless. It was quite interesting, but we all survived it. Then Ratelle came up here before me—I had a serious injury when I was 19 and took a year off. Gilles wound up in Buffalo with Fred Shero.

*Rod Gilbert and I played junior hockey together
in Guelph, Ontario. (New York Rangers)*

"In those years they didn't believe in the two-goalie system. A lot of the teams only had one goalie who was so superior to the other one—they wouldn't spend the money to secure a second-string goalie. Our team, having Eddie Giacomin, Emile Francis's protégé because he had given seven players to acquire him, it was very difficult for Gilles to break in here. Had he been with another team, I think Gilles would have been a superstar, because I think he was equal to Giacomin in ability to stop the puck. But Eddie was here, Eddie was flamboyant, and he could handle the puck like another defenseman out there and made it to the Hall of Fame, and he could display his ability because he was playing the majority of the games. But if Gilles had played as many games as Eddie, he would have been as successful, for sure—so you could see the combo of the two of them playing for us, the one year we were invincible with those two guys.

"Gilles was a very sound, cool goaltender—he didn't get excited. The position of goaltending probably requires more than any other position as far as not being jumpy, because you make a wrong move and the puck is behind you. Gilles was settled all the time, played his angles, and was a student of the game. He was the hardest for me to score against in practice. We used to have these bets, and I'll tell you what, he beat me a lot."

On the change from losers to winners:

"It was basically Emile Francis's doing by transforming the team into a younger team. I was really sad when I got here, and I got to play three years with Andy Bathgate, when they traded him to Toronto along with Don McKenney. I was kind of apprehensive about that. He was my mentor; I was learning a lot from him, and I guess Emile Francis decided it was time to rebuild the team, and he got Rod Seiling and Arnie Brown and Bobby Nevin and Bill Collins, young players. They came here, and I think it was the beginning of the ascension.

"Getting Gilles to come up here with Eddie Giacomin was another major move. Then, of course, we had two of the best players who played for the Rangers. Brad Park, who went to the Hall of Fame, was on defense, and he was rated not far behind Bobby Orr, and then you had Walter Tkaczuk. And then Emile complemented the team with Pete Stemkowski and Teddy Irvine, Bruce MacGregor, and Davey Balon. I think we jelled quite well together. He kept the team as a group for a number of years. We all had the same common goal, and it was fun.

"Why we didn't win? There's only one team that wins at the end, and the reason we couldn't beat Boston in 1972 was mainly because of Bobby Orr."

On this group being close:

"We were extremely tight. We all lived in the same area, Long Beach. Emile Francis had this about him—he made sure that everyone on the team was treated the same way, whether it was Vic Hadfield or Gillies Villemure. Everybody was the same. His philosophy was you're only as strong as your weakest link, so, therefore, if the last three or four guys, the guys who didn't get as much ice time, didn't feel as much part of the team as I did, he felt the team wasn't going to be successful."

Dave Balon (above), formed the "Bulldog Line" alongside Walt Tkaczuk and Bill Fairbairn. (New York Rangers)

How crazy was Pete Stemkowski?

"Stemmer was wonderful. He was a practical joker, and he had all these one-liners. He enjoyed life to the fullest. He used to keep the team loose. He remembered everything, and he saw the humor sometimes in very serious moments. He saw the humor of it, and he used to use it and keep the team loose.

"I used to dress well, and every time he'd see me with a new suit and stuff, he'd say, 'Hey Rocky, nice suit—who shines it for ya?' He used to get me all the time.

"Stemmer was a very special individual."

On a French-Canadian kid falling in love with Manhattan:

"When I was 19 and 20, I stayed on here with Emile Francis and Harry Howell to do hockey camps at the old Madison Square Garden. I met all the kids that were coming to the camp, and I met their parents. So now the parents are enjoying what I'm doing for their kids, and they're treating me to the best restaurants in Manhattan, taking me to Broadway plays, taking me to Wingfoot in Westchester to play golf, and I kind of enjoyed that. I developed some strong relationships and friendships, and that was it."

On being one of the two retired numbers at the Garden:

"That's a big honor. You think about all the players—there should be a lot more. They should have some of the great players that played before me, like Andy Bathgate, and some of the other Hall of Famers, like Harry Howell, should be up there. Certainly, Brad Park made a big contribution here. But Eddie and myself—I'm sure he feels the same way.

"When the kids go there, they can relate to me now. I try to help them. I go to after-school programs and take them to the Garden and I think that's one of the things that impresses them the most. 'Oh, they retired your number and it's hanging there at Madison Square Garden, it's wonderul, Wow!'"

On almost becoming coach of the Rangers:

"I left the Rangers for a while to open a restaurant and work on Wall Street. I was a little disappointed. Sonny Werblin, rest his soul, had promised me the coaching job, and I went to New Haven to coach for one year, rode the buses, and prepared myself. He had asked me to coach the Rangers, and I told him I wasn't ready yet, but I asked him to promise me that I could go down there for a year and then come back up and coach the Rangers. I said, 'That's the only team I want to coach—I don't want to move out of New York.' He promised me I would get the job.

"I did my apprenticeship at New Haven and gave a course at Yale, and I did pretty well, made the playoffs, and then I was ready to come up here. Fred Shero was leaving, so the position was open, but I didn't hear from Werblin after the season. So I stormed into his office and said, 'Why aren't you returning my call or why aren't you talking to me—we have a deal.' He said, 'Well, did you like it down there?' I said, 'I liked it, but it's over—I'm ready to take over the Rangers.' He's squirming, he's not even looking at me and he says, 'Well, you know the success of the Olympic Team in Lake Placid ...' I said, 'No, you didn't, did you?' He hired Herb Brooks. I said, 'How many years?' He said, 'Four years.' I said, 'Well, I wish you well, I wish the Rangers well, but here's my resignation, and you can't count on me for anything around here anymore.' I was angry."

On coming back to help the Alumni Association:

"In 1989, Steve Vickers and Bill Chadwick were very active, and I helped them, but not as much as I'm helping now. It has grown tremendously. But the problem with the area of New York is there's not that many players that live here. I can count on Gilles, but we used to have Pierre Larouche and Marcel Dionne and Ulf Nilsson; all these guys left. Now we just have a few guys. But we do things; we have a golf tournament, and we raise money, and we have the Man of the Year, and we bring the guys in. We're still active, we keep in touch with a lot of them and try to help them in any way we can.

"Most of the guys are doing well. There's not that many requests. We helped Davey Balon, he had MS, but all in all, I think the majority of the guys are doing pretty well. Some could do better, but that's confidential, of course."

On the breaking up of the team, and adjusting to life with Phil Esposito, hardly his best friend:

"It was very difficult, I'm sure it had some effect on me. It wasn't only Espo. The loss of Brad, my closest friend, with Ratelle, my roommate who I've known since I was 10 years old, and Vic Hadfield on my left side—those were my bread and butter. We had a tremendous amount of success together and as a team. You sort of expect something—I had gone through Andy Bathgate, so nothing surprised me. I had seen the greats get traded from the Montreal Canadiens. Think about Jacques Plante and Doug Harvey coming to the Rangers, and I had the pleasure to play with them. I knew there was always that possibility that things would change, but I didn't think Emile Francis was going to be put in that situation to make those moves. I think he was forced to do it, by this guy Michael Burke, who has passed away.

"It must have been more difficult for Emile because those were his proteges, and he had built this, and to see it disintegrate like that ... and then the fact they brought Ferguson here to team up with Espo, and Espo becoming the captain ahead of Walter Tkaczuk or myself just didn't make any sense.

"It was a different team, let's put it that way. It was a different era, it was a different Rangers and life goes on. I was very affected by it. I was sad and depressed at times. I have a pretty strong will to accept a lot of conditions. It wasn't death, it wasn't sickness, it was just an organization that was trying to survive."

On rooming with Ratelle the day of the trade:

"Jean is a very unemotional person to start with. They were all in a state of shock. I remember them sitting on their suitcases. I don't think it was handled very well. They were just told, coldly, but I remember them just being beyond belief. They didn't expect that. I don't remember much; I probably chose to block it out. Ratelle was very nondemonstrative. It was almost like the news turned into anger and inward silence. It wasn't until we played in Boston (the following month) that I got to share with him a little bit of his feelings.

"They both went on and did well. They're true professional players, and the reason this took place was Harry Sinden. He had Jean, Brad and myself on Team Canada, and we were successful in Russia. All three of us played the four games in

Russia, and Brad and Jean were tremendous. Sinden was our coach, so he knew the quality of these two guys. He just pulled the trigger and that was their gain. Getting Vadnais and Esposito here didn't change too much, but the worst trade was Rick Middleton for Hodge. Those consequences were very serious.

"Phil did well when he came here, and Carol held his own. But for Ferguson to trade Rick Middleton—that's gotta go into the Rangers' history as the worst. I think Ricky led the Bruins for 10 years. Ferguson caught him one night, I think he was off guard somewhere with maybe a few drinks, but you know where it came from, it came from Esposito. He wanted Hodge. Imagine if Esposito didn't want something? You give a 21-year-old kid who was a wizard on the ice—why would you give him up for a 32-year-old guy? Does that make sense to you?"

On being there for the Cup in '94:

"That was the most incredible experience. I had been really close to that team that year. I started with them in London, England, when they went there to play a couple of exhibition games against Toronto. I got to travel with them and got to know Mark Messier and Brian and Beukeboom and all those guys. It's just like all the pieces were falling together, and it was almost like, 'Could it be? Could it be?' I went to Vancouver for the sixth game, and I was really hurt. We should have lost 10-2 there. We got beat up real bad and then we're coming back here for the seventh game. I had to shoot a commercial that afternoon for Prodigy, and I think I had a little bit of a stroke in the middle of my shoulder blades, I was so nervous. I couldn't even read the teleprompter, I was that nervous.

"When we scored the two goals at the beginning of the game, I relaxed a little bit. Then there was celebration."

 **Rangers Trivia**
 # 6

Brian Leetch has had six of the top eight point-scoring seasons by a Ranger defenseman—Nos. 1, 3, 4, 6, 7 and 8. Who are the other two who cracked that list?

7

Derek Sanderson

Toward the end of my days with the Rangers, we picked Derek Sanderson from the rival Bruins. Derek scored 25 goals for us his first year in New York, where he was perfect for the lifestyle.

Good hockey player, good guy, Derek Sanderson. He was outspoken, and the media was after him all the time. He had all his stories. I'll never forget that he was the first one nearest the door in the dressing room and all the media was there. Nineteen other guys, no problem, there was nobody around. They wanted Derek. He had that personality. He was a natural with the media. He got all the attention. We didn't have to say anything because they all wanted to talk to him.

He was making big money, and he was a good hockey player. Off the ice, he was a little wild. He was a young guy with money in New York. That can be a dangerous combination.

We heard stories about his past, how the Bruins would leave for road trips and Derek would park his car in front of Logan Airport, just leave it there. It would be towed, and he'd come home from the trip and bail his car out. They got to know him at the impound lot. He didn't care about the money—he had tons of it because of the World Hockey Association, where he only played eight games but got a lot of money up front. That's the way he was in those days. He had a good time.

When he was with the Bruins, he was a pain. We had a big brawl with them in the playoffs one year that started with Eddie skating out and saying something to him. Derek was always instigating, and those Bruins teams had a lot of guys who could help back him up. But he was a tough guy, a pest, and a great, great penalty killer and defensive player. That team was known for the Orrs, the Espositos, and the Bucyks, but Derek, Eddie Westfall, and Don Marcotte were great checkers and penalty killers.

We traded Walt McKechnie to the Bruins to get Derek, who never played much with Boston after his WHA experience. He played only one full season with the Rangers and was also gone from New York the same week Emile traded me and Eddie just before the big deal with the Bruins. Derek was traded to St. Louis and scored 24 goals there the rest of the year, actually finishing the season with a career-high 67 points, all in the 65 games with the Blues after he went scoreless in eight games with the Rangers.

For his career, Derek played 13 seasons and had 202 goals. He wound up doing a lot of broadcasting with the Bruins. Great guy.

No one will ever forget Derek Sanderson's rather brief stay with the New York Rangers. He was a special kind of guy, and everyone seems to have a Derek Sanderson story.

Says Peter Stemkowski: "He was a beauty. Derek was the kind of a guy that if you got him in a group, Derek had to be the center, and Derek had to tell a story, and Derek could top anything that you had. But you got Derek one on one, he was a good guy.

"I always remember the cute story about Derek Sanderson. He lived in Manhattan and practiced in Long Beach. I guess he woke up and missed his ride out to the Island. I remember a hundred stories about Derek Sanderson, but this one comes to mind. I guess he was in Manhattan, his ride was supposed to pick him up and honked and honked, but I guess he was late getting out of bed so the guy took off, and he ended up taking a cab from Manhattan to Long Beach. He got to Long Beach, and it was like 60, 70 bucks—whatever it was and Derek didn't have the cash.

"So he came in the locker room, and here's this little guy, the cab driver, typical cab driver—the Danny Devito look, with the cap, and I guess Derek said, 'Well, I don't have the cash, but just park here and I'm gonna go in and get some money off the guys in the locker room.' He walks in the locker room, and here's this little guy following him. Now, we pick up on what's going on, right? So, Derek said, 'Hey, I need 60 bucks to pay this guy,' so we were all like, 'Aw, payday's next week, I don't have it.' We were like really breaking his horns here for about 15 minutes. He needed 60 bucks to pay this guy; this poor cab driver was going from stall to stall.

"I said, 'Derek, I got four bucks on me, I didn't bring my wallet.' Polis caught on and said, 'Derek, I don't have it.' We just let him hang there for about 10, 15 minutes, then he finally got the money and gave it to the guy. That was Derek Sanderson. You never knew what to expect from this guy."

More Derek

Stemmer continues with the Derek Sanderson stories. "He was something else. He got a lot of money from the WHA, but that wasn't his role. Derek was a good role guy, third-line, penalty killer. You can't take Derek Sanderson and say, 'Derek, you're going to be my Wayne Gretzky, you're going to be my main man, you're our leader.' Derek's not a leader. Never was a leader. He made a lot of money, spent a lot of money.

"There are so many Derek Sanderson stories. I remember when he was here and Rick Middleton was playing with us. I guess he called up Rick Middleton right after the season and said, 'Rick, I'm gonna pick you up in about 15 minutes.' Derek had this limousine kind of thing—I don't know what he was driving, a Jaguar or whatever he's driving.

"Rick said OK, Derek picked up Rick Middleton, they got in the car and Rick asked, 'Well, where we going?'

"Derek said, 'We're going golfing.' Rick said, 'Derek, I don't have any of my stuff here. Why didn't you tell me we were going golfing?'

Derek said, 'Don't worry about it.' I guess they pulled up to the golf course, they go right to the pro shop, and he said to him, 'what do you like? Grab a set of clubs and grab a pair of shoes, and that's it.' I guess Derek had the gold American Express card at that time, picked something out, shoot, I don't know, three, four hundred bucks, threw the card on the table, paid for it and they went and played golf.

"Golf was over, they got in the car, headed home, and I guess Rick Middleton said, 'Hey, hold it—I think I left my shoes and my clubs back there against the fence, left them for the guy to clean off when we went to get something to eat.' Derek says, Nah, forget about it,' left the clubs back there and that was it. That's the way Derek lived.

"Derek would throw the card down. Derek would take his buddies to Hawaii, throw a gold American Express down. Bob Wolff was his agent, and Wolff would get these bills at the end of the month, 25, 30 thousand dollars. He went to Hawaii, took five friends, flew first class, United. That was Derek [laugh].

"I only spent a year with him, but, boy, there's more things that that guy did ... he lived in Manhattan. He wasn't going to live in Long Beach, that's for sure. He liked the lights. I don't know what he did away from the rink, because I was out here and he was there, but he got along with everybody. There was no one who didn't like him. You just put up with him and just kinda shook your head at the way he was."

And Even More Derek

Rod Gilbert chimes in with the following Derek Sanderson story:

"I recall Derek coming to the Rangers, and we would always go out after practice and after games we'd stay in town and go to il Vagabondo, this old Italian restaurant on the east side. On the road, Brad and myself and Vic and Glen Sather we were always together.

"I recall being at this place and having to share the bill. I think there was six or eight of us together. It didn't come to too much—maybe 10 dollars apiece, and Derek Sanderson was brand new, and he said, 'You guys are so cheap, let me pick up the bill.'

"I said, 'No, Derek, just put your 10 dollars in the middle of the table there.'

"So he had one hundred dollars out, and he wanted to give it to the waitress.

"I said, 'No, just put the money in because we all share.'

"So he took a lighter and lit the hundred-dollar bill on fire. We all watched him burn it, and none of us stopped him.

"He was really upset. Then, after he burned it, I said, 'OK, now put the ten in.' That was to tell him we all share."

Eddie Giacomin, who was there, recalls it differently. He says Derek burned *two* hundred dollar bills, not one. "Dale Rolfe was there," Eddie says, "and he turned to Derek and said, 'You say you have a lot of money, watch that sucker *burn*.' The first one went, and the waitress was right there, and her eyes just went crazy—that was a hundred dollars—and he turned around and lit the second one, of course with the intention of putting it out, but Dale Rolfe grabbed his wrist and said, 'Watch that sucker burn.'

 **Rangers Trivia**
 # 7

Before winning the Stanley Cup in 1994, the Rangers' last visit to the finals was in 1979, when they lost to the Montreal Canadiens. Can you name the three teams the Rangers beat to get to the finals that year?

8

A Little Help From My Friends:
Brad Park

"My first two years in New York we were just in the transition of really going into a two-man system[of goalkeepers]—the first year, Don Simmons was the second goaltender, the next year it was Terry Sawchuk. Unfortunately, Terry passed away. I played a little bit with Gilles in Buffalo before I got called up in '68. He was an impressive goaltender, and they went on to win the Calder Cup that year. Then, they brought him back up. We saw him in training camp, and then he was up a little bit if Eddie got hurt. It wasn't really until he came up after that, and you're seeing him every day in practice, and the first thing that hits you in practice—and this is my third or fourth year in the league—is you can't beat this guy. Probably the best angle goaltender that I've ever seen—his angles and his quickness were impeccable. You started to appreciate the things he could do. Also, handling the puck—he prob-

Brad Park was an All-Star six seasons in a row for the Rangers, from 1969-70 through 1974-75. (New York Rangers)

ably didn't shoot it as well as Eddie Giacomin, but handled it in tight very well. He was basically a good standup goaltender. I think in practice is when it really started to sink in what a great player he was.

"When I saw him in Buffalo, he had a great attitude because he was the consummate professional. He worked every day, he played all the games, he played hard all the time. So when you looked at him, even though he was down there, he never really took a day off. He didn't look forward to day off. [His attitude] was, 'This is my job, this is how I do it and I'm going to do it the best I can.' I believe he was out to prove a point that if the Rangers weren't going to use him, somebody else would. He was out there to impress other people."

On being part of a team that won the Vezina Trophy in front of Giacomin and Villemure in 1970-71:

"Emile Francis had always prided himself and made the team have pride in their defensive game. He set goals for us to keep the goals-against under 200. The year that we went with Gilles and Eddie, and Gilles was getting more games in, it was a nice fit. Between him and Eddie, they had a common goal, and that was for the team to win, regardless of who was in net, there was no jealousy on either part—whoever was in net we were going to play for him and he was going to play for us. That was a great attitude and that was just a fun attitude. There was no pettiness involved. The success of the team is what really mattered, and it started in the goal and moved out to your defensemen, and we, as defensemen, were more than happy to play in front of these guys."

On the goalies having competition with the other players:

"They would challenge us all the time in their own way. Eddie was much more vocal in his challenge in practice when you were shooting on him—probably much more of an extrovert than Gilles. But Gilles would very quietly say, 'Hey, I own you.' We used to do shootouts and things like that, and they were always challenging us, as well as each other, and that was very successful. We played shootout for money after practice with Gilles and Eddie, and if you got two out of five on breakaways, you won. After I got traded to Boston, three of five, you won. These guys in New York were that confident. They knew you and what you did, and they challenged you. They had to stop four out of five to win, and that's how highly they thought of themselves."

On Peter Stemkowski:

"Stemmer was a beauty. They don't make them like Stemmer anymore. Stemmer was a character. Every day he was the lively voice in the dressing room. A lot of the humor came from Stemmer, the fun times. He could break guys' chops in a fun way without hurting them."

On the Rangers being perhaps the best team that never won a Stanley Cup:

"I think it was probably the best and the closest, yeah."

On the chances of that '71-72 team winning the Cup if Jean Ratelle didn't break his ankle:

"Pretty good chance, yeah. He was having a banner year, and when a guy has a banner year, it carries right into the playoffs."

On his fondest memories of his Rangers years:

"Probably the way we hung out together. It didn't matter what age you were, if you were 30 or you were 20, nobody was ever excluded. On the ice, I guess one of the most satisfying things was the year after we lost in the finals to the Bruins, and the next year we went back and we beat the Bruins in Boston. There was a great deal of satisfaction there because that rivalry was so strong."

On switching sides in that rivalry after The Trade in 1975:

"It wasn't my fault. It was a shock. I had kinda moved along, I had been in the organization for seven years and moved up to where I was the captain. Getting to that point, I was Ranger blue through and through and to go to Boston was such a shock to my system, especially to my nervous system. I cried. I was very disappointed and very upset when that happened. I remember calling my wife, and I had to hang up on her because I couldn't talk to her anymore. But I went to a very stable organization, and the Rangers got very unstable."

On Emile Francis:

"I think a great deal of the man, even though he traded me. I think a great deal of him because he was honest, he expected you to play, expected you to participate. He was appreciative of the way you went about your job. The guy, in management, he was the consummate professional."

On criticism of the team after players signed big contracts not to go to the WHA. Many said the Rangers were soft:

"I don't believe that. I think we were fighting two things —we were fighting a little bit of age and we were fighting a little bit of toughness. Philadelphia came in after that, and they changed the way the game would be played, and that was difficult. There was a whole new set of rules coming in. Philadelphia came in as the Broad Street Bullies and initiated a lot of physical play, a lot of fights, things like that, and that was a whole new concept we hadn't seen. We ended up playing that seven-game series against them in 1974. We had more points than them, and they had the home-ice advantage, and I think that hurt us a little bit [the Rangers lost Game Seven, 4-3, and the Flyers won the Stanley Cup]. But we were still a strong team. The two out of three series, which was kind of a fluke, against the Islanders, that dictated, a little bit I'll bet, the dispersal of that team and that kind of brotherhood.

"It kinda started in the summer when we traded Jerry Butler, Teddy Irvine, and Bert Wilson to St. Louis for John Davidson and Billy Collins, and that was a lot of character off that team. Then we got into training camp, and in October, Derek Sanderson was off to St. Louis, Giacomin was waived, which was an unbelievable situation that he would go on waivers. [The night] he came back was probably the only game we ever threw. We threw that game, we can say we didn't, but we did."

"This was a dispersal of that team. I think if you talk to Emile, basically Gulf & Western told him to get rid of the high-priced guys who were not producing. I believe he went to Bill Jennings and didn't get any support from him. He knew his days were numbered. I think Harry Sinden in Boston had inside knowledge, and the reason I say that is that Ratty and I played for Team Canada in '72 and he knew what kind of people we were, how we practiced, and how we played."

 Rangers Trivia

 # 8

In 2001-2002, Brian Leetch became the third player to play in 1,000 games as Ranger, moving into third place on the club's all-time list at 1,021. Harry Howell (1,160) is the leader, followed by Rod Gilbert (1,065). Who is next on the list, sitting in fourth place?

9

Breaking Up is Hard to Do

There were a lot of people who thought the Rangers became soft after the money came in and players started to get paid more because of the World Hockey Association being there to try to steal players away. We used to see people calling the Rangers The Cat's (Emile Francis) "Fat Cats." I don't agree with that label.

Even though we didn't win the Stanley Cup, we still played well for a year or so. I don't know what happened after that; just before they traded everybody, we went flat! The whole team went flat. For what reason, I don't know. I never found out why. It just happened, and it sadly led to the end of our days together in New York.

But soon after that, they started trading everybody and began breaking up a great team that just never managed to win it all. It should have ended better than the way it did, with all of us taking our memories to different cities around the National Hockey League. We all knew this was a business, but when you're as close as we were as a team, it's tough to see it all end—one of the toughest things that ever happened to me in the game.

Traded

I never could really imagine not being a New York Ranger, or at least part of the only organization I ever knew. But after we lost a first-round playoff series to the Islanders in 1975, it became more and more apparent that the gang wasn't going to stay together much longer. I decided to tell Emile Francis something I never imagined myself ever saying.

I asked Emile to trade me. Nothing was working; I hadn't played in a game to that point, and I told him, "If you can get somebody for me, then go ahead and do it." The next day, I was gone, off to Chicago for defenseman Doug Jarrett.

The whole team was getting traded—upper management traded everybody because it just wasn't working anymore. Derek Sanderson was traded the same day I was; Eddie Giacomin went three days later, and then came the big deal with the Bruins in which Brad Park and Jean Ratelle were swapped for Phil Esposito and Carol Vadnais, a deal that fans of both teams will never forget.

Not long after, Emile Francis was gone, too, and a wonderful era of the New York Rangers came to an official end.

When I finally did get to Chicago, it felt very strange putting on that sweater. Very strange. What a weird feeling—when they took a picture of me, I couldn't believe it. Oh my God! I got scared. Really. From 16 until 35 years old, I'm a Ranger. All of sudden, I'm not any more—I'm going to Chicago now. I'm divorced; I'm by myself.

When I was traded to the Chicago Blackhawks in 1975, it felt very strange putting on that sweater. (Gilles Villemure)

I didn't know anybody on the team, but those guys were great. Dennis Hull, Stan Mikita, Tony Esposito, they used to invite me over to their homes all the time. But there were two French guys, Alain Daigle and J. P. Bordeleau, who were there and helped me a lot. Alain Daigle came from my hometown, which also helped. He was a young kid; he was 22 years old, I think.

I played quite a few games my first year with the Blackhawks. My second year, I broke my finger twice and didn't play that much. Then it was time for me to retire. I could tell that the reflexes weren't there anymore. I was getting slower, and the puck looked a little smaller. That's the truth—guys used to shoot from the blue line, and I'd say, "What the heck, I can't see it." Time to quit and that was it. I had had enough.

Wheeling and Dealing

I was traded to Chicago on Oct. 28, 1975. Derek Sanderson was shipped to St. Louis two days later and Eddie Giacomin was off to Detroit a day after that. But this was all just a prelude to what would happen only a week later.

Talking years later, Emile Francis told my coauthor, Mike Shalin, how "The Trade" came about. Emile and Harry were talking about trading 13th players for 13th players, and Emile finally just said, "Let's do something big." Something big? The Rangers traded Brad Park and Jean Ratelle to the Bruins for Phil Esposito, Carol Vadnais, and a defenseman named Joe Zanussi, who always called himself "The Fifth Wheel."

What a trade! Three Hall of Famers, Park and Espo, and Ratty, one of the greatest players ever to wear the Ranger uniform. Fans in both cities were in shock. But it was starting to become clear, in New York anyway, that it was time for a changing of the guard. We had lost to the Islanders in the first round of the playoffs the year before, and Emile was crushed by that. It was clear the great years of the Rangers, at least *those* great years, were over.

A little background. The Cat dealt Ted Irvine, Jerry Butler, and Bert Wilson to St. Louis after the previous season for a young goalie named John Davidson and Bill Collins. The overhaul was underway. Ron Stewart, our old defensive specialist during his playing days, was the new coach. Then came the two goalies' move and "The Trade" with the Bruins.

The Bruins were in Vancouver when the trade was made. Later on, in his 75th anniversary book about the Rangers, John Halligan wrote that Bruins executive Nate Greenburg said Sinden received death threats after making the deal. Wayne Cashman, Espo's left wing in Boston, was so upset he threw the television set through the window of his Vancouver hotel room, and it went crashing to the street below. Halligan also wrote that Cashman ordered 100 sandwiches from room service and charged them to the Bruins.

It was truly the end of an era in both cities. The hated rivals had essentially swapped their heart and soul to each other. Fans in both cities were confused and didn't know how to act. Park had ripped the Bruins heavily in a book he had written, and Ranger fans hated Esposito.

But it all worked out. Park and Ratelle became stars in Boston, Espo wound up taking over the Rangers after his playing days ended, and that young goalie, Davidson, took the Rangers to the Stanley Cup finals in 1979. Emile was fired soon after "The Trade," but his hockey career wasn't over—he still had work to do with the St. Louis Blues and Hartford Whalers.

One more thing about "The Trade": when Espo came to the Rangers, Rod Gilbert was still there, and he was No. 7, the same number Phil wore in Boston. Phil first wore No. 5,

Dale Rolfe's old number, with the Rangers, then switched to No. 12 (Ron Stewart's), before finally settling in as No. 77.

Stan Mikita

When I think about the colorful people I played with in the National Hockey League, Derek Sanderson's name comes to mind. But Derek was kind of in his own world when we played together with the Rangers—he was a young guy with a lot of money, so he didn't hang around with the rest of us too much.

When I think of funny guys, I keep coming back to Peter Stemkowski and another guy I played with in Chicago, Stan Mikita. He was funny.

Somebody told me before I went to Chicago, "He's an asshole; he's not a nice guy," but when I got there, it was a completely different story. The guy was great for me—*great!* He and his wife were unbelievable—I was over at his house all the time. "Come on, Gilly, we'll go for dinner." On the road it was the same way. And what I heard before that, before I got there, was "This guy ain't nothing." I couldn't believe how good this guy was. And I'd say he was a character.

We used to go to races together. I was single then, and many nights I was by myself, and he'd say, "C'mon, let's go, we're going out for dinner." And he was one of the great players. He was a great player—tough, chippy, but a good hockey player, a Hall of Famer. One year he was a tough guy, and the next he won the Lady Byng Trophy for gentlemanly conduct, because he wanted to show he could do it. That's the kind of guy he was—whatever he wanted to do, he did, except score against us with the open net in New York in the second overtime in 1971.

He was a good hockey player, though—over 1,600 points in his career, including playoffs. I had the chance to play against

Stan Mikita and was glad to get the opportunity to finish my career with No. 21 on my team.

Hull of a Shot

Hockey fans today have enjoyed watching Brett Hull star in the National Hockey League all these years. And Hull has been a great offensive player. In my day, I got to face his father, the great Bobby Hull, the Golden Jet, and his uncle, Dennis.

Some people felt Dennis actually shot the puck *harder* than Bobby, even though Bobby had the reputation. But Dennis had a different shot; Dennis had a hard time controlling where the puck was going. It was fast. He broke my finger once in practice. I went to catch the puck, and you have the stick against your finger, and, boom, I broke it.

What I remember about Bobby Hull is he took a slap shot on me from the blue line—years ago they used to have that big curved stick, before they really clamped down on them. Well, Bobby took a shot from the blue line, and the puck was waist high. All of a sudden, it was a foot off the ice and went right through my legs. I'll never forget that.

Another thing I remember about Bobby Hull is that he used to take a slap shot while he was skating. He's going a hundred miles an hour, and all of a sudden the big swing. And he used to come down the wing all the time—like outside the faceoff circle to my right. The goaltender has no place to go now—you have to stay there and face the wrath of that shot. You don't have much of the net covered, and he's coming in there so fast, and you can't move. That could get very scary because you had no place to hide. And I had my glove on my right hand, which made it tough because he had more of the wide side to shoot at it. It really was an intimidating thing. You knew he wouldn't pass it, so you just had to get ready for it the best way you could.

He had the hardest shot I ever saw—he and this one guy who hurt me, a guy from Philly, Reggie Leach. He hurt me. I tried to catch it, and he had a heavy shot. I used to catch the puck away from the webbing, on the outside, so a hard shot could hurt me.

We had a guy who came up to the Rangers who could fire the puck—a defenseman named Larry Sacharuk. But no one shot it harder than Bobby Hull.

The thing about the great shooters was that it was no different to play them than it was to play anyone else. You knew they were going to score more, that's all. You couldn't let them intimidate you, because that could get inside your head and cost you your focus. One lapse in focus can cost you a hockey game.

For their careers, the brothers wound up with over 1,000 goals against innocent goalies like me, counting playoffs. Toss in the 800 or so that Brett, the "Golden Brett," has scored, and you have, if I can say it, a "*Hull* of a family." Sorry about that.

My Style

When I was traded to the Chicago Blackhawks in 1975, I became the backup for future Hall of Fame goaltender Tony Esposito. I had some things in common with Tony—we were both wily veterans, and we both caught with our right hands, which is unusual for goaltenders. But our similarities really ended there—on the ice, anyway.

Our styles were different. I was a stand-up, angle goaltender. Tony was a flopper, playing the style the kids are playing now, butterfly style. But he was good at it, very good.

I was always a stand-up, angle goaltender. (Gilles Villemure)

There were not too many like him. Most of the goaltenders in those days stood up; Jacques Plante, Terry Sawchuk, Johnny Bower—he would never fall down. Never. And I was the same way. I believe, because I was small, I had to stand up, or they would have killed me on top. I lasted 20 years doing it, 20 years of pro hockey.

Nowadays, it's a different style. They all play the butterfly style. Some of them are good at it, some of them are not (it's like anything else, I guess). Tony was good at it—maybe the best ever. I guess that's why he's in the Hall of Fame along with his brother Phil.

Tough Nights

One of the keys to being a successful goaltender in the National Hockey League is the ability to forget what happens in one game and go on to the next—especially when that previous game is a disaster. We all have them; we all have to recover.

I was watching the playoffs recently and saw Jose Theodore give up five goals on five shots to the Carolina Hurricanes in the deciding game of a playoff series. That's tough—here's a guy who carried his team into the eighth and final Eastern Conference playoff spot and then beat the No. 1 Boston Bruins in the first round of the playoffs. Then, his season has to end like this, he has to live with it all summer rather than being able to come right back in the next game— same thing happened to the great Patrick Roy. That's the life of a goaltender—but he has to tell himself, and others have to tell him all summer, that he was the main reason they got as far as they did. Sometimes, you can say the words, others can say them, too, but you're the one who gave up the goals.

I had many tough nights during my playing career. And even though this is a book about the New York Rangers, one of my worst came in Pittsburgh after I left the Rangers and was traded to the Chicago Blackhawks.

The score was 11-1, and I wouldn't be telling this story if we were winning. There were about three minutes left in the game, and I was not playing well, to say the least. They left me out there because they didn't want to bring Tony Esposito off the bench in a game he was supposed to be sitting out and resting. So, I was in there for the duration.

After a whistle, I notice the linesman coming toward my net. What he was doing was checking the net to see if there were any holes in it. Linesmen do that from time to time during a break just to make sure the net is all right.

I couldn't stop every puck that came my way, especially one night after I left the Rangers and was playing for the Chicago Blackhawks. (Gilles Villemure)

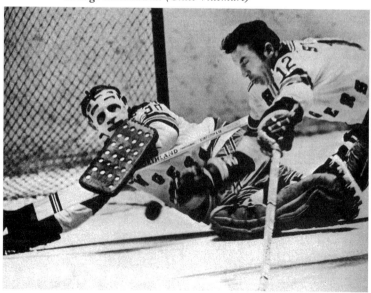

Well, the linesman was behind the net, and I was in front. I yelled to him to come to the front of the net, and when he came around, I said to him, "You see the big four-by six-foot hole in front of the net? Would you repair it, please?"

I got a big laugh out of him.

I never let myself get too down after a bad game. There's always the next game to redeem yourself. And it's the same thing when you get a shutout—it means nothing once the next game starts, so you can't go out there thinking you're ready for the Hall of Fame. This can be a very humbling game, even if your name is Dominik Hasek or Patrick Roy.

 **Rangers Trivia**
 # 9

Two players share the Ranger record for fastest two goals by one player. Can you name the two Rangers who have scored goals eight seconds apart in the long and proud history of the team?

10

A Little Help From My Friends:

Peter Stemkowski

"Back then, when Gilles was breaking in, there were six teams, 12 guys, and the backup really didn't play very much. Does anybody remember Glenn Hall's backup in the glory years, or Terry Sawhuck's backup? You don't remember these guys. Expansion helped a lot of guys.

"We had six teams up until 1967; we went to 12, and that opened up some doors, and in the seventies, they expanded again, but at that time you did what you had to do. Nobody went to college or graduated or had something else to fall back on. Back in those days, you played hockey as a kid, and if you were good, you progressed into the juniors, you came, and you signed a pro contract. The money was like $5,500 the first year and maybe $6,000 the second year with a couple thousand signing bonus—that's what you were making and you just didn't know anything else.

"If you didn't play hockey, what would you do? Nobody had any kind of a trade or anything like that. Now guys are coming out of Boston College and schools like that, and have something going, and if they turn pro now, they make so much darn money—a million bucks, and that can carry them the rest of their lives. I remember the year we won the Cup, I made $9,000—and I think we made like [another] six or seven [thousand, as a Cup share]."

On coming so close with the Rangers:

"Ratelle went down one year. That didn't help. We had the ingredients. We beat teams we shouldn't have beaten, and we lost to teams we shouldn't have lost to. Bobby Orr? That hurt, but what are you gonna do? It's like Peter Forsberg today, one of the greatest players, and he goes out and wins games. When Bobby Orr was on the ice and they beat us in six for the Cup, that was the year. I think we were at our peak then. Guys strarted getting a little old after that. And then that series against the Flyers—losing that ... then we started to dismantle, then the pieces started to break off a little bit.

"That was some series. When I go back and think, I have never been involved in a best-of-seven series like that, even from a broadcaster's point, which is what I'm involved in now. That was a hell of a series, that one. We lost in seven, we got called for too many men on the ice by John D'Amico, we lost by a goal, we got one late in the third period—I think I scored it—and Hadfield was serving the penalty, and they caught him with a chuckle on his face in the penalty box. He was gone after that—Emile took exception to that. Then Hadfield went, and the team started to dismantle. We had Vic and Walter and Billy Fairbairn and Eddie and Villemure there—we had our team, we had our chances. I was there through the thick and thin, and then when John Ferguson came on the scene, he didn't really care much for me. He and I ran into each other quite a few times in my early going when he was with Montreal and I was with Toronto, and I don't think he ever forgave me for some of the run-ins we had. It was just the beginning of the end—they brought in Wayne Dillon and Pat Hickey and ...

On Villemure's contention that Stemkowski fired pucks at his head in practice:

"Yeah. Well, I didn't do it on purpose, but, occasionally, one would get away, and he'd chase me around the rink. Everybody would stop and say, 'Oh, ho-hum, there's Stemmer and Whitey going at it again.'

"I used to call him Whitey because guys used to come to training camp in the fall and at least spend an hour or two on the beach and get a little bit of color. But he was just white, and I asked him what he did in the off season—did he work in a flour mill, or what? So I nicknamed him Whitey, and I think we all called him Whitey after that. I still call him Whitey to this day.

"He never caught me. Listen, I was big; I wasn't the fastest guy, but I could out-skate him, a little short, stubby guy who played goal.

"We used to practice at New Hyde Park, and one would get away, and he'd get a little upset and chase me around the rink a couple of times and get back in the net and practice. Emile Francis would say something, and I'd say, 'Hey, it's not the first time it's happened, it won't be the last, so get it out of your system, Gilles, and let's get back to practice.' He says maybe it wasn't an accident when it happened, but you've got a puck, and you've got a stick, sometimes you've got a two-iron in your hand and keep it low and hit it off your back foot, and sometimes you've got a wedge in your hand and it kinda gets away on you. It always depended on which way the wind was blowing.

"New Hyde Park was quite a place. It had that chicken wire around the boards. It was cold, ice-cold. It wasn't exactly the spacious and beautiful practice facility that the guys have today. We used to walk downstairs, and I think we had nails to hang up our coats that were knocked into the wall. Now, you walk into the locker room and there are15 treadmills and 20 stationary bikes, a fitness guy—we never used to have that.

"It was nice when we moved to Long Beach because all the guys lived down here. A couple of guys lived in the City, like Bob Nevin and Rod Gilbert, and I think Eddie Giacomin ended up living in Manhattan, but we were all here on Long Beach. These were all summer rentals back then. It was ideal for us. I'm in Atlantic Beach now, right next door."

On Villemure saying Stemkowski is the funniest guy he ever played with:

"Really? That's quite a compliment. That's quite a reputation to have to live up to. I don't know how many funny things I did. I used to do impersonations and things like that. Sometimes people tell me I did things that I don't even remember. I mean, Emile Francis says, the triple overtime goal, I walked into the locker room—I guess I must have said it—'The concessions have run out, bars are going to be closed, let's get this thing over with,' and lo and behold, I'm the guy who goes out and scores the winning goal, gets it over with so we all go home around midnight.

"Gilly was the kind of guy you could kid around with, call him short and Whitey, and he took a good ribbing. I was a kind of a jokester where I could poke nicknames at guys. Like, Gilles Marrotte drove this small, little car and I called it the Batmobile and he kinda took exception to my calling it the Batmobile—it looked like the Batmobile—but with Villemure, you could kid around with him and he wouldn't mind. He always had trouble with the first shot on goal. I don't know what it was with him, but I'd say in the locker room, 'Jesus, Gil, let's get a beach ball and somebody shoot the damn beach ball, stop the first shot, then you're OK.' He had a tendency to always let the first shot in for some reason, I don't know why."

On winning that game with one of the biggest goals in Ranger history:

"Both teams were just running on fumes. You're at the point where nobody's any fresher or nobody's more tired than the other guy—you're all at just about the same level at that point. You're numb, actually, just numb, and you're just thinking, 'I don't want to make the mistake that's gonna cost this game.' Everybody was pretty cautious.

"I think [Tim] Horton dumped it in, and that was his last point as a New York Ranger. I just followed up the play. A lot of people think I was a slow guy getting in there last, and I tell people I was the first guy in, that's how I got to the puck. I just tucked it in the short side. Irvine took the shot, the puck was lying there, and I just put it in.

"I think we went to Gallagher's, across the street there, after the game, and we sat there until about 2 in the morning and I think I came out here to Long Beach, and there was a place that stayed open until about five o'clock; you couldn't sleep after something like that. I remember me and Dale Rolfe— he was rooming with me at the time—just stayed up until about six or seven o'clock in the morning, just sitting, talking, and nobody seemed to want to go home. I remember finally leaving this place, and there were kids getting on the school bus. I said, 'This is a bit strange—I haven't been home yet and these kids are getting on school buses.' It's not like we went out and celebrated, there were no celebrations, no wild drinking, we just sat and talked and ate. Finally, the exhaustion kicked in— you just didn't feel the exhaustion after something like that. Then, a couple of days later we went into Chicago, and we lost."

Have you ever had a bigger thrill in hockey than that goal?

"Well, yes—I would have to say winning the Stanley Cup that we won in Toronto in 1967. That was in my early years as a professional. The turning point in that year was when Punch Imlach got sick. We were on a losing streak, Imlach got sick, and King Clancy took over and we kinda put it together. They put Pulford, Pappin and me together. I was the center guy who knocked people down, got the puck. Pappin had some speed down the wing, Pulford was a pretty tenacious guy, and we just clicked and everything worked out, and we ended up winning the Stanley Cup."

On his old boss, Emile Francis, and how no one ever seems to say a bad word about the guy:

"What can you say? I can sit here and say call me back in 24 hours, and I'll try to think of something, and I can't. He was just an honest hard worker, and he treated everybody the same—if you were the 50-goal scorer on the team or you were the guy on the fourth line and didn't dress, there were five, six rules, whatever, and you followed them. And I don't think anybody that ever was traded by Emile would have anything negative to say about him. I think those teams back then were his favorites; he comes back for alumni things. I was in Florida, called him up, said hello ... I just feel he's very special. He's a very special person in hockey and a pretty special person in my life. I don't think I'm the only guy to say that. I have the highest respect for him.

"The only thing I feel bad about is we never won a Stanley Cup for him. It would have just been terrific. You just admired the guy. He practiced here in Long Beach, he jumped on the train, went into Madison Square Garden, probably got back seven, eight o'clock at night. He deserved the championship, and I really feel if there's one disappointment being with the Rangers it's that we never won one for the people in New York and for Emile Francis."

Does Francis get shortchanged historically because he didn't win a Cup?

"I think, what do you say, [something is missing] if a guy's involved 20 years in the major leagues and never wins a World Series or never wins a Super Bowl. It's always nice to win one. I think if Mario Lemiuex went through his entire career with all the numbers he put up and didn't win a Cup, I would think there would be a little bit of—maybe a little asterisk next to him. I don't think "Cat" got shortchanged because of that, but I certainly don't think he didn't win because of lack of effort.

"Maybe he made some bad trades, but this is New York, and they're pretty demanding here. As far as I can see, I don't know how many bad trades he actually made, but he's respected. You never heard something that he said about you behind your back. If he didn't like the way you were playing or didn't like you, you knew right away. I mean, he'd call you in, and he'd look you in the eye, and I always respect anybody who's truthful and doesn't deny—like, 'I didn't say that.' He's a very highly respected guy.

"I still get a chance to see his son, Bobby Francis, in Phoenix, and I always ask how Emile's doing, and his son is just very much like him. You can see, when I talk to Bobby, you know where he's coming from. He's got his father's input in him.

"No, I can't think of anything bad I could ever say about Emile Francis."

So, The Cat was different from other guys you dealt with?

"Well, I had Punch Imlach in Toronto, and everything with him was fear. He'd yell and scream at you. With Punch Imlach back then, that was old school. Now, with Emile, if we got on the ice at 10:30 a.m., we knew at 11:30 a.m. we were coming off. With Punch Imlach, you got on at 10:30 a.m., you might be there until noon. If he didn't like the way you were practicing, he would just throw the pucks in the pail and say let's go do some skating. "He was a real yeller-screamer, and Emile was more of an even-keel sort of guy. From Punch Imlach, what did I know? Then I went to Detroit and played for Sid Abel—I went from Toronto, which was Alcatraz, to Club Med, Sid Abel, we practiced 20 minutes. Alex Delvecchio, Gordie Howe, those guys were seasoned pros, and we didn't practice much there. Then we came to New York, where we worked hard, but it was just different."

On winning the faceoff that led to a Ron Harris overtime winner in Montreal in the 1974 playoffs:

"That faceoff win was against Pete Mahovlich. It was me against him, and I think that just as they went to drop the puck, Pete was distracted by something, whether he looked back to see whether the goalie [Bunny Larocque] was ready, or went to adjust his elbow pads. I just won the puck to Ronnie Harris, he just one-timed it, and it was over. It was one of those clean draws, right on his stick, in the net, and, hey, we went home. We were happy.

On the differences in the game now:

"Our trainer in New York was Frank Paice—a lovely guy, I think the world of Frank. Frank has passed on, but he wasn't an athletic trainer. He wasn't certified. I remember we used to have to take our own stitches out. A guy gets stitched up during a game, and they have to stay in five days or whatever, and Frank had a little bit of the shakes, so after five days, nobody wanted to go all the way to the doctor's office, sit there, and have him put the hydrogen peroxide on and get the scissors and cut them out. I remember Glen Sather used to take our stitches out for us. Trainer? Frank Paice was an usher between games. He'd go up in Madison Square Garden—he was an usher. Now, in any sport, you have to be certified. If something happens on the ice, you have to be able to jump out there and save a guy."

 **Rangers Trivia**
#10

Oh, good, another goalie question. During the 2000-01 season, the Rangers set a team record by using six goaltenders. One of them appeared in only one game, another in two, a third in four. You're a real Ranger fanatic if you can guess all six.

11

Fun and Games

_____

You always have to be alert in a hockey locker room. Let your guard down, and you are likely to become a victim of a practical joke.

In the locker room, there would be 20 players and trainers and coaches. Anyone is capable of playing tricks on you, so you have to be ready.

Shaving cream in your skates, laces cut on your skates, and if you had false teeth, you had better make sure they weren't switched with somebody else's.

But any guy who pulled one of these pranks also had to know, in the back of his mind, that payback is a you-know-what. It's all part of being a team, and we were a team when I was with the Rangers. It was a great bunch of guys.

Creatures of Habit

Hockey players are very superstitious individuals, and our team showed it in the locker room.

First, there was the way some guys put on their hockey equipment before a game. Left skate on first, right skate on second. I myself had a routine—same routine every time I got dressed. I, too, would put my left skate on first, then my right—and I would do the same thing with my goalie pads.

After we dressed, Emile Francis would come in, shutting the locker room door. If the door was already closed, he would open it and shut it just to make sure everything was the same so he wouldn't disrupt anything. He was a creature of habit, too.

Now, the guys all knew of Emile's routine, so they would make sure to shut the door before he came in just to make him go through his little ritual. Everybody would laugh, including Emile.

The Cat would give us his little speech before going on the ice for the game, and we would leave the locker room in the same order—same order all the time. The goalies would go first and then the rest of the guys. It had to be the same every game. We didn't want to do anything to break our rhythm.

Shuffling the Deck

Peter Stemkowski remembers how much we used to all play cards together.

"Everybody today on the backs of planes plays cards, and we had our group that played cards. Sanderson used to play, Rolfe, Villemure, Brad Park—the card players. I remember very distinctly that we got stuck in Minneapolis with a big storm, and we were at the Thunderbird at the old stadium there, we had a half-day there. We didn't have a lot of time on the road then—the road trips weren't as big as they are now.

"Well, they played for half of a day, and I think Ron Greschner ended up just endorsing his paycheck and handing it to Villemure. And I know he used to take Greg Polis—he and Polis used to play cards all the time. I think it was gin rummy. Villemure used to tell me, 'I own that guy, I own that guy.' He loved playing with Greg Polis. I think he used to take Sanderson a little bit, too.

"Villemure liked the horses, and he liked to play cards, but it sure didn't bother his goaltending."

Slats and the Safe

Peter Stemkowski remembers a funny story about Glen Sather, one of our teammates and the guy running the show with the Rangers these days.

"We used to leave our belongings in our pants pockets at Madison Square Garden. There was the Rangers locker room, then there was the medical room in the middle, and the other room was the Knicks' locker room. We used to just leave our wallets and our rings and watches in our pants pockets. I guess guys were starting to complain a little bit, whether it was the Knicks, or us, maybe there was a couple of bucks missing now and then.

"What they decided to do was put a wall safe in the medical room. Big enough to fit everybody's stuff, you could put your wallet and your ring and your watch in there during the game. Then, if somebody did get in, there would be nothing to steal in the room. So the first day we got it, the thing was open and only the trainer, Frank Paice, knew the combination. He was fiddling with it, closing it and opening it to make sure it worked all right.

"Well, Glen Sather walks in there, and said, 'So, this is the new wall safe, huh, Frank?' Frank said, 'Yeah,' He shut it, and within five minutes, Sather opened it. Somehow, he figured out the combination, opened it, and that was it for the safe.

"I don't know what that safe cost, but it was of no use anymore. He somehow figured it out.

"I guess right then and there we should have known that he was destined for bigger and better things."

New York's Finest

Bobby Orr once told my coauthor a story about the night the Bruins won the Stanley Cup at Madison Square Garden.

After they beat us, the Bruins needed some help getting out of the Garden. Ranger fans in those days didn't like the Bruins and would let them know it—inside and outside the building. So, after they won, they were given a police escort through the streets of Manhattan on the way to the airport.

Orr said they got as far as the Midtown Tunnel, where the police were no longer needed. So, as the police cars peeled off to turn around and go back, the Bruins players waved thank-yous out the window and were greeted by one New York cop's salute—with one of his two middle fingers.

Hell hath no fury like a Ranger fan scorned.

The Streak

Rod Gilbert says nothing was off sides when it came to Peter Stemkowski.

"When I married my first wife in Florida, she had a shower," Rod recalls. "It was in 1974. Stemkowski and I were both getting married in June. About 10 couples from the team had gone to Acapulco to the opening of the Acapulco Princess, and we all went there. We came back to Miami where my future wife was living, and she had about 10 girlfriends over celebrating a shower. All the guys had dropped their wives and girlfriends, and we had two limousines, and we all went out to dinner ourselves.

"When we came back, Stemmer said to me, 'Hey, Rod, this has never been done before, in 1974, streaking is in the future groom's thing at your future wife's shower.' I said, 'Are you crazy? I don't even know three of the girls there. I can't do that.'

"Then he talked me into it. I said, 'OK, if I do it, then will you do it with me?' He said, 'Fine.'

"So we come into the apartment, and I see all these gifts, you know, the Frederick's of Hollywood negligee. I picked that up, and I stuffed it into the back of my jeans, and I took him into the bedroom, and I said, 'Let's go.'

"He took all his clothes off, and I took all mine off. I put this negligee on with pompoms all over the place. I opened the door, and I pushed him out, and he was bare-assed. The girls were screaming, and I went real quick around the room, and I came back with my jeans and my shirt and it was a streak, right? Well, he didn't make it—he made it to the other side of the room, and he sat on the stereo there. He was like sitting down.

"Now, the girls were uncomfortable, and his future wife said to me, 'What's this all about?' I said, 'Gayle, it wasn't my idea.' So she said, 'Well, get him out of there.' I said, 'Stemmer, come on—you're not streaking now. Come on, you gotta end this.'

"He finally got up, looked at all the girls and said, 'What's the matter, girls? Didn't you ever see a 220-pound rocket with a one-inch fuse before?'

"That was funny, but that's the kind of humor he had. He was crazy. He could do a lot of stuff, but all in good fun. Nobody got hurt."

Another Streak

Eddie Giacomin relates the following story about Emile Francis getting the fellas out of trouble in, of all places, Colorado Springs:

"We had a week off and we went to Los Angeles," Eddie said. "We played a game, and we didn't fare too well, and he couldn't visualize us spending one whole week in Los Angeles. So he decided to take us to the Broadmoor Hotel in Colorado Springs. He had all the rules, that you can't drink in the building and all that. Of course, needless to say, we as a team broke every rule, and one of the players decided to streak down the hall.

"Well, this guy ran down the hall, and Walter Tkaczuk and I were at the end of the hall, and we reached out and pulled him in. The security people came, and they wanted to haul all three of us off to jail. Bill Jennings, the CEO of the Rangers then, was the one who had us go to the Broadmoor, and he got the black of it all from Emile Francis and the people at the Broadmoor, but Emile stuck by us and said, 'You're taking me to jail before you take those guys to jail. He was a battler—small in stature but certainly big in heart, and they weren't taking his players anywhere.

"The next morning, at breakfast, you could hear the waiters saying, 'Did you hear about the Ranger player who was streaking down the hall last night?' It was hilarious.

Deli Day

Monday was usually our day off, and it was usually what we called our "Deli Day."

Said Eddie Giacomin: "If I got a shutout, in those days they used to pay you a hundred dollars, and if somebody got a hat trick, they'd get a hundred bucks. I would throw the hundred dollars into the pot, and we would go to practice at New Hyde Park. The majority of the time the coach wasn't there, so we would have Deli Day, and we would order beer and some sandwiches and whatever else. After practice, we'd go into the locker room and just BS. Sometimes, we'd have our children with us.

"The irony of it all, is that I can remember having 13 or 14 shutouts one year, and I was getting a hundred dollars, and [defenseman] Arnie Brown was getting two hundred bucks a shutout. At no time did we ever know that. Yet I was always throwing my hundred dollars in the pot, and he was always keeping his two hundred bucks in his pocket.

"We found out a long time down the road, and it was no big deal. But here I was willing to give up my hundred bucks for Deli Day, and somebody else was taking the bonus. I didn't expect him to give up his 200, but he could have contributed to the pot."

Spiderman

Eddie Giacomin remembers one of his teammates turning into a cartoon character.

"We were at the Executive House in Chicago," Eddie says, "and we had a few drinks. We wanted to go down to the next floor to one of the other guy's rooms, and he wouldn't open the door. So, I think we were on the 11th or 12th floor and Fairbairn decided to play Spiderman. He just went over the balcony, down to the next balcony.

"If anything happened, he would have just splattered on the pavement down below. But, sure enough, there he was, and the guy had no choice but to open the door. He was out on the balcony. Needless to say, we got the door open, but thank goodness that Spiderman Fairbairn was the one that did it.

"This was in downtown Chicago. I'll never forget that as long as I live. We've told that story so many different times, it's unbelievable."

A Toothy Story

As you know, most hockey players lose some or all of their teeth. Eddie Giacomin is proud of the fact that he never lost any. Harry Howell never did, either. But teeth, especially missing ones, are an important part of any hockey team's lore.

"I happened to sit beside Walter Tkaczuk, and Fairbairn was there, and they were all getting ready," said Giacomin. "I would see eight or nine or 10 guys get ready for the game, and they always had their little plastic containers—they would take their teeth out and put then in the little plastic container, and I would watch these guys do it all the time. So I decided, 'I'm gonna change those teeth around.'

"So I would go through all those things and change everybody's teeth around. The game would be over, and we'd come back in and the guys would put their teeth in and say 'Eddie, you son of a B.' And, of course, the next day in practice, where are they going to shoot the puck? All at my head, hoping to hit me in the teeth.

"This went on constantly. But at no time, though, in my 10 years in New York, did anyone ever hit my face. They came close a couple of times, they tried hard, but I had so much fun mixing those teeth up."

Wanting to Be Me

I can't imagine why anyone else besides me would want to be me, but that's exactly what happened to me when I was playing for the New York Rangers.

There was a guy driving around the New York area in a van that had the words: "Paul Villemure, New York Rangers Scouting Department," written on the side. He claimed to be my brother, but was also passing himself off as me. Apparently, he was trying to convince young hockey players to tour colleges with him, and there was a feeling he was doing it for sexual reasons.

Frank Torpey, the head of security for the National Hockey League, was made aware of what was going on and set up a sting that saw him accompany a kid to a meeting. Torpey, a great guy who passed away recently, was accompanied by a couple of FBI friends, and they did a good job of scaring the imposter, whose real name was Paul Kostofsky.

They peeled the words, which were actually stuck on, off the van, and sent him on his way with a strong warning and a good scare. But this wasn't over.

Kostofsky was using my name to get dates. Now, Rod Gilbert was known as the lady killer on our team, but this guy was saying he was Gilles Villemure, and I think he even had a helicopter that he used to pick up women. He went all the way with this thing.

Did it work? Well, I was doing a card show in New Jersey, and a girl approached me at the table. She said, "You're not Gilles Villemure—I'm going out with Gilles Villemure, and you're not Gilles Villemure. I'm going out with him, and I should know."

I said, "Lady, here's my driver's license," and showed it to her. She almost fell on the floor. She kept looking at me and saying, "You're not Gilles Villemure." Isn't that something?

I guess this was going on for a long time, because the card show was after I finished playing. I guess he had money to be able to pull something like this off. He used to fly in to meet girls on this helicopter.

As Rodney Dangerfield used to say, "It ain't easy being me." Little did I know it took the work of two of us to get the job done.

12

A Little Help From My Friends:

Vic Hadfield

"It always seemed to me that Gilles was just a special guy. By that I mean he was so dedicated, he really wanted to help the hockey club in any area that he possibly could. We could see that he had a tremendous amount of skill and determination. He wanted to win. He was very much a team type of a player who would do anything. He didn't have an opportunity to play a lot because Ed Giacomin was our main goalie, but we as players felt very comfortable when Emile did make a change and put Gilly in. It didn't really matter to us because we had so much confidence in Gilly's ability.

"He was a fiery kind of guy, great off the ice, great with his teammates, and I think he's just turned out to be one of the nicest fellas that I've had the opportunity to meet.

"He did get started late but didn't give up. Back then there were only six teams with six goalies, and there was a

*Vic Hadfield became the first Ranger to score
50 goals in 1971-72. (New York Rangers)*

tremendous amount of other players in the same position as
Gilly. Denis DeJordy came to mind—he played in the minors for a lot of years before he went up, and with Gilly it just
showed what type of individual he was. We had a pretty strong
goaltending duo there with Eddie and Gilly. They won the
Vezina Trophy that first year together, and when we started
out the first of the year, we tried to keep our goals down to
less than two a game. A lot of years we were able to do that
with the type of team that we had and strong goalkeeping.
Gilly was right up there and equal to Eddie Giacomin.

"They both came from the same mold. Gilly had a little
different temperment than Eddie. Eddie was the one who
played most of the games, but Gilly was preparing himself for
whenever he was needed.

"Gilly was a great guy back then, and he's still the same type of guy today. He helps me in some of the golf tournaments I run in New York for different foundations. He's always readily available with a big smile on his face, and the people just love him."

On Emile Francis:

"No one ever worked harder than Emile. I used to call back in July to New York and say, 'how's everything?' He would have just had his lunch—he brought his lunch from home because he didn't want to leave the office. He wasn't out in all the restaurants around New York City. He stayed right in the office, and, being a player and hearing those types of things, you see just how dedicated he was to having a winning team. And that rubbed off down to the players—the guys would go through brick walls for him. It was just unfortunate that we weren't able to win the Stanley Cup back then, but we certainly tried, and Emile couldn't have been a better coach or general manager in New York. It's a difficult city, as most people know, and he certainly gave it his 100 percent."

On the Rangers perhaps being the best team ever that didn't win a Stanley Cup:

"It was unfortunate that Jean Ratelle broke his ankle, and we just didn't have anybody to replace him, which would have been difficult on any team because he meant so much to us. I would have to say that that was probably one of the better teams that didn't win."

On whether there was a feeling that year that the 1971-72 team was special right from the start:

"All the teams went to training camp with the thought that, 'Geez, you know, we have a pretty good squad here, and our main objective is to win the Stanley Cup.' Personal goals meant nothing to any of the players back then, whether you scored 30 goals, 50 goals or 10 goals. We dedicated ourselves to winning that Stanley Cup. We were always reminded that New York hadn't won in so many years, and you look around the room, and you see the squad that we had there, with All-Star defensemen and centermen and two top goalkeepers and with a little luck we could be there. We came awful close, but it just wasn't good enough. You have to be very lucky and not have the injuries, and we were just unfortunate to lose a player of Jean Ratelle's capabilities. He meant so much to us, and we just couldn't recover."

On his fondest moment:

"I don't want to sound corny, but coming from Canada, I wanted to be a hockey player. In my little hometown there of Oakville, Ontario, there were about 15 or 20 guys that had shown some ability when they were 14, 15 years of age. That's all I wanted to do—play hockey. I neglected school because I wanted to grab as much ice time as I possibly could, and I was one of the very fortunate ones to come out of Oakville and have a chance to play pro hockey. So when you're asking me what would be the most important thing, I'd have to say it was putting on that New York Ranger sweater back in 1960.

"On the ice, with that team, there's a few things. I mean, your ultimate goal is to win the Stanley Cup. Personal things don't mean anything if you don't win. That's how everybody felt. I know I was very fortunate to have the opportunity to play with guys like Gilly and Eddie Giacomin, Brad Park,

Emile Francis, playing on a line with Jean Ratelle and Rod Gilbert. That was a big thing. And I was lucky enough to score 50 goals in 1972. That was also a highlight, but they were all secondary as far as I'm concerned, and I don't dwell on it even today because we didn't win. If we had won and I had scored 50 goals, that would have been great, but we didn't win, and so you feel like you cheated, and you didn't give enough, but we certainly tried, and it just wasn't meant to be."

On the Rangers being a very close group:

"Oh, very tight. Very tight—you don't see that today. There was a tremendous bond. We have our alumni golf tournaments, and you might not have seen an individual for 10 years, but as soon as you sit down, it's like you were with him yesterday. We always traveled together in New York. Bruce MacGregor and Glen Sather and I drove to practices and to the games. The three wives would drive in together, and then the six of us would go out and have dinner afterwards. It wasn't just us six—half of the team would be at an Italian place, and the rest of the team would maybe want Chinese, so we were always together after games and as families. We were very, very tight."

On whom he has stayed in closest contact with over the years:

"I'm in touch with Rod Gilbert a lot in New York, and Gilles Villemure. Bobby Nevin's here, Andy Bathgate, and Harry Howell. We have a pretty good group right here in the Toronto area. Rod Seiling's here, working for the hotel association."

13

Life Away From the Ice

Harness Racing

Besides playing hockey, I was a harness racing driver, trainer and owner—something, like hockey, that is in my past, even though I still enjoy going to the track.

I started to drive horses when I was 17 years old. The hockey rink and the racetrack were side by side in my hometown. After the hockey season was over, I would go back to my hometown and drive horses. It used to keep me in shape. In 1970, I won the driving title.

I could have easily made a career for myself in harness racing, but I chose to play hockey full-time and make harness racing a part-time thing.

No one in hockey ever bothered me about driving horses during my off season, not even Emile Francis. When we reported to training camp, he would always ask me how I did driving over the summer, and if I had won many races.

For me, it was the perfect setup—hockey in the winter and harness racing in the summer. I was involved in sports all year round.

I raced at many of the major racetracks—Montreal, Quebec, Trois Rivieres (my hometown), Roosevelt (which is now gone), Monticello, Freehold and The Meadowlands. I had a lot of fun driving horses.

I got out in 1990. The game was changing. I had only one horse left, and it was very expensive to buy horses. So I just decided that's enough, and I stopped.

This is me behind my first New York horse, Guy Bristol. My son Bobby and daughter Denise's favorite. They played with him all the time. (Gilles Villemure)

When people ask me if harness racing is fixed, my answer is simple—"fix" is a big word. Fix is a very, very big word. You can get help in the race, but I don't think you should call that fixed. You have eight drivers; you might get help, but I don't think that's fixed. There were some fixed races, but the guys got caught, and they don't have a license anymore. They're out.

When I was driving, I wasn't aware of anything. But I knew one thing—in the race, the guys pop on the outside of you, and there's two things you can do. You let him go or you park him. If you want to help yourself win the race, if it's better to let him go, you let him go. If it's better to park him, you park him. And people say, "Oh, he let him go, he let him go," and they say it's fixed. It doesn't go that way.

It's an athletic competition. You have to do the best you can, and every race is different. There were some fixed races, of course, but the guys got caught and got thrown out, and they're still not racing.

I still go to the track. I go out to Belmont to watch thoroughbreds almost every Saturday. I go to The Meadowlands three or four times a year. They closed Roosevelt down. Yonkers is up, but barely—but if they get the slot machines it's going to come back, it's going to come back big time. They did it in Ontario and the game is big. They did it with Dover Downs; the purses are great, people are working—and I know New York State will do the same. They need those slot machines. The slots will make the difference.

Near Return

After I left the Rangers, I played only 21 more games in the National Hockey League with Chicago over two seasons. We didn't make the playoffs. But as it turned out, John

Ferguson almost brought me back to New York after he took over as head of the Rangers. Almost.

I can't remember who got hurt for the Rangers, but Fergie had me traded back to New York. Our third goaltender in Chicago got hurt, and they couldn't trade me anymore. As a matter of fact, I was back on Long Island for a week; we had a week off and I was hurt or something, and I heard Fergie said I was traded back to New York.

I was coming back, and I would have been happy to come back. I settled in New York after my playing career ended, so it would have been great to finish my career here. The Rangers were struggling at the time, but it still would have been nice to end my career where it all started, with the people I knew.

Why I Stayed

Even though I'm a French-Canadian, I decided to stay in the New York area after my playing days were over, and it's been home ever since.

I married an American girl. I've been married twice. My first wife came from East Northport, Long Island, which is why I stayed here. Then, my second wife came from Levittown. When I got divorced, my kids were young, and I could have gone to Edmonton. Glen Sather was in the World Hockey Association at the time, and he called me and said, "Gilly, I have a job for you. If you want to come out with us [as a player] for a year or two, you have a job." I said, "Glen, I can't do it. I have two young kids here, and I can't move away." I retired, but that's why I stayed here. It was because of my kids.

My kids and their ages: Denise, 37, Bobby, 36, Therese, 23, Natalie, 18 (she's the baby, just starting college).

Hall of Fame

One of the greatest things that ever happened to me just took place in January, 2002. I was inducted into the Trois Rivieres Sports Hall of Fame. There was a special ceremony, my wife, my kids and I went home, and about 700 people were there. All my friends were there, my family was there, my mom, my brothers. It was great thrill for me.

There are other names you might remember in that Hall of Fame. Andre "Moose" Dupont was selected a few years ago. I was in the Ranger organization with Moose before he went on to bigger and better things in Philadelphia. Rene Robert, one-third of Buffalo's French Connection line, is another name in there. Leon Rochefort, another ex-Ranger, who also played for a half-dozen other teams, is in there.

It was a very nice thing.

Rangers Alumni

Steve Vickers, Bill Chadwick and John Halligan are the three guys who started the Ranger Alumni Association. Now the Rangers have taken it over.

It was started to help former players in trouble. We had a golf outing, we had old-timer's games. Management of the organization would change every two or three years; it got put on the back seat for awhile, when nobody took care of it. Now we have a corporation, and we have people working for the Alumni now.

I do things connected with the organization, but I wish I could do more. We have golf outings once a year, a couple of games. We have the legends box at the Garden, and every game they sell this box to 20 or 30 people, and I go sit with the fans, sign autographs. I wish I could do more. I'm retired —just call me and I'll do it. I don't mind going places to represent the Rangers.

The Alumni events help me keep track of where the guys are now, and it's not easy.

As I've said, this was a very close group, on and off the ice. I could talk about 20 guys, all great guys. We used to have parties—Rod Seiling used to invite us all over to his house. We were a great bunch of guys who stuck together. Time and distance have separated us, but we still love getting together whenever we can, for whatever function.

Rod Gilbert is in New York working for the Rangers as the director of special projects and community. You knew when he was a player that Rod loved New York City and would never want to leave. He and New York got along well from the start.

Jean Ratelle was working for the Bruins but is retired now and has homes in Cape Cod and Florida.

Brad Park went back to work for the Rangers last year and is a pro scout covering seven other NHL teams and the minors. He'll be great at that.

Steve Vickers is living in Toronto.

Walter Tkaczuk owns his own golf course, River Valley Golf Resort, in the Toronto area.

Vic Hadfield owns two driving ranges in the Toronto area.

Billy Fairbairn is in the western part of Canada, Brandon, Manitoba. I see him once in a while.

Bruce MacGregor worked in Edmonton for all those years with Glen Sather and there was talk of him coming to New York with Slats, but that didn't happen.

Seiling works for the Toronto Hotel and Convention Bureau. Like me, he was in the horse game but is out of it now.

"The Chief," Jim Neilson, is living in the Winnipeg area.

Dale Rolfe is retired and living up north in Ontario, in

Gravenhurst, where they have about 20 feet of snow every winter.

Emile The Cat Francis is retired and living in Florida, playing a lot of golf.

Eddie Giacomin spends his time out west in Utah and Montana these days. I don't see him much. He comes around a couple of times a year for card shows and golf outings.

Peter Stemkowski lives on Long Island during the off season but is a broadcaster for the San Jose Sharks during the season, working their games on radio.

Bobby Rousseau is in Montreal, Bob Nevin in the Toronto area.

Ron Greschner, who joined us in 1974, is living in Florida.

Perhaps—no, certainly—the most unusual where-are- they-now on this team is Teddy Irvine. His son is a famous wrestler, Chris Jericho. The guy's a big deal in World Wrestling. Big name, one of the top guys. Teddy is in Winnipeg, in the financial planning business.

Three years ago, we had about 15 guys back here for a hockey game. It was great. A lot of stories. It's always great to see the guys whenever I can.

They Never Forget

One thing about New York Ranger fans—once you're in their hearts, they don't forget you. People still remember me around New York. I go on the train to go into the Garden, and people say, "Hey, Villemure?" They're looking at me, they know me. I go to restuarants or bars sometimes with my wife and they remember. They remember who we were.

It was a special time for hockey. It was a special time for the New York Rangers, and those people don't forget. A lot of them were right there when the Rangers finally won the Stanley Cup in 1994, and that's a special thing about hockey in New York.

14

A Little Help From My Friends:

Rod Seiling

"Gilles, through no fault of his own, took a long time to get to the National Hockey League. He was always a very good goaltender and certainly showed that during the years he was with the Rangers. He was much different than Eddie in style and temperment, and they complemented each other. Eddie got much more publicity, but I've always felt that Gilles was his equal. They both contributed to our overall success.

"Gilles's personality was much more easy going, kind of laid back, took things in stride, great temperment for a goaltender, was a great team player."

Rod Seiling and I spent a great deal of time together—both on the ice and at the racetrack. (New York Rangers)

On Villemure's love of horses and harness racing:

"I must have spent more time with Gilles than anybody on the team. We spent a lot of time at the racetrack. I'm out of it now—I retired to work in the horse racing industry. I had my own farm and owned horses but also ran a racetrack and did some things, and when I moved on, I was with the Ontario Jockey Club, which was the largest operator in North America. I wasn't allowed to own horses when I worked there, so I had to sell my horses, and I've just never gotten back into it. I bought my first horse (Gilles and I knew a guy at Roosevelt Raceway) and shipped it up here.

"We used to kid Gilly. Gilly was always buying horses, and we'd say, 'You sure you know how many horses you've got, and where are they and what are they doing?' Before we went to practice every morning, he and I would go to Roosevelt and jog and train horses. We had a great time—it was a great outlet from the wars of hockey. We really enjoyed it, and we got to know some people there. Gilles was responsible for my involvement with horses—if it wasn't for him, I wouldn't have gotten involved to the degree I did."

Is this the best team that never won a Stanley Cup?

"I would think so, but who knows—there are others that may disagree. But 'should have, could have'—all those markers apply to us, I guess. They're reasons, excuses, and at the end of the day, I guess that's all they were—excuses, because the simple fact is we *didn't* win. We were certainly good enough to win and should have won but did not win, and at the end of the day, I guess that's all that counts.

"There are players who never get as close as we did, but that still doesn't take it away. I think if you talk to the players on that team, the vast majority of them never did end up winning a Stanley Cup. If there's one missing element of their career, that would be it. It certainly is mine. I mean, I'm not lying awake at night crying over it, but certainly we all would love to have been able to say we were Stanley Cup winners, and we can't. To say we could is just it—the hockey gods were not kind to us."

Was there a feeling among guys on the team at the time that something would always happen in March to mess up April and May?

"I don't think so. You put that out of your mind. You think if we're good enough to win, we'll win, and you do your best, and, unfortunately, something came up during all those things that took away from the ultimate victory. The Ratelle injury and other factors certainly hurt, but you can also say good players play through those things."

On his feelings about Emile Francis:

"The Cat demanded—with reason—respect and was a very good hockey man, a tough taskmaster, but fair. He expected his players to be as competitive and as dedicated as he was. He never let up, and we went as hard the last day of training camp as we did the first day. That's the way he went at it. No one put more in the team on a personal commitment than he did. On the other hand, he expected his players to be the same.

"I've never seen a dressing room yet where the coach and general manager are universally loved, that's the nature of the beast. But, on the other hand, to give him his due, I think he was respected by all. Some may not have agreed with everything he did—I don't see how you can run a team and have every person on that team agree with everything you did. That's an impossibility. But I think it's equally truthful to say he was respected by everybody within that room."

On what it meant to him when the Rangers finally won the Stanley Cup in 1994:

"From my perspective, being an ex-Ranger, people stopped asking: 'When are the Rangers ever going to win a Stanley Cup?' From that perspective alone—I was pleased for the players that were there, don't get me wrong. But from a personal perspective, those questions stopped immediately. There's never been a question since, which is *nice*.

"I was watching [Game Seven against Vancouver] at home. I had the opportunity to go to New York to watch the game, and I just couldn't get away. It turned out to be quite a wise decision because they did pan down and show a whole bunch of ex-Rangers at the game. They had them stuck in their own corner there, and I would have had to dodge out of an important business meeting, and it would not have been a wise career move to have my picture flashed at the game at Madison Square Garden when I was supposed to be back here in Toronto at a meeting."

On his life as one of the Garden fans' whipping boys during his stay in New York:

"They weren't [nice to me]. I respect fans and their right to have opinions. I think it goes within reason, and I thought toward the end of my career in New York they far out-stripped that, and that's why I reacted back. I knew The Cat wasn't in a position to do anything—his own position was tenuous at best, and I just took matters into my own hands. I just made a few comments about the fans.

"It got nasty and very personal, and it got personal for my wife and kids and that's where I drew the line and said, 'Enough is enough.' I didn't think they had any right—do what you want, say what you want about me, but when you go at my family, that's where I draw the line.

"They were looking for someone to be a goon, and that wasn't me, nor would it ever have been me."

On missing New York in spite of the way the fans treated him:

"I still have friends there. I go back to New York on a regular basis. I think it's a great city. I love New York. I almost came back and worked there 10 or 12 years ago. But for reasons, nothing to do with New York, I'd be back there now. I actually accepted a job and then some other things came up. I love the city, I like what it has to offer and was just back two months ago with very good friends, other ex-players, for a surprise birthday party. I had a great time."

On his proudest achievement in hockey:

"I think the 1972 [Summit Series] team— Team Canada beating the Russians would be right up there. It's still marked as the greatest event in hockey, at least in [Canada], and I suspect anywhere. I just came back from Russia, and it's still the major topic over there."

15

A View of the Game

Best of the Blue

With the New York Rangers having passed the 75th anniversary of the start of the great franchise, I have seen some all-time Ranger teams pop up. Two lists came out at the turn of the new century, and we'll throw two more in here for you.

One list was by John Davidson, who came to New York to take over the goaltending from me and Eddie Giacomin and carried the Rangers to the Stanley Cup finals in 1979—another near miss.

Writing in John Halligan's great book, *New York Rangers, Seventy-Five Years*, J. D., who is now a great TV commentator, picked Mike Richter as the all-time Ranger goaltender, with Brad Park and Brian Leetch on defense, Mark Messier at center, Rod Gilbert on the right wing and Adam Graves on the left.

The game may be quicker today, but goaltenders had to make more saves back when I played. (Gilles Villemure)

The other list I saw in print appeared on NYRangers.com, as voted by the fans. There was only one difference from the Davidson picks—Vic Hadfield, the first Ranger to score 50 goals, was the left wing, instead of Graves, who also had a 50-goal season and now plays in San Jose.

Emile Francis, our great coach when I played with the Rangers, picks Chuck Rayner as the goaltender, Park and Leetch on defense (over Tim Horton, who wasn't with us that long but made quite an impression on The Cat while he was) and the GAG Line up front, all three of them.

Rayner? "I saw Rayner the year that the Rangers could have won the Stanley Cup [1950], and he carried them on his back," The Cat says. "He played there with hardly any support at all, as did Gump Worsley for a number of years."

My picks? Remember, I don't have the background going way back with the franchise. But I'll take a shot. And I'm only picking retired players.

How can I not go with Eddie Giacomin in goal? It wouldn't make sense. I had the pleasure of playing with that man for five years, and I know what he did to help put the Rangers at the top of the National Hockey League. True, Richter was able to win a Stanley Cup, and he even stopped Pavel Bure with that unbelievable penalty shot save, but Eddie's my choice as No. 1 overall.

On defense, my choices would be Brad Park and Harry Howell. Of course, Brian Leetch is still playing.

Up front, I have to go with the GAG Line—Rod Gilbert, Jean Ratelle and Vic Hadfield, with Gilbert in a close nod over Andy Bathgate, one of the greatest Rangers of all-time.

The Best I've Seen

We've talked about my all-time Ranger team. Now, it's on to the best I've seen overall.

In goal, I'd have to go with Kenny Dryden, Eddie Giacomin, Tony Esposito, Bernie Parent and Gerry Cheevers. In no particular order. It would be very, very tough to pick one guy out of that list.

Oh, by the way, they're all in the Hall of Fame.

Defense? Well, Bobby Orr. That's an easy one. Then I'd go with Brad Park and Denis Potvin, the great Islander defensemen.

Yes, these three are in the Hall of Fame, too.

On left wing, I'd have to go with Bobby Hull, the man with the incredible shot. Behind him, I'd have to name Frank Mahovlich.

Two Hall of Famers.

On right wing, Yvan Cournoyer was great. So was Rod Gilbert.

Two more Hall of Famers. I guess I have an eye for the better players.

Bigger Bodies . . . But

People are always telling me how the game has changed since I was playing. Remember, I left the National Hockey League a quarter of a century ago, so you know a lot of things have to be different. Heck, sometimes I have to read the standings in the paper every morning just to catch up on how many teams there are now. The league has grown 500 percent since I came in, and the players have grown, too.

The kids are more physical; they're bigger, stronger. You have to give them credit—they are. We didn't have all the stuff they have—the weight room, bicycles. We didn't have anything. And we had to work at other jobs during the off season. Now, they can work out, and they have their own personal trainers to help them stay in shape. These kids are in terrific shape these days. They work at it.

But I think the skill level in our day was better. Maybe people will disagree with me. But we had guys like Jean Ratelle, Stan Mikita, Guy LaFleur, all those guys, making plays. These days, very seldom do they make plays in the center. They shoot the puck in and go get it, play dump and chase. In our day, players carried the puck and made plays—we never shot the puck in. We just carried it in. That was a big difference, but now, because the kids are so big, they can't carry it in anymore. They take up the whole ice, some of these guys playing today.

We used to make more plays. We had more shots on goal. Many games were 40-45 shots. Now, if you see 25 shots a game, 30? ... that's a lot. There was more action back then, more shots—I mean, Phil Esposito had 15 shots on goal against me in one game. But I've seen some games in the last couple of years with the Rangers, in which there were 18, 15, 12 shots on goal. We handled the puck more, we took more chances, and maybe had more room to move which led to chances.

As the generation of new buildings grew in the NHL, they had the chance to make the surfaces bigger, which would have allowed the game itself to grow at the same rate as its players. The door was open, and they didn't walk in. Now, you've got these huge men playing this game on the same surface we played on, and there's just no room. This is a much bigger game now.

The game was better to watch then—the goaltenders had to make more saves. But now, it's quick—my God it's quick! Especially in the playoffs—you have no chance to do anything. You have to get rid of the puck because if you don't, you'll get in trouble. It's dangerous now, the kids are so strong —and there's not enough room on the ice.

Better? I was playing then, in the seventies, so I would ask the fans what was better to watch. It's hard for me to tell because I played the game. But more shots, more saves, more goals, more chances—I think that's the name of the game.

The game has changed in the way players settle things, too. Years ago, they used to drop the gloves. They have visors on their helmets now and that's changed everything. When I played, you fight, you fight for five minutes, 10 minutes, you're so tired you can't lift your arms up, you can't do anything. Some guys got hurt—cut, not hurt—but not usually.

There was one time that Bobby Hull had a broken jaw, and John Ferguson, one of the toughest there ever was, ripped the football helmet Hull was wearing off and broke the jaw again. But there was one time John Ferguson was good to Hull. Bobby was on the ice, and Fergie was on top of him and really could have pounded him. And he said, "Get up." He could have killed him, but Fergie backed out.

16

A Little Help From My Friends:

Bill Fairbairn

"Did anyone tell you about the thing that happened in Oakland?

"We flew into Oakland, and we had a practice. We had won a game, and we were going to have a practice in the morning, around 10 o'clock, and we all got to the rink, and Stemmer's idea came: 'let's get The Cat.' So, they filled his whistle up with shaving cream so it wasn't working, and then Stemmer got his gloves and filled them up; Dale Rolfe found a hammer and beat the crap out of his blades so it was hard for him to stand up, and then on the way out, we all headed out to the ice, and Stemmer put Vaseline all over the door handle so he couldn't really turn that.

"What Stemmer had done really made The Cat mad. He was in a bad mood in the first place, and he comes out on the ice, and he's madder than heck at what we had done, and he's going to really skate us, eh? But the thing was that Stemmer had talked to the rink guy to tell him after about 10 minutes to shut off all the lights. Well, Cat started skating us, and all the lights went off, and we had to leave the rink and there was no practice.

"We had a blast there. That was just part of a team—we knew what was going to happen. The Cat was mad, and he started skating us, and we knew the lights were going out.

"[Cat] just kinda giggled and that was it. He says, 'OK, you guys have had your fun—until the next practice.' That's the way he was."

On being part of such a close group:

"I wouldn't give up the years I played in New York with that team for anything. It was like one big family. We stuck together, not just on game days. When we had days off, we all got together, the wives got together, and everybody enjoyed each other. After practices we even hung around together. It's something that doesn't happen now in the game. I think it's more of a business than it was back then. I can really appreciate it because I have a lot of friends from back then. I don't get to see them that often but when we do it's just like we've never been apart. I don't know what I can say about that team, but it was a great team."

On the craziest guy he ever played with:

"Oh, I would think Stemmer. He was a case, that guy. He was a fun person that kept everybody laughing, all the time."

On The Cat:

"He worked so hard at it, and hard at it, and hard at it, and he had all the respect of all the players. He wasn't very big, but I'll tell ya, most of the guys were scared of him—I would say all of them—and really did want to win for him. I couldn't have had a better coach in hockey, ever. He got you going. He did a lot to get the team built up and everything else. He would do anything for the team and expected it back. Everybody respected him and would do anything for him."

On the Rangers' goaltending duo:

"I thought we had two of the best in the league. I think they competed against each other, even in practice, to see who would be the game goalie. They really had to work hard in practice, too. They were both exceptional goalies, and you don't usually get that on a team. Usually you have one that is quite a bit better than the other. We were lucky there to have two really exceptional goalies, even one who would come up big in a game. It was great for the team."

On Canadians living in New York:

"It was different. I have to admit that. Coming from a small town, like I did—Brandon, Manitoba—and going right into New York was kind of a shock. I think the big thing that really relaxed me and a lot of the players was the fans. The fans we had there were just great. They were just part of the team, too, and it kind of relaxed you on the ice. Outside the building, it was a different situation altogether, a little scary in the big city, but as soon as you got into the Garden and all the fans were there ... and we had good players and had winning teams there, and it made a difference. The fans and their backing just helped everybody fit in and work together. I couldn't have gone to a better city to play hockey."

Do you remember your first day in Manhattan?

"I don't remember the first one, but I remember back when Martin Luther King was shot. I was staying in a hotel and went outside. I think there were 10 policemen at every corner of the streets down there, and I was just going for a walk. I turned around and stayed in my hotel the rest of the day. It was a scary moment, and I think that was the first time I was brought up from Omaha to play. It was a scary time.

"As I said, though, once I got into the Garden, the fans kinda took care of you—they took you under their wing. They looked after you. You played well for them, they appreciated it. If you gave a 100 percent effort, they liked that. New York fans don't like to lose, I know that, but in those days when I first came up, we were winning, and we didn't lose too many at home that year, so that helped out a lot. It took a lot of the pressure off and made you feel more at home; just being in the Garden was a different matter than being outside."

On taking a hit to make a play:

"Even from my junior days, I was more or less kind of a hitter and a grinder. Nothing really bothered me. I felt more comfortable along the boards than the way the game's played now, with criss-crossing and everything else. And playing with Walter [Tkaczuk] was a big factor, too. We kinda read each other, and that helped a lot. He would give me the puck, and if I had to take a hit, he would be there to pick up the puck and vice-versa. Playing with a solid guy like him was a great help, too."

On the great Tkaczuk-Fairbairn penalty killing duo:

"When we first came up, The Cat came to us and just said we would be doing most of the penalty killing, and he wanted us because we were young, had a lot of speed and could take the bumps and grinds and it wouldn't wear us down. That was one of the main reasons, I think, he had us killing penalties."

On the Rangers finally winning the Cup in 1994:

"Once a Ranger, always a Ranger. Anybody that was ever on the Ranger team, even if they played for other teams before that ... I don't know, I think it's because of the city and everything else and the fans and everything. Just being part of a winning team is just great. Maybe we never did win the Cup while I was playing, but to be part of the Rangers when they won it is an honor."

On his fondest memory of his Ranger days:

"There are so many of them, but I guess going to the Stanley Cup against Boston. I guess that was the biggest feat and most important in my hockey career. Losing was a big disappointment, a real big disappointment. Every time I watch TV now, I just wonder if maybe there was a little more I could have done to get that Cup. But you can't, and it's hard when you see the Stanley Cup on there, and they show different teams winning and pointing to the Cup, and your name isn't there. It's pretty disheartening when you know you could have won that year.

"We had a few years there, even when the Islanders beat us out in overtime. We could have had a chance that year and the other year when Philly won it, and we had a chance, we were there. We were right there, three years in a row we could have won, but we didn't."

17

A New Beginning

———————

Sometimes, a guy you've played against and hated, in a hockey sense, anyway, winds up becoming your teammate. Sometimes, guys identified with one team suddenly wind up playing for that team's biggest rival. Derek Sanderson, Phil Esposito and Carol Vadnais all became Rangers; Jean Ratelle and Brad Park moved to the Bruins. It's the nature of the business.

On June 6, 2002, the Rangers named Bryan Trottier as their new head coach, replacing Ron Low. Bryan Trottier, Mr. Islander!

"He was a hard-working player. I would imagine that's the reason they got him," my old teammate, Billy Fairbairn, said of the new coach. "I had a lot of respect for Trottier, a lot of respect in those years. He wasn't a chippy, or a cheap hockey player. He was a hard-working hockey player. It would be a little different if it was somebody that didn't earn it, but he did, I think.

"He deserves it. He's a proven part of hockey as a player and a coach. I just hope he can swing the team the right way. We need to get into the playoffs."

No. 99, Wayne Gretzky, told the New York *Post*: "I think the Rangers made a great choice. I think they have a great coach ... he's very sharp. I'm sure he's going to succeed there."

Anyone who has ever worn the Ranger sweater hopes "The Great One" is right! And, you know, as soon as he does succeed, Trottier will be adopted by the Madison Square Garden faithful as one of their own.

18

A Little Help From My Friends:

Ted Irvine

Teddy Irvine took the shot that Peter Stemkowski converted into the winning goal in the third overtime period of that incredible game against Chicago in 1971.

"When you get in situations like that, you wonder where you get the adrenaline from to hang on. You just do. The conditioning pays off. I remember it more because I remember the picture more than anything else. The puck thrown into the corner—and what I remember was the explosion. I threw it out front, and Stemmer had deflected the puck in, and I think the explosion from the fans with that goal going in and then the reaction of the guys all jumping together—I think it was a relief that we were finally off the ice after a long game.

"The fans' explosion and roar—things like that happen so fast. It's a shot in the corner, it's out front and it's in the net, just like that, and you think, 'Why didn't you do that earlier?' That's what I remember more than anything else."

On how good that team really was:

"It was an outstanding team. To this day, people still talk about that team. I found, being on the line I was on, with Stemmer and MacGregor, and then Jerry Butler ... we all had a role on that hockey club, whether it be Bard Park, to Gilles Vullemure, to Eddie Giacomin, to Stemkowski or Irvine. That's what I found to be the biggest strength of that hockey club— we all respected each other and the role we had to play and what type of game that individual had to play well and do his job.

"There's no greater thrill in my life than being able to sit here and, say, Jean Ratelle would come to me and say, 'What a great goal you got, Teddy,' when he's one of the great goal scorers ever, or somebody would come to you and say, 'nice fight,' or 'way to backcheck,' and then you'd be going to those superstars and saying, 'Brad, nice play,' and 'Rod Seiling, nice defensive play.' I found it an unselfish bunch of guys. We all had a role to play, Emile Francis played us equally, and there was a lot of pride on that team, as far as respect for each other."

On wanting to win the Cup for Emile Francis:

"To this day as I sit and talk to my own family of all the things we don't have, there's that Stanley Cup ring. And when you get 30 years out of the game, you look back and say, 'What was it all about—yeah, it was fun and it was great playing New York and it was fun playing in front of the fans.' But you can't look at that finger and say you have that Stanley Cup ring. And Emile Francis was such a gentleman and a true ...

he was almost like a father to me. I remember that when I got traded from Los Angeles, he lent me money for my first house, and we look back now, all the things he did for us personally, how he protected us and how he stood up for us and how he scolded us and how he skated the heck out of us and taught us lessons. If you look back, there was such a relationship there with Emile, I think every one of the players would say the same thing. It would be nice to have a Stanley Cup ring, but, just ego-wise, it would be nice for Emile Francis to go into Boston and Montreal and say, 'Hey, I got one, too.' I think that hurts him more than anything, not having the ring. And us not giving Emile his day. I remember we played in Chicago against Billy Reay, and we had a team meeting before and Emile said, 'You guys go out and you'll fight your hearts out, and I'll stand up for you,' and during the game he was yelling at Billy Reay and he was going to fight Billy Reay. We just looked at him and said, 'Hey, this guy's on our side,' and not getting him the ring is just as important and sad as us not getting one either."

On what the players did to The Cat, as jokes:

"I remember a lot of things the boys did to Emile, and that's why I say what a man he was. We knew how far we could go with him as a coach and as a man. He let us go so far, but then there were other days, too, where you just stayed out of his way. When Emile wasn't happy with us ... we'd get off the plane, you talk about discipline, if we'd played a bad game, he'd get the ice somewhere, and we'd have to go from the airport right to the rink and he would skate the heck out of us. In Oakland, they turned the lights off, and Emile said, 'I don't care, these guys are still skating.'

"I remember a time we lost in Los Angeles, and they took us into Toronto. We got off the plane at four or five o'clock, and he skated the heck out of us for two hours and just wouldn't stop. No pucks, and he skated us and skated us and we were just dragging ourselves. I remember Walter Tkaczuk yelling, "One more time, Cat,' and away we'd go again. We're saying, 'Walter, SHUT UP!' But Emile, he skated us and skated us, but also there were times when he knew to let up a little bit, too.

"We used to do things to him. I remember what Vic Hadfield did to him. Emile had a habit of coming into the dressing room and picking up a piece of tape and throwing it in the garbage. That was kind of a routine he had. We were winning a little bit, so Vic just tied a string on to the tape and Emile bent over to pick it up and he just pulled it away from him. We had a great laugh and Emile was a good enough sport to laugh, too. But when we lost, he didn't think it was funny—he came after us pretty good."

On his rather famous son, wrestler Chris Jericho:

"Chris Jericho, Y2J, was born in Jericho, New York, a Ranger fan, still a huge Ranger fan, has an opportunity to play in Madison Square Garden in the Christopher Reeve Foundation game. He just absolutely loves his hockey, so he's played at the NHL All-Star Game and he's played at Madison Square Garden. This past year I had the chance to play against him, and he and I had a full-scale brawl at center ice, and I'm proud to say I gave it to my son."

How did the wrestling thing get started with Chris?:

"When we came back to Winnipeg when Chris was 15 or 16, he started lifting weights. He just said, 'Dad, I want to give it a try.' So we took him up to Calgary, and he went to wrestling school, and that's been his dream and love. He worked very, very hard at it, and now he's one of the top wrestlers in the world."

And he's making more money than hockey players of his dad's era ever dreamed of:

"He says to me every day, 'I calculated out what you'd make now—that one year you got 26 goals, you'd be worth about $4 million today.' But, you know, I never regret anything. Emile Francis paid us very well. In those days, with inflation, we were paid very well, we were treated very well, and you couldn't give me the money in trade for the memories we had or the closeness of that hockey team. For six years, I'd died and gone to heaven, to play in the Big Apple with that group of guys—you can have all the money in the world, that's one of my greatest memories ... the Billy Fairbairns and the Stemkowskis, and Eddie Giacomin and Whitey Villemure. All the guys. Brad Park always says to me, 'Why don't you write a book, Teddy?' because I can tell stories about all those guys and the fun we had on and off the ice."

On negotiating with Emile Francis:

"My first negotiation, I was on the second year of a contract. I came from Los Angeles, they weren't paying me a lot, and Emile renegotiated right away. He paid me $19,000 for two years. I had a pretty good year that one year, and I went in there in training camp, and I said, 'Emile, I'm making 19 this year, but I think I deserve more, I had a pretty good year.' He says, 'Yeah, Teddy, you did, but you're under contract,' and he says, 'What are you gonna do if I don't sign you?' I said, 'I have a standing offer to go back home and work for another company.' He says, 'They're a great company and good luck to you,' and I went, 'Uh-oh.' He says, 'What do you think you're worth?' I said, 'I think I'm worth $25,000.' He says, 'Teddy, I'll give you $27,500.' I walked out of there, and I said to Billy Fairbairn, 'I think something's wrong, I think I was supposed to ask for $30,000, and they gave me $27,500. I don't think I'm supposed to ask for 25 and they give me 27-5.' He was more than fair with me.

"The following year he did the same thing for me and said, 'We want to keep you here,' and ripped up my contract. I got real bold and said I wanted points bonuses and stuff like that. He said, 'Teddy, I'll tell ya what, I'll give you an extra thousand dollars, forget the point bonuses." He was a good, fair man to all of us."

On his greatest moment with the Rangers:

"I think the game we beat Boston in Boston, the fifth game [in 1972] when they had the Stanley Cup in the dressing room, and we came back. I was so proud of the guys when we left that building. I was proud of them there. I was proud of them some of the nights in Philadelphia, when we went out of that building and the fans were rocking our bus—I was proud of that. Those are memories I have—the year I got 26 goals, but more team stuff.

"I think the biggest thing is, I can remember games where we played in Vancouver, Los Angeles and Oakland, any place we went everybody wanted a shot at the Big Apple, and the guys had to perform to another level. I remember we lost to Los Angeles, and we flew all the way to Montreal, and Montreal had a heck of a hockey club, and we had a brutal practice and we went into Montreal. I always thought, 'How the heck did we do that—right in the Montreal Forum, we beat them.' There were so many things I remember, but I think [playing for] the Stanley Cup was probably the highest moment of my career and the lowest at the same time. To this day, I can relive that game over and over again, with Bobby Orr taking that puck and the spin-a-rama. But the game before, when Bobby Rousseau scored, and we beat them in the Boston Garden, and they had the Stanley Cup in the dressing room and their napkins made up and everything else. I was really proud of the guys.

"That's the biggest thing I found about the Rangers— the guys stuck together and came up with some huge wins— and how guys fought back. Rod Gilbert wasn't the toughest guy in the world, Rod Seiling wasn't the toughest guy in the world, and they went into some buildings and guys ran the heck out of them. I know guys came looking for them."

On the things the players did to Emile Francis:

"We played in Los Angeles, and we were brutal. We flew all the way from Los Angeles to Montreal, and I'm afraid the guys had a little too much to drink on the airplane. We got to Montreal, we had a night off and a day off, but we hadn't played well, and Emile also knew we had a few drinks on the airplane. We're in Montreal, we went out for a nice dinner and a few more beers, and the next day at practice it was embarrassing. Emile stopped the practice, it was so embarrassing. We went and beat Montreal that night, and we were just quiet on the bus. Emile came on the bus, and he just said, 'Don't you guys ever do that to me again, play that bad and be so stupid off the ice.' As he sat down, his hat was crushed again. The guys used to crush his hat all the time, but that was a tough time to do it. Emile turns around and says, 'Chiefy

Ted Irvine's famous son, wrestler Chris Jericho, loves to play hockey too. Here, father and son get into it during a 2002 charity game. (Ronald Asadorian /Splashnews)

or Rolfy, whoever did this,' and we all looked at these guys and said, 'Guys, don't get us in more trouble.'

"Then there was the time in Montreal, the reporters were looking for Emile Francis in the lobby of the hotel, and Stemmer said, 'Emile Francis is the only guy that goes up to his room with next year's draft list, compared to the rest of us— we go out looking for women.' But he got his hat crushed so many times. He knew it was going to be squashed, but he didn't say anything about it."

On the Rangers finally winning the Stanley Cup:

"For years, on the golf course, when I putted, I used to say to my partners, 'Don't put any pressure on me, we haven't won anything since '40.' Then, when these guys won it, I was very proud of them of. You're happy for the franchise. It's nice for the players, and Messier was so important, but the Ranger fans and the franchise, it takes the pressure off, because it's been a glorious franchise. Yes, you're proud. I went down in '98 and got an Alumni ring, and I wear it to this day. My son Chris said, 'Dad, you don't wear jewelry.' I said, 'This one I will.'

"I remember the year we lost, 1971-72, the following year they had the Team Canada thing, and Team Canada came through here with Brad and Rod Seiling and Rod Gilbert and Vic Hadfield and Ratelle. I remember Don Awrey came over to our table when they played in Winnipeg and he stuck out his hand with this Stanley Cup ring, kind of 'just what you guys lost,' and we were all ready to deck him, but it was a Team Canada type of thing. And we lost, that was the difference—they had it and we didn't."

GILLES VILLEMURE'S CAREER RECORD

REGULAR SEASON

Year	Team / League	GP	Min	W	L	T	GA	GAA
58-59	Trios-Rivieres Reds QJHL							
	Troy Bruins IHL	3	180	1	2	0	18	6.00
59-60	Guelph Biltmores OHAJr	35	1980				128	3.66
60-61	New York Rovers EHL	51	3060	16	34	1	223	4.37
61-62	Long Island Ducks EHL	65	3900	25	39	1	242	3.72
	Charlotte Checkers EHL	1	60	0	1	0	7	7.00
	Johnstown Jets EHL	1	60	1	0	0	2	2.00
62-63	Vancouver Canucks WHL	70	4200	35	31	4	228	3.26
63-64	Baltimore Clippers AHL	66	3960	31	33	2	192	2.91
	New York Rangers NHL	5	300	0	2	3	18	3.60
64-65	Vancouver Canucks WHL	60	3676	27	26	6	212	3.46
65-66	Vancouver Canucks WHL	69	4178	32	34	3	223	3.20
66-67	Baltimore Clippers AHL	70	4180	34	27	9	238	3.42
67-68	New York Rangers NHL	4	200	1	2	0	8	2.40
	Buffalo Bisons AHL	37	2160	18	13	6	89	2.47
68-69	New York Rangers NHL	4	240	2	1	1	9	2.25
	Buffalo Bisons AHL	62	3674	36	12	14	148	2.42
69-70	Buffalo Bisons AHL	65	3714				156	2.52
70-71	New York Rangers NHL	34	2039	22	8	4	78	2.30
71-72	New York Rangers NHL	37	2129	24	7	4	74	2.09
72-73	New York Rangers NHL	34	2040	20	12	2	78	2.29
73-74	New York Rangers NHL	21	1054	7	7	3	62	3.53
74-75	New York Rangers NHL	45	2470	22	14	6	130	3.16
75-76	Chicago BlackHawks NHL	15	797	2	7	5	57	4.29
76-77	Chicago BlackHawks NHL	6	312	0	4	1	28	5.38
TEN (10) NHL SEASONS		2 051	1581	100	64	29	542	2.81

POST-SEASON

Year	Team	GP	Min	W	L	GA	GAA
59-60	Guelph Biltmores OHAJr	5	300			19	3.80
62-63	Vancouver Canucks WHL	7	429	3	4	27	3.78
64-65	Vancouver Canucks WHL	5	309	1	4	17	3.30
65-66	Vancouver Canucks WHL	7	420	3	4	27	3.86
66-67	Baltimore Clippers AHL	9	569	4	5	39	4.11
67-68	Buffalo Bisons AHL	5	247	1	3	15	3.64
68-69	New York Rangers NHL	1	60	0	1	4	4.00
	Buffalo Bisons AHL	6	360	2	4	19	3.17
69-70	Buffalo Bisons AHL	14	875	11	3	31	2.13
70-71	New York Rangers NHL	2	80	0	1	6	4.50
71-72	New York Rangers NHL	6	360	4	2	14	2.33
72-73	New York Rangers NHL	2	61	0	1	2	1.97
73-74	New York Rangers NHL	1	1	0	0	0	0.00
74-75	New York Rangers NHL	2	94	1	0	6	3.83
SIX (6) NHL POSTSEASONS		14	656	5	5	32	2.93

NEW YORK RANGERS PLAYOFF RESULTS DURING GILLES VILLEMURE'S TIME WITH THE TEAM

1971

Game	Date	Opponent	Score	Result
1	Apr. 7	Toronto	5-4	W
2	8	Toronto	1-4	L
3	10	@Toronto	1-3	L
4	11	@Toronto	4-2	W
5	13	Toronto	3-1	W
6	15	@Toronto	2-1	W (ot)

Rangers win quarterfinals, 4-2

1	Apr. 18	@Chicago	2-1	W (ot)
2	20	@Chicago	0-3	L
3	22	Chicago	4-1	W
4	25	Chicago	1-7	L
5	27	@Chicago	2-3	L (ot)
6	29	Chicago	3-2	W (3 ot)
7	May 2	@Chicago	2-4	L

Blackhawks won semifinals, 4-3

1972

1	Apr. 5	Montreal	3-2	W
2	6	Montreal	5-2	W
3	8	@Montreal	1-2	L
4	9	@Montreal	6-4	W
5	11	Montreal	1-2	L
6	13	@Montreal	3-2	W

Rangers won quarterfinals, 4-2

1	Apr. 16	@Chicago	3-2	W
2	18	@Chicago	5-3	W
3	20	Chicago	3-2	W
4	23	Chicago	6-2	W

Rangers won semifinals, 4-0

1	Apr. 30	@Boston	5-6	L
2	May 2	@Boston	1-2	L
3	4	Boston	5-2	W
4	7	Boston	2-3	L
5	9	@Boston	3-2	W
6	11	Boston	0-3	L

Boston won finals, 4-2

Cont.

1973

Game	Date	Opponent	Score	Result
1	Apr. 4	@Boston	6-2	W
2	5	@Boston	4-2	W
3	7	Boston	2-4	L
4	8	Boston	4-0	W
5	10	@Boston	6-3	W

Rangers won quarterfinals, 4-1

1	Apr. 12	@Chicago	4-1	W
2	15	@Chicago	4-5	L
3	17	Chicago	1-2	L
4	19	Chicago	1-3	L
5	24	@Chicago	1-4	L

Blackhawks won semifinals, 4-1

1974

1	Apr. 10	@Montreal	4-1	W
2	11	@Montreal	1-4	L
3	13	Montreal	2-4	L
4	14	Montreal	6-4	W
5	16	@Montreal	3-2	W (ot)
6	18	Montreal	5-2	W

Rangers won quarterfinals, 4-2

1	Apr. 20	@Philadelphia	0-4	L
2	23	@Philadelphia	2-5	L
3	25	Philadelphia	5-3	W
4	28	Philadelphia	2-1	W (ot)
5	30	@Philadelphia	1-4	L
6	May 2	Philadelphia	4-1	W
7	5	@Philadelphia	3-4	L

Flyers won semifinals, 4-3

1975

1	Apr. 8	Islanders	2-3	L
2	10	@Islanders	8-3	W
3	11	Islanders	3-4	L (ot)

Islanders won prelinary round, 2-1

ALL-TIME RANGER SHUTOUTS,
INCLUDING PLAYOFFS

GOALTENDER	REGULAR SEASON	PLAYOFFS	TOTAL
Ed Giacomin	49	1	50
Dave Kerr	40	7	47
John Ross Roach	30	5	35
Mike Richter	24	9	33
Chuck Rayner	24	1	25
Gump Worsley	24	0	24
Lorne Chabot	21	2	23
John Vanbiesbrouck	16	2	18
Andy Aitkenhead	11	3	14
GILLES VILLEMURE	**13**	**0**	**13**
John Davidson	7	1	8
Glenn Healy	7	0	7
Johnny Bower	5	0	5
Jacques Plante	5	0	5
Wayne Thomas	5	0	5
Jim Henry	4	1	5
Steve Baker	3	0	3
Cesare Maniago	2	0	2
Eddie Mio	2	0	2
Marcel Paille	2	0	2
Hal Winkler	2	0	2
Glen Hanlon	1	1	2
Bill Beveridge	1	0	1
Bob Froese	1	0	1
Ken McAuley	1	0	1
Jack McCartan	1	0	1
Terry Sawchuk	1	0	1
Doeg Soetaert	1	0	1
Steve Weeks	1	0	1
Joe Miller	0	1	1
TOTALS	**304**	**34**	**338**

Trivia Answers

 # 1 *Vic Hadfield has the Ranger record for power-play goals in a season, with 23 in 1971-72.*

 # 2 *Frank Boucher suffered the most losses by a Ranger coach (243), while Lester Patrick was third (216).*

 # 3 *The Chicago Blackhawks are the only one of the original six the Rangers haven't faced in the finals. The Blueshirts have met Toronto three times, Detroit and Boston twice each, and Montreal once. Toronto is the only one of the group the Rangers have beaten in a final series, and it happened twice (1933 and 1940).*

 # 4 *John Vanbiesbrouck, "The Beezer", has the only other Ranger Vezina, winning it in 1985-86.*

 # 5 *Walter Tkaczuk has played in more playoff games than any other Ranger, 93.*

 # 6 *Sergei Zubov's 89 points in 1993-94 (the Stanley Cup season) ranks second on the Rangers' all-time list for points in a season by a defenseman, while Brad Park's 82 in 1973-74 was fifth.*

 # 7 *The Rangers beat the Los Angeles Kings, New York Islanders and Philadelphia Flyers to reach the 1979 Stanley Cup finals, going 10-3 before winning the first game of the final series against Montreal and then losing four straight to come up short again.*

 # 8 After the three members of the 1,000-game club, defenseman/center Ron Greschner is next on the Rangers' all-time list, playing in 982 games.

 # 9 Pierre Jarry and Don Maloney are the two Rangers who scored goals eight seconds apart. Jarry scored at 11:03 and 11:11 of the third period against California on Nov. 21, 1971 at Madison Square Garden, and Maloney tallied at 12:48 and 12:46 of the third at Philadelphia, March 12, 1987.

 # 10 Mike Richter played 45 games during the 2000-01 season, while Kirk McLean appeared in 23, Guy Hebert in 13, Vitali Yeremyev in 4, Johan Holmqvist in 2, and Jason LaBarbara in 1.

Get a JOB!

10 Steps to Career Success

KATHLEEN BRADY

PORTLAND • OREGON
INKWATERPRESS.COM

*Scan this QR Code
to learn more about
this title*

Publisher: Inkwater Press

Paperback
ISBN-13 978-1-59299-918-7 | ISBN-10 1-59299-918-2

ePub
ISBN-13 978-1-59299-826-5 | ISBN-10 1-59299-826-7

Kindle
ISBN-13 978-1-59299-827-2 | ISBN-10 1-59299-827-5

Printed in the U.S.A.
All paper is acid free and meets all ANSI standards for archival quality paper.

1 3 5 7 9 10 8 6 4 2

Contents

From the Author

Dear Job Hunter,

GET A JOB! These three powerful words often leave people paralyzed. Whether you are looking for your first job or a new job, the process can be daunting.

While there are many books and resources available to assist you with specific aspects of job hunting, like self-assessment, writing resumes, interviewing and negotiating offers, **GET A JOB!** provides a comprehensive game plan that shows *how* all these pieces work in tandem. It offers practical instructions to show you exactly *how* to conduct meaningful self-assessment and *how* to craft a winning resume and cover letters. It describes *how* to network, *how* to interview effectively and *how* to negotiate and evaluate offers. The advice is specific, yet generic enough to be applicable across industry lines and experience levels.

My vision is for you to use this publication as you would a travel guide. Like a travel guide, you will want to skim through **GET A JOB!** to get a lay of the land. Next, you'll want to zero in on the chapter related to where you are on the job hunting continuum. As you work through the various exercises and activities, the book will direct you to other areas that will be helpful to you as you work your way through the process. I have left ample space for you to make lists, take notes and highlight information. The book is designed so that you can jump around to reference the information you need at any given moment in your search.

Keep in mind, there is no one-size fits all approach to job hunting. The world of work is evolving every day; so is the hiring process. Worry less about doing it "right" and focus more on how your job search actions impact the image you are trying to project. Do your actions scream "confident" or "desperate?" Review these best practices, add your own wisdom and creativity, and be fearless in your approach!

GET A JOB! is the travel guide for the most important journey of your life. Refer to it repeatedly throughout your career. Add notes and build on lessons learned and successes achieved. But most of all, enjoy the ride!

Wishing you great success,

Kathleen Brady, CPC
Brady & Associates, Career Planners, LLC
www.careerplanners.net
www.Facebook.com/KBCareerPlanners

CHAPTER ONE

Introduction to Career/Life Planning

TO BE SUCCESSFUL AT LANDING YOUR DREAM JOB, YOU MUST first consider the impact your work will have on your life. Every job choice you make will impact the quality of your career, which in turn will affect your entire life. These choices will impact your long term earning potential, your social circle, where you will live, if and who you will marry... everything. Therefore, the sooner you decide what you want long term and what you are prepared to sacrifice short term, the happier you will be. Whether you are 25, 45 or 65, whether you are looking for your first job or a career change, the rest of your life starts right now!

The good news is that despite current economic conditions there ARE jobs to be had at EVERY level. It does not matter if you are looking for your first job or a mid-career change, the job search process is exactly the same. The people who are going to be successful at landing their dream jobs are the people who know how to conduct an effective job search and are willing to put in the time and effort to get them. Reading **GET A JOB!** and completing the exercises throughout the book will enable you to be one of those successful people.

Job hunting is like learning to drive a car. No one is born knowing how to drive or how to conduct a job search--yet both are very learnable skills. It is simply a matter of learning the rules.

Most people spend more time planning a weekend road trip than they do planning their career or life. Think about the last trip you planned. You likely chose a destination based on specific criteria about how you enjoy spending your time and selected the best route to get there. Before you started your trip you probably made sure your vehicle was operating at optimal performance and gassed up the tank. Perhaps you bought maps or invested in a GPS system, stocked a cooler with bottled water and snacks and made sure your jumper cables were in the trunk, just in case of an emergency. You packed your suitcase with everything you would need for your time away to ensure a safe and pleasant journey.

Why not apply the same process towards mapping out a career/life strategy? Think about what you like to do and where the best place to do it might be. Gather the tools you need (skills and education), plan for possible emergencies and you will have a safe and pleasant journey.

Some of you may be thinking, *"I haven't got time to be thinking about this stuff. I need to find a job!"* But unless you pause to consider your options and map out your strategy, the choices you make today may take you in a direction you don't want to go.

Too many people choose the path of least resistance and end up living an unfulfilled life. As a career coach, I've seen it countless times. For example, a finance major encountering a competitive job market opts to accept Uncle Lou's offer to work construction at his company. A perfectly fine job for someone who wants to do construction, but limiting for a person interested in working on Wall Street. Short term, the money may be good, but long term, this job does not take that finance major any closer to the ultimate goal of working on Wall Street.

Similarly, some people avoid facing a tough job market by enrolling in graduate school, believing the added credential will ensure success. However, unless graduate school fits into your predetermined career plans, hiding out in graduate school until the economy improves simply exchanges one set of problems for another. While it allows you to avoid any timing gap on your resume, it also forces you to incur additional debt. Graduate school could add upwards of $100,000 to your debt burden, which would seriously limit your career options. An unpaid internship in your field/industry of interest which allows you to expand your network and develop industry knowledge or volunteer work at any not-for-profit organization to build your skill set may be better options. They provide you with an opportunity to gain valuable experience without incurring any additional debt.

Any action that takes you towards a goal you are not interested in achieving, is not worth taking. It is better to put your energy into finding a job that you actually want. HOWEVER--and this is huge--that does NOT mean you can hide out indefinitely playing XBox until the job market improves. You MUST be taking action towards achieving your goals every day. That's why it is so important to first *define* your goals.

Career theorists have examined a multitude of variables that influence career choice at different points throughout the life cycle and remind us that career planning is a continuous process of choices and adjustments. Career planning requires a focused but flexible plan that allows you to move towards your goals while at the same time positioning yourself to be prepared to react to changing circumstances that are inevitable through the course of your life.

Studies suggest that during your twenties and early thirties, you are likely to:

- commit to an occupation, lifestyle, spouse;
- focus on "establishing" yourself within your chosen profession;
- concentrate on your career "advancement," with a vision toward the future.

Typically, the career trajectory during this phase is a steep incline with well defined benchmarks to assess growth.

Sometime during your late thirties and early forties, you may:

- discover your choices are no longer rewarding;
- experience a "period of crisis" as the result of some life altering event (death of a parent, birth of a child, divorce, etc.)
- become more specific about your needs, focusing on the here and now;
- reassess your choices;
- accept your current situation or opt for change

The trajectory during this stage is less steep and in some instances even flat. At this stage you have proven what you can do and now you are deciding if you still **want** to do it. For some, this period provides an opportunity to reap the benefits of years of hard work; they allow their careers to operate on automatic pilot while they tend to other facets of their life. For others, it is a time of discontentment and frustration as they try to determine what lies ahead.

By the time they reach their late forties and early fifties, most people are old enough to have acquired considerable life experience and to have learned from it, yet young enough to act on it and make the necessary course corrections by readjusting goals and shifting priorities. People may opt to change careers, change lifestyles or change both. They may also opt to do nothing. Recognize that opting to do nothing is a choice too.

Whatever stage you are at, ask yourself, *what do I really want to do?* Not what makes sense or what your spouse, parents or friends want you to do, but what do YOU really want to do? What do you want to accomplish, what roles do you want to have and what possessions do you want to acquire during your lifetime? During the next five years? The next year? Allow yourself to dream at this stage. Dreams foster hope and open our minds to the possibilities. Do not allow limiting beliefs, previous disappointments, criticisms or failures to stifle your dreams. Ask yourself, *"what might I attempt if I knew I could not fail?"*

With the dream firm in your mind, the next step is to think about what you need to do to make those things happen. You will be amazed at what you can accomplish when you are clear about what you want and have an action plan in place to guide you. Your goals must be measurable and should have both long and short term components that are time, task, and resource specific. **Write this information down.** Written goals make dreams physically real. They provide a long term vision of the kind of person you want to be and the kind of life you want to lead.

If your goals do not move you, if they do not inspire and incite you to action, they are not the right goals. Too many people try to alter themselves to suit their "should" goals. That is a bit like wearing the wrong size shoe because it goes with your outfit. It can work for a short time, but eventually it becomes uncomfortable and ultimately unbearable. Therefore, don't "should" all over yourself.

The right goals outweigh any excuses you have to achieve them. It won't matter if you don't have any experience or have too much experience or went to the "wrong" school or selected a "useless" major or are male or female, black or white, gay or straight. Your passion and commitment to your goal will fuel your efforts.

Do not underestimate the power of passion throughout this process. The world is filled with examples of people who achieved their goals—against all odds—because of their passion. Consider Neil Parry, the San Jose State football player whose right leg was amputated below the knee after a horrific injury in a game during the 2000 season. Hours after his leg was removed, Parry vowed he would play football again, an unlikely proposition under the circumstances. Yet, in September 2003, Parry was back on the field and fans were hard pressed to notice a difference between his abilities and those of his two-legged teammates. It wasn't easy but he had the drive and passion to withstand 25 operations and countless hours of rehabilitation and physical therapy to achieve his goal. If you allow yourself to be fueled by your internal drive instead of any external pressures, your shortcomings will have little or no impact on your ability to succeed. They may present hurdles, but your passion will galvanize your abilities, skills, strengths and talents so you can easily clear the bar.

EXERCISE #1: Develop Your Dream Action Plan

1. List the 10 to 12 most important things you want to accomplish during your lifetime. Invest the time to seriously think about this. Do this over a period of a few days or even weeks. Do not worry about whether or not these things are practical or even possible just yet. Allow yourself to dream. When you are satisfied with your list, date it. These are your **LIFETIME GOALS.**

_____

_____

_____

_____

_____

_____

_____

_____

_____

_____

2. From that **LIFETIME** list, select the 4 or 5 things you want to accomplish in the next 5 years to create your **5-YEAR PLAN.**

_____

_____

_____

_____

3. Review your 5-year plan and choose the 2 or 3 things you want to accomplish during the coming year. These are your **ANNUAL GOALS.**

_____

_____

_____

_____

4. For each **ANNUAL GOAL** listed, write down the answer to the following questions.
   - WHAT is the goal?

- WHY do I want to achieve this goal?

- WHEN will I achieve this goal?

- HOW will I achieve this goal? (Or: *What 3 things do I need to DO?*)

- WHO can help me achieve this goal?

Repeat this process once a year, referring back to your LIFETIME GOALS and 5-YEAR PLAN. Revise each list as circumstances warrant. Once you are clear about what you want and have an action plan in place to guide you, you will see just how possible the "impossible" can be.

By following the steps outlined in this book, you will be well on your way to securing the job—and ultimately the career and life--you want. These pages provide guidance to assist you in evaluating your natural abilities and transferable skills, drafting resumes and cover letters, identifying opportunities, perfecting your networking skills, preparing for interviews, negotiating and evaluating offers and starting your new job successfully.

A job search does not have to be overwhelming. You simply need to be DRIVEN to succeed.

Define your "product" through self-assessment exercises (Chapter Three)

Research the world of work and possible career paths (Chapters Five, Six and Seven)

Inform others of your talents by crafting effective resumes and cover letters (Chapter Four)

Verbalize you talents by perfecting your interview skills (Chapter Eight)

Evaluate offers and their impact on your long term goals (Chapter Nine)

Navigate the journey. (Chapter Ten)

To get yourself started, decide how much time and effort you are willing to devote to your search. Maintaining a steady and consistent effort throughout your search will be one of the most important elements in determining your success. Accept that there will be peaks and valleys in the process. There will be days with a great deal of activity and positive feedback and there will be days when you feel like you will never find a job. Those are the days it is important to find a way to reenergize and motivate yourself. Spend time with friends and family, tackle a long overdue project, volunteer your services, whatever you need to do to remind yourself of your gifts, talents and competencies. And remember, this is a temporary situation.

Because each job choice you make throughout your career is likely to have an enormous impact on your life, getting started can be scary and overwhelming. Do it anyway. I promise, the rewards will be worthwhile.

CHAPTER TWO

PLOT YOUR COURSE: How to Launch Your Job Search

TYPICALLY JOB SEEKERS START THEIR SEARCH IN THE MIDDLE OF the process instead of at the beginning. They start by drafting a resume, simply listing all their experiences in reverse chronological order. But a resume needs to be more than just a laundry list of your education, employers and job titles. A resume is a sales document; it is your marketing brochure. To ensure you design an effective one you have to know what you have to sell AND you have to understand who your target audience is. That is why the chapter on resumes comes in the middle of the book and not at the beginning.

The job search is not a linear process; it is typically not even a logical process. It is more complex than that. It involves three phases that sometimes overlap with each other:

Phase 1   SELF ASSESSMENT
During this phase, the focus is inwards. You have to know
what *value* you have to offer employers, so you must invest
time to:
- identify your values, skills and abilities
- recognize your special knowledge
- evaluate your experiences
- list your accomplishments
- acknowledge your educational level
- recognize your preferred work styles
- consider your temperament
- examine your interests
- evaluate your motivations
- set goals

Phase 2   MARKET ASSESSMENT
The focus during this phase is outwards. Knowing what
value you have to offer, you now must learn which employers need your abilities, skills and talents. During this phase
you must:
- review job postings
- research individuals, organizations and communities
- talk to business associates, friends and family members
- read trade papers, blogs, websites
- develop contact lists
- conduct informational interviews

Phase 3   IMPLEMENTATION
It is only after you understand what you have to offer and
who needs what you have to offer that you can focus on the
mechanics of the job search. Now it is time to:

- draft resumes, cover letters and applications (revise as needed)
- interview for positions
- negotiate salaries
- evaluate offers

But remember, the job search process is not as linear as these steps suggest. It is circular and continuous. For example, information discovered during market research may require you to revisit Phase 1 and revise your goals or rework your resume. An unsuccessful interview in Phase 3 may point you back to Phase 2 to do more in-depth market research. Every step along the way is meant to teach you something about yourself or about the world of work. It can be overwhelming and disorienting, like being lost on a road trip, but, you may just discover a path you had not even considered. Be open to the journey.

Implement the winning formula:

Self-Assessment + Market-Assessment = Career Success!

Phase 1: Self-Assessment

Ask yourself: *What is my dream job?* Don't worry, *for the moment,* if the job makes sense or if you are overqualified, underqualified, too young, too old, etc. Don't worry about pay scales or additional training needed. For the moment, just think about what you would like to **do**. Once you identify the dream, the practicalities will come into play to shape the direction of your job search. The trick is to not let those practicalities stifle the dream prematurely. There may be ancillary careers that can put you in the arena of your dream job.

For example, let's suppose the dream job is to be a pitcher for the New York Yankees. Rather than simply dismiss that as an impractical dream, brainstorm what other positions might be available that incorporate a passion for baseball with your current skill set. Are there positions at organizations such as Major League Baseball, Tops Baseball Cards, Spalding, Nike, the players' union, etc.? What firms/companies do work with or for the owners, players or specific teams? Have any of the players established youth baseball camps, restaurants or clothing lines? What role could you play in those ventures? Think creatively. Think big. Once you have a general direction, it will be easier to strategize how to get there.

Some people are unclear what the dream is. If that is where you are stuck, try to imagine it is six months from today and you are in your dream job. Do not worry for a moment what the job IS, just try to identify how things would be different in your day to day life. Think through the details; what time are you waking up, how are you dressing, what is your commute like, are you in an office or in the field, are you meeting with people or dealing with data, what time are you getting home, how do you feel? The more details the better. The answers to those questions will offer some insight into the types of positions you ought to research further.

You have the power to create the career—and the life—you want. It is simply a matter of deciding *what* you want and then *choosing* to invest the necessary time, energy and resources to move you in that direction. You *can* accomplish everything you want and you *can* achieve life/work balance, providing you are willing to do what it takes to achieve your goals.

We all have some idea of what we *want*—a better job, more money, love, a bigger house, a nicer car, etc. Yet we don't often think about *why* we want it. The answer to why is really the goal. We also neglect to ask what we need to *do*, what actions we need to *take* or what *choices* we need to make to get those things. We get caught up in things that keep us busy but do not contribute to our life's happiness; we confuse activity with accomplishment. We don't pay attention to the choices we are making that may hinder our success.

Think about success for a minute. What does it look like? Odds are, every person reading this has a different answer. However, there are four common elements in every vision of success. They are:

1. being content about your life;

2. achieving measurable accomplishments that compare favorably to others with similar goals;

3. believing that you have a positive impact on people you care about most;

4. leaving a legacy.

Each element contributes to the way you experience success **right now**. Success is NOT merely a future event or something to aspire towards. Think of it also as a current state of being: the ability to pay full and undivided attention to what matters most in your life at any given moment. Recognize that what matters most evolves over time and may require making different choices.

Everything you do requires a choice. There are the big choices: where to live, what career path to follow, who to share your life with, your faith, etc. Then there are the small choices: what time to wake up each morning; what to eat, what to wear, how to spend the day, how to respond to people and events. The small choices seem inconsequential. Some people would argue they aren't really choices at all, but rather decisions dictated by life's external pressures or requirements.

But they are choices.

You choose to get up at 6 a.m. to catch the 7:09 train to get to work despite the fact you'd rather sleep till noon because you know that the price you would have to pay to sleep till noon is too high. If your goal truly is to sleep till noon each day, you would choose a different job and lifestyle to accommodate that goal. The seemingly small choices you make day in and day out ultimately determine the quality of your life. These decisions reflect your character, your values, and your purpose.

Some people construct a reality out of the world around them where success and happiness is impossible because they focus on the obstacles that exist to thwart their efforts rather than the *choices* available to overcome or manage them. They fixate on the problems and assign blame. They tell themselves, *"I can't because..."* They blame their boss, spouse, lack of money, the weather, etc. for their inability to achieve their goals. They can't see the choices available to them to overcome the obstacles. They become paralyzed and get caught in the "loser" cycle.

Happy, successful people on the other hand, focus on solutions to problems. They assume responsibility for future outcomes and take control of their fate. They are able to identify the choices they have, understand the price tags attached and design a course of action to achieve their goals.

Their faith in their own abilities is undeniable. Unquestionable. They succeed simply because they *believe* they can.

But how can you train your mind to believe it is possible to be happy and achieve your goals when you really truly in your heart of hearts don't believe it?

You do it by altering your *perspective.* Instead of thinking *"I can't because..."* think *"How can I..."* That change in perspective allows you to see the action steps necessary to achieve your goals. It allows you to focus on **what you need to do** to make it happen, no matter what is happening around you.

The secret to success all boils down to the *choices* you make. The question then becomes, are you willing to pay the price for the choices you make?

It is not easy. The road to success is paved with detours, roadblocks, speed bumps and potholes. The average American will work for 10 employers, keeping each *job* 3.6 years, and change *careers* 3 times before retiring. Sometimes the change will be voluntary; sometimes the change will be instigated by outside forces. Either way, you will experience challenges and transitions along the way. Whether you label each transition as positive or negative will influence the choice you make to respond.

Most people experience transitions as something that happens TO them rather than as something they can plan for and control. By anticipating transition points throughout your career, you can develop effective strategies to manage them.

Transition may be brought on by a major event, disenchantment with current choices, recognition of more satisfying possibilities, etc., at any stage. It can come in the form of a layoff, or while morphing from an entry level role to a manager or from manager to director/vice president. It may involve switching offices or industries, or going from a full time to a part time schedule. Then there are the transitions in other areas of life that will impact your career path. Consider the impact becoming a new spouse or parent could have on your career, or the death of a parent or an unexpected illness or a change in the economy. While you may not be able to control the event, you can strengthen your coping strategies to respond effectively to them. Learn to navigate the terrain and you'll not only reach your destination faster, you will also enjoy the journey. Don't view such changes or course corrections as a sign of weakness or as a lack of commitment. Rather, see them as an opportunity for personal and professional growth. Once you recognize you always have a choice in how you frame a situation and respond to it, you will gain confidence in your ability to achieve your goals.

EXERCISE #2: Reflect

To help you get started with the self-assessment process, consider your responses to the following questions. Consider the choices you made. Jot down your responses. Note any patterns, themes and inconsistencies. These are not easy questions. Take time to truly think about them.

1. How do you **describe your current job/career** to others?

2. At the **start of your career**, what were your ambitions/long range goals?

3. Thinking about your **first job**, why did you make that choice? What were you looking for and how did it advance/contribute to the achievement of your ambitions/long range goals?

4. Consider your **first job change**. How did it come about? Who initiated the change? What were the reasons for the change? How did you feel about it? What impact did the change have on your ambitions/long range goals? (Repeat this question for each additional job change.)

5. Reflecting upon your career to date, can you identify times when change seemed more than routine? What **life event(s)** served as the catalyst(s) for change? How did you feel about it? What impact did the change(s) have on your ambitions/long range goals?

6. Are there periods of your career/life that stand out as particularly **happy/enjoyable times**? What made them enjoyable?

7. Are there periods in your career/life that stand out as particularly **unhappy/difficult times?** What made them unhappy/difficult?

8. What **messages** did you receive about work during your formative years?

9. What did your **parents/significant adults in your life do for a living?** What were their views towards work?

10. What did your **parents/significant adults in your life want you to do** for a living?

11. What do your **siblings do** for a living? What are their views towards work?

12. If you **are struggling** to make a career/life decision, can you describe **why**?

13. **Have your goals changed** since you started your career? When? Why?

14. How do you see your **career/life progressing** over the next decade?

15. Without worrying about qualifications, education, salary, security, etc., describe your **"fantasy" job/career.**

16. BONUS QUESTION: **Why** do you work?

Chapter Three will offer you further opportunities for self-assessment.

Phase 2: Market Assessment

Market assessment enables you to understand and ultimately articulate the value you have to offer employers. The internet makes it easy to conduct market research. Review job descriptions on job boards like www.hotjobs.com or www.careerbuilders.com. You could also google *"jobs for math majors"* or *"jobs in sports marketing"* to find niche websites. (See appendix for a list of useful websites.)

EXERCISE #3: Conduct Market Research

Review a variety of job postings and notice your reaction to them. Do they sound interesting and exciting? Is it something you think you would enjoy doing? If so, print those out and put them in a folder. Do this over the course of a couple of days or even weeks. Once you have 20 or 30 postings, review them and consider what they have in common. For example, do they all involve working with people or data; are they all various roles within a particular industry; are they concentrated in a specific geographic location; do they all require a specific skill or talent? Pay attention to the words they use to describe the position. (These will be important when you are crafting your resume and cover letters.) A career coach or other objective person can help you see what they have in common if you can't see it clearly. With 2 or 3 directions to pursue, you can investigate further.

There is a wealth of information beyond simple job listings that can assist you in keeping abreast of marketplace trends and understanding how to highlight the abilities and skills you have—or need to acquire—to ensure employability. There are databases containing information about industry trends, specific company profiles, relocation information, salary levels, etc. With over 40,000 employment related sites in existence, you are sure to find the preliminary information you need. But it can be overwhelming. With so many resources and so many different things you can do on the web, it's hard to know just where to begin.

EXERCISE #4: Bookmark Useful Websites

Identify 10-12 sites that are most likely to serve you best (see appendix). Remember to save them to your "Favorites" for easy access. To help you assess which are the best ones to use, consider:

- the number and kinds of jobs posted on the site;
- the primary salary levels of the posted jobs;
- the cost of using the site;
- the availability of other job search information, such as interview preparation, negotiating tips, etc.

You also want to make sure the site is well maintained, regularly updated and easy to navigate.

Consider using electronic "job agents" and joining "talent communities." These are functions offered by some websites that allow you to enter your employment objectives and be automatically notified whenever there is a match. As powerful and convenient as they are, job agents should not be a substitute for the host of other activities involved in an effective job search; they are just one of many resources available to you. Remember, you are NOT ready to apply to any positions just yet. At this stage you are looking to uncover information.

Because you need to be prepared to have the salary conversation whenever the employer brings it up, before you meet with anyone, consider how much money you need to earn in order to maintain your current life style. Write out a detailed budget for yourself and your family. This preliminary investigation into salary will help you later on as you negotiate opportunities.

EXERCISE #5: Review Your Budget

It is important to do the math and know what your monthly cash outflow is. Multiply by 12 months to come up with a target NET annual salary needed. Keep in mind that the stated GROSS salary is the amount of money that your employer pays you. The NET pay is the amount of money that you receive after deductions. Aim for a GROSS salary that is approximately one third more than your net needs

Monthly Budget Worksheet

$_____ Mortgage/Rent
$_____ Gas & Electric
$_____ Telephone
$_____ Cable/Internet
$_____ Loans (Student, Car, Personal/Home Equity)
$_____ Car Expenses (gas, parking, maintenance)
$_____ Public Transportation/Tolls
$_____ Personal Care (haircuts, etc.)
$_____ Groceries
$_____ Savings
$_____ Professional Membership Fees
$_____ Charitable Contributions
$_____ Child Care
$_____ Tuition
$_____ Pets/Pet Care
$_____ Insurance (Health, Homeowners , Disability, Life)
$_____ Medical/Dental Expenses
$_____ Health Club/Gym Fees
$_____ Clothes (Laundry/Dry Cleaning)
$_____ Entertainment (Eating Out, Vacation, Magazines/
         Newspapers/Books, Movies/Theater, Hobbies)

$_____ Home Expenses
$_____ Gifts

$_____ Total Monthly Expenses x 12 = _____ Annual Net
Salary Needed
(Add 1/3 of Net Salary to determine Gross Salary)

If your monthly net need is 4000 x 12 you need a net salary of $48,000 + $16,000 (1/3 of $48K) for a gross salary of $64,000.

It is important to recognize that what you *need* is not necessarily what employers will think you are *worth*. While the seller may set the price, it is ultimately the buyer who determines the *value*.

Review annual salary surveys published by trade magazines and associations to get a ballpark figure of the going rates. Keep in mind that these numbers are not absolute figures; they should be used to help you calculate an appropriate salary range for positions based on a realistic assessment of what the market will command. This information will be critical during the negotiating phase of a job search campaign. Check out www.payscale.com; www.vault.com; and www.salary.com. Also google *"salaries in XYZ industry."*

Finally, you must understand what you can expect from the internet. Sitting home in your pajamas applying to jobs on-line is not likely to yield the results you want. Studies indicate that approximately 4-6% of new hires come from job boards. The percentage is higher for company websites, but it is still under 25%. If you dedicate 90% of your time to an effort with such a low rate of return, you will be missing opportunities. While the internet is a great tool, you must use it in conjunction with every other resource available to you in order to be effective.

Phase 3: Implementation

Chapters Seven through Nine outline in greater detail how to draft resumes and cover letters, prepare for interviews and negotiate and assess offers. But you must spend time doing self assessment and market research first in order to articulate your storyline and create effective materials.

A job hunt does not have to be a devastating experience; it does not take guts so much as it requires thought, persistence and a willingness to make choices to achieve a long term goal. Keep in mind that job searches take time, effort and creativity. It is not necessarily the most qualified person who gets the job; rather, it is the person most skilled at finding a job. Focus on the *PROCESS*.

Allocate a Specific Amount of Time

To get yourself started, you must decide how much time you can realistically devote to your search. If you are currently working, consider 2-3 hours per week; if you are unemployed, consider 5-7 hours a day. Maintaining a **steady and consistent** effort throughout your search will be one of the most important elements in determining your success. A "start and stop" approach almost always leads you back to square one at each juncture. Working in bursts of activity will ensure failure. Sending out a stack of resumes 6 months ago does not entitle you to say *"I've been looking for 6 months"* if you have done nothing to follow up.

Adhere to a Schedule

Regardless of how many hours you have allocated to the process, work out a schedule and make a personal commitment to stick to it. During those reserved hours, your job search must be your primary focus. This is the time committed to self-assessment exercises, making phone calls, conducting research, etc. Do not allow yourself to be interrupted by running errands, baby sitting, etc. By adhering to a schedule, you will reduce the insecurity most job seekers feel because you will be in control. You will also be able to chart your progress.

Select a System to Record Your Activities

Whether you opt for a notebook and pen, an elaborate computer based system or an app, you must develop a system for recording your activities in order to easily retrieve important data and to ensure appropriate follow-up actions. Be sure to include:

- Target Employer (name, address, phone, email)
- Primary Contact
- Date Contacted
- Follow-up Action (5-7 days after initial contact)
- End results
- Additional info (i.e., source of lead)

Use All Available Resources

Many people are unaware that they can schedule individual appointments with a counselor at their school's Office of Career Services. An initial appointment with a career counselor (generally free of charge) can provide information about the type of services your school offers its alumni. For example, nearly every school has created a newsletter or intranet job board containing job listings of positions. These offer a wealth of information and possible job leads because many schools receive listings from their alumni that are not published elsewhere. Every school's Office of Career Services contains a mini library for graduates to research job opportunities, jot down listings, and read directories, books and periodicals relevant to the job search. By utilizing their career library, you can save a lot of expensive subscription costs and have access to a multitude of resources.

Also, look for industry associations that offer job search assistance for a specific target audience. Google *"Job search resources for lawyers/dancers/veterans/mechanics/etc."*

Tend to Your Emotional Well Being

Your emotional well being deserves attention and care throughout the process. In fact, your productivity and ultimate success depend on it. This is the hardest part for most people. A job search creates a tremendous sense of anxiety. The things people typically fear most about a job search include:

- financial considerations
- self doubts
- loss of status/identity
- disruption of familiar and comfortable routines
- fear of the unknown
- not getting along with new co-workers/supervisors

Analyze the panic. How real are these fears? How can you prepare for, minimize or render any of these scenarios temporary? Share your anxieties with friends/family. Hire a career coach. Not only can these people be great sounding boards but they can also help you spot flaws in your approach. However, if you believe a well meaning spouse or parents will drive you crazy by trying to be helpful or asking too many questions or by just plain nagging, politely ask them to leave you alone while you sort through things. Keep in mind a change in your life naturally means a change in the life of your family members. They may be scared or have questions too. Do not try to protect loved ones by acting in control. They will be more supportive if they know what is going on and understand how they can be helpful.

Because the very nature of the job search process invites rejection, it is important to design strategies to work through the rejection so that you have the energy to move on to the next call or meeting or interview, which may be the one where you land the perfect job. Allow yourself time to be with the important people in your life who can provide support, encouragement and perhaps a few laughs during this challenging time. Do not feel guilty about enjoying something or goofing off periodically. Exercise, take a short trip, tackle a project or read a novel. A short time away from your job search may allow you to return with renewed vigor and energy.

Finally, in order to maintain a sustained, consistent effort, break the job search process down into small, manageable steps. If you wake up each morning and declare, *"Today I will find a new job,"* you are setting yourself up for failure; you will become overwhelmed and subsequently paralyzed. Ask yourself instead, *"what can I do today?"* and then do it!

EXERCISE # 6: Develop Your Weekly Action Plan

Create a Weekly Action Sheet to establish short term goals and monitor your progress. Be sure to include:

• The specific number of hours you can commit to your job search.

_____

• The tasks you will **accomplish.**

_____

_____

_____

_____

• The things you must **do** to accomplish these tasks.

_____

_____

_____

_____

- Possible **obstacles** and **challenges** to prevent you from accomplishing the tasks.

_____

_____

_____

_____

- Strategies to **overcome** obstacles and challenges.

_____

_____

_____

_____

Finding the courage to forge your own path and construct a personal definition of success in the face of external obligations and pressures isn't easy. Focus on the action steps, trust the process and you will arrive at your destination.

DEFINE YOUR "PRODUCT":
Know What You
Have to Offer

BY NOW YOU REALIZE THAT SELF-KNOWLEDGE GAINED THROUGH self-assessment exercises like those found in Chapter Two is the most reliable tool you can use to run an effective job search and ensure career success. It is your job to know what you have to offer in order to meet the needs of your target employers.

People in Los Angeles often joke that "you are your car." We select what type of car we drive based on which car best meets our needs. That is exactly how employers selected candidates. Therefore, job seekers must be able to demonstrate exactly how they can meet employers' needs. They must be able to articulate their skills and abilities, temperament and preferred work style, passions and values, motivations and goals, and accomplishments and knowledge base in order to interview successfully and land not just *a* job, but the *right* job. These are the ABCs of job hunting:

Abilities (catalogue your natural talents, skills, accomplishments and special knowledges)

Beliefs (acknowledge your motivations, passions, values, goals and ideals)

Communication (consider your temperament, work style and communication patterns)

In tough economic times, job seekers dismiss the importance of self-assessment, viewing it as a luxury that must be sacrificed to obtain a job. Instead, they allow the market to dictate career and job choices. That is the exact wrong way to approach your job search. It's *especially* critical in a tumultuous job market to focus on self-assessment. Your challenge is to explain how what you can do and what you know is of value to the employer. Jobs are joint ventures in problem solving. The idea is to find a match between an employer's needs and your abilities and skills. Therefore you need to have a keen understanding of how you process information, solve problems, make decisions, and communicate.

Two basic questions apply to every career (and thus every career plan): (1) What needs to be done? (which you uncover through market assessment) and (2) What can *you* do?

Let's start by identifying what *you* can do.

EXERCISE #7: Discover Your Abilities and Skills

STEP 1: Review the following abilities and skills and indicate the extent to which you believe you possess each one on a scale of 1 to 5. (1 = Very Little...5 = Very Strong). Highlight the ones you would rank yourself 5.

Rank your ability to:

___ Accept responsibilities

___ Adapt to change

___ Adhere to deadlines

___ Analyze data

___ Assemble deals

___ Assimilate new data quickly

___ Be responsive, reliable and conscientious

___ Be self-directed

___ Build internal/external networks

___ Collaborate with colleagues

___ Communicate well orally

___ Communicate well in writing

___ Compete

___ Conceptualize

___ Conduct research

___ Confront

___ "Connect the dots"

___ Counsel/advise clients

___ Decide/act in pressure situations

___ Delegate

___ Demonstrate commitment

___ Demonstrate good judgment/common sense

___ Demonstrate political judgment

___ Develop business

___ Develop rapport and trust

___ Digest large quantities of material

___ Draft documents

___ Edit

___ Empathize

___ Explain complicated ideas in simple terms

___ Facilitate

___ Follow through

___ Formulate strategy

___ Gather facts

___ Initiate

___ Inspire confidence

___ Interview

___ Keep confidences

___ Lead

___ Listen critically

___ Maintain "systems"

___ Manage complex tasks

___ Manage details

___ Manage people

___ Mediate

___ Motivate

___ Negotiate

___ Organize

___ Persuade/promote/sell

___ Predict/forecast trends

___ Prioritize

___ Produce quality work

___ Put in long hours

___ "Read" people

___ Research

___ Resolve conflicts

___ Retain information

___ Schedule deadlines, set goals

___ See "big picture"

___ Solve problems creatively

___ Speak persuasively

___ Strategize

___ Summarize

___ Supervise

___ Synthesis

___ Take risks

___ Tell stories

___ Theorize

___ Tolerate delays/wait

___ Train/teach

___ Troubleshoot

___ Understand objectives and work standards

___ Use technology proficiently

___ Work well under
pressure

___ Work efficiently

___ Write persuasively

___ Write technically

STEP 2: For each characteristic you ranked 5, go back and add the phrase "for example," and provide a specific example or story illustrating when you used that ability or skill well. You will be able to use these stories to demonstrate to an interviewer that you are the ideal candidate for a job.

Example: I have the ability to organize. For example, I organized a job fair coordinating 200 employers, and 900 students from 14 different schools. My job was to make sure that every student was in the proper place every 20 minutes and that the employers had the correct resumes.

FOR EXAMPLE:

FOR EXAMPLE:

FOR EXAMPLE:

FOR EXAMPLE:

FOR EXAMPLE:

FOR EXAMPLE:

(use additional paper to add more stories)

Identify Your SUCCESS Patterns

Transferable/functional abilities are ways that we characteristically react to problematic situations throughout life. As a child, if confronted with a puzzle or task, your reaction may have been to organize the pieces and then examine alternative solutions. As a teenager repairing a car engine, the same problem solving abilities may have been utilized. These problem solving patterns are known as "success patterns" and tend to become set during the teenage years. Over the years, we tend to become more proficient in the use of our favorite abilities, but because they seem innate, we do not always recognize them as marketable skills.

To help you identify your success patterns and marketable skills, think about what you have already achieved or accomplished. Include things related to work, leisure and education. An accomplishment can be something big like planning a fundraising event, winning a jury verdict or landing a big client. Or, it can be something very simple, like receiving an A on a school project or hosting a surprise birthday party for a friend or managing a personal crisis. Your abilitiy/skill patterns will emerge no matter which accomplishments you select. Divide your life into segments to ensure you cover the entire spectrum of your life (i.e., "High School, College, Graduate School, Job #1" or "Teens, 20s, 30s, 40s" etc.) Review files and look through yearbooks and family photo albums to help jog your memory. You may not be able to complete this exercise in one sitting. Consider doing it over the course of a few days, adding accomplishments as they occur to you.

EXERCISE #8: Catalogue Your Achievements

STEP 1: Define the segments of your life and then list a total of 10 accomplishments, with representation from each segment.

SEGMENT A   **SEGMENT B**   **SEGMENT C**

_____   _____   _____

ACCOMPLISHMENTS

1. _____

2. _____

3. _____

4. _____

5. _____

6. _____

7. _____

8. _____

9. _____

10. _____

STEP 2: Select three or four accomplishments on your list that you would like to examine more closely. Describe the accomplishment, answering the following questions:

What was the subject matter?

What was the environment like?

What abilities/skills did you use?

What did you do best?

What did you enjoy most?

What was your key motivator?

Concentrate on HOW you did it, but do not analyze. Have fun with this—do not worry about grammar, spelling or punctuation. At the end, note how you felt at the conclusion of each event. Insert additional pages to explore more stories.

SAMPLES

#1 In the fourth grade, every student had to do a presentation on a specific country. I was assigned Guatemala. I went to Funk & Wagnalls encyclopedia to do my research on the population, climate, etc. I also went to the library and took out all the books I could find on that country to ensure I knew all there was to know about Guatemala. I copied information onto index cards and organized the cards into categories. Unlike my classmates, I was excited about standing in front of my classmates and showing off how much I knew. My teacher told me I did a good job and gave me an A+. I felt proud.

#2 In senior year of college, I took an elective course that required an oral presentation at the end of the semester. Because the course was in my major, I was well versed in the subject matter and not overly concerned about the presentation. The day before the presentation, I spent about 15 minutes organizing my thoughts. The following day in class, another student asked if she could deliver her presentation first because she was very nervous and wanted to "get it over with." She had handouts and diagrams, and despite how prepared she was, she appeared flustered and unorganized. When it was my turn, I walked to the front of the classroom with my half page of

notes feeling slightly worried that I did not have all the supporting documentation she had. But I delivered my presentation—barely referring to my notes—in an interesting and engaging way. The audience applauded and I received an A. (They didn't applaud for my classmate and she only got a B.) I remember feeling surprised at how easy it was and feeling slightly superior to my classmate who had clearly invested more time in preparing than I had.

#3 I am extremely proud of having my nonfiction book published. I spent several months researching the topic, drafting the chapters and putting the information together in a way I believed would be useful to the reader. A friend of a friend presented the draft to a small, independent publisher who agreed to publish it. In order to boost sales, I scheduled several presentations on local TV & radio shows, Barnes & Noble bookstores, etc. The publisher printed twice as many copies as he expected and told me how pleased he was to find an author who wrote well and who enjoyed the marketing component of the book business.

From the sample stories, one might assume that the author enjoys being recognized as an expert and has an innate ability as a public speaker. The author demonstrated research and writing abilities as well as oral presentation talents. This information is important to know and easy to translate to employers during the interview process. (*"Ever since the fourth grade, I knew I enjoyed researching topics and was comfortable speaking in public. Those skills will serve me well as a trial lawyer."*)

STEP 3: Review your stories, circling all skills mentioned. Read the stories aloud to a friend, colleague or career coach and ask them to note the skills they heard. (This is a great way to learn how you are perceived by others.) Note any themes and patterns.

In addition to knowing what you can do, choosing the right career path also requires insight into your personality. Understanding your temperament will enable you to select an environment compatible with your preferred work style.

For example, introverts and extroverts thrive in different work environments. Introverts are often quiet and reflective. They like to have time to process information before articulating their thoughts. They like a more stable, consistent work environment. Extroverts get their energy through external events and other people, so they generally like a faster paced environment. They tend to think "out loud" and enjoy lots of interaction as well as variety in their tasks. An extrovert forced to sit at a computer alone all day would be unhappy (and ultimately unsuccessful) just as an introvert forced to interact with others all day would be unhappy. Of course, some people fall in the middle of the introvert-extrovert scale and find they need a workplace that provides a combination of such activities.

Knowing where you fall on this scale will enable you to consider what types of bosses, colleagues, clients, and subordinates you work well with and in what environment you are likely to feel most comfortable.

You also need to understand which of the following you prefer:
- Dealing with facts and data or people and emotions
- Solving problems in a linear, logical manner or holistically

- Making decisions intuitively or deductively
- Working in a structured or unstructured environment

There are a variety of self-assessment tools designed to help increase your understanding of yourself. While no one test is going to provide you with all the answers to guarantee career success, any one of the tests described in this chapter, in conjunction with a trained career coach, can provide useful insights to help you design a focused but flexible career plan.

The Highlands Ability Battery (www.highlandsco. com) is a tool that offers insight into your temperament as well as your natural abilities. While the words "abilities" and "skills" are used interchangeable throughout this book, there is an important distinction to be made. A true ability is demonstrated when a particular task comes easily, quickly, and effortlessly; it is the way a person is "hardwired." Skills, on the other hand, are learned through training, practice, and experience. Knowing your natural abilities can help steer you toward tasks and roles that use your best talents and steer you away from tasks that would be difficult and unfulfilling for you to learn. Many smart people acquire and employ skills that play against their natural abilities and become quite successful in doing so. Yet they are never completely satisfied. Similarly, if you don't have an opportunity to use your natural abilities in your job, you may become frustrated in your work.

Based on the work of research scientist Johnson O'Connor, this online assessment tool uses 19 different timed work samples to measure the speed with which a person is able to perform a particular series of tasks. The scores, shown together on a personal profile and bar chart, reveal patterns or "clusters" of abilities that highlight your natural gifts and talents in relationship to how you learn, how you solve problems, how you communicate, and even which type of work environment best suits you. A certified provider offers a skilled analysis of the written report and helps individuals explore the best career options based on their natural abilities.

Strengthsfinder is another excellent resource. This book by Tom Rath provides a code to take an assessment on line that measures the presence of 34 talent themes. It offers insights into your top five themes, describing your naturally recurring patterns of thought, feeling, and behavior and the impact on your behavior and performance.

The online **Self-Directed Search** (SDS) (www.self-directed-search.com) provides an individualized interpretive report describing what you like—your favorite activities and interests—as well as information about potentially satisfying occupations. The SDS was developed by Dr. John Holland, whose theory of careers is the basis for most of the career inventories used today. According to Dr. Holland's theory, people are most satisfied in their careers when they are surrounded by people with similar interests because it creates a work environment that suits their personalities. People are more comfortable and ultimately more successful in a work environment that rewards the traits and behaviors that come most naturally to them. Holland's theory states that most people can be loosely categorized with respect to six types:

> **Realistic:** likes to work with things more than with people

Investigative: likes to explore and understand things or events rather than persuade others or sell them things

Artistic: likes creating original work and has a good imagination

Social: likes to be around people, is interested in how people get along, and likes to help people with their problems

Enterprising: likes to persuade or direct others more than work on scientific or complicated topics

Conventional: likes to follow orderly routines and meet clear standards, avoiding work that does not have clear directions

Occupations and work environments can also be classified by the same categories. The interpretive report provides a list of career options that match your results and offers direction about where to focus your market research.

Another assessment to consider is **The Myers-Briggs Type Indicator (MBTI)**. It is based on the theory that individuals are either born with, or develop, certain *preferred* ways of thinking and acting. By examining your responses to a series of questions, the MBTI defines 16 possible psychological types. These combinations indicate your preferences for the following:

Extroversion and Introversion: whether you get energy from being around people or from time spent alone

Sensing and iNtuition: whether you enjoy working with facts and concrete details or prefer to focus on hunches and the big picture

Thinking and Feeling: whether you tend to make decisions based on logic and the principles involved or on your values and promoting harmony for the people involved

Judging and Perceiving: whether you prefer your life to be planned and decided or prefer to go with the flow and like keeping your options open

This test is offered online (www.mbticomplete.com) without the assistance of a qualified counselor or can be administered through a qualified MBTI career counselor who will help interpret the results.

Finally, the **DiSC Sort**, offered online (www.disctests.com), classifies four aspects of behavior by testing a person's preferences in word associations. DiSC is an acronym for the terms below:

Dominance: People who score high in the intensity of the D styles are very active in dealing with problems and challenges, while those with Low D scores want to do more research before committing to a decision.

Influence: People with High I styles scores influence others through talking and activity and tend to be emotional. Those with Low I scores influence more through data and facts, not feelings.

Steadiness: People with High S styles scores want a steady pace, security, and do not like sudden change. Low S intensity scores are those who like change and variety.

Conscientiousness: People with High C styles scores adhere to rules, regulations, and structure. They like to do quality work and do it right the first time. Those with Low C scores challenge the rules, want independence, and are uninhibited by details.

Both MBTI and DiSC provide an individualized written report. While you don't need a certified career counselor to interpret the results, someone trained in interpreting these tools would be extremely useful in terms of guiding you toward the practical application of the information on designing your career plan. Check with the career development office of your college or graduate school to see if anyone on staff is certified in these instruments. They are typically willing to meet with alumni on a limited basis.

Take advantage of these various assessment tools to help you clarify your goals.

People tend to be motivated by what they *like,* not by what makes sense. Yet, they allow "what makes sense" to pull them in a direction they'd rather not go, which ultimately leads to burnout or unhappiness. The job market, which is conservative and myopic by nature, wants you to keep doing what you have been doing. You are most understandable to potential employers in terms of your past choices and your tenure in prior settings. Understandably, your most recent position is the clearest indication of your highest level of competency. The mere fact of change can raise questions about your motives. Are you running toward something or away from something? It is important to stay in control of your search to ensure that these market forces do not dictate your choices.

Internal motives combine the forces of **mind, will, resources and heart**. When you are truly motivated you have the **MENTAL STAMINA** to focus and concentrate no matter what is happening in the world around you. Sheer **WILL** provides the necessary drive and determination, commitment and dedication, as well as discipline, persistence and endurance to achieve your goals in the face of seemingly insurmountable obstacles. Motivation enables you to capitalize on your internal **RESOURCES** such as your abilities, skills and talents as well as strategize how to use external resources to your advantage. But most importantly, motivations capture the forces of the **HEART** and fuel your efforts through enthusiasm, excitement, and passions. When your heart is committed, NOTHING can deter you.

Success is a subjective perception based on what YOU as an individual value. Values are those intangible principles and standards that bring meaning to your work and motivate your involvement and commitment. You need to ask yourself what your values are and which hold the most meaning and importance to you. People tend to feel most comfortable when surrounded by others who hold similar values and in situations where their values are appreciated. The following exercise will help you further identify career/ work values and factors crucial to your job satisfaction.

EXERCISE #9: Identify Your Values

Step One: Consider the importance of each item. Highlight the ones you believe are VERY IMPORTANT.

Achievement	Diversity
Advancement	Economic Return
Aesthetics	Education
Affiliation	Effectiveness
Altruism	Emotional Growth
Authority & Power	Ethics
Autonomy	Excellence
Being Needed	Excitement & Adventure
Boss You Respect	Fairness
Challenge	Family
Change	Flexibility
Closure	Focus
Commitment to Goal(s)	Fringe Benefits
Competition	Friends
Competence	Harmony
Complexity	Health/Physical Fitness
Control	High Profile
Courage	High Risk/High Reward
Creativity	Holistic Approach
Direct Impact	Honesty
Discovering New Things	Improving the World

Independence

Individuality

Influencing People

Innovation

Integrity

Intellectual Stimulation

Interesting Work

Job Security

Justice

Knowledge

Leadership of Others

Leisure Time

Lifestyle Integration

Location

Mentoring

Morality

Nurturing

Physical Appearance

Physical Challenge

Physical Environment

Pleasure

Popularity

Power

Recognition

Relationships

Religious Observance

Respect

Responsibility

Routine

Salary

Security

Social Relevance

Specialization

Spirituality

Stability

Status

Structured Environment

Supervision

Supervision of Others

Training

Traveling

Upward Mobility

Variety

Working Alone

Working on Teams

Other

Step Two: Rank all the things you highlighted on a scale of 1-10 with 1 being the MOST important and 10 being the least important. Refer back to this list whenever you are confronted with transition decisions.

It is important to consider the competencies and personal qualities you want to live by and see reflected in the workplace. Value your unique gifts and talents and you will, in turn, be valued by others. Catalogue your skills, abilities and special knowledges continually and be prepared to tell people about them. Don't think of it as shameless self promotion; instead think of it as sharing relevant information with people who can help you achieve your goals.

EXERCISE #10: Draft Your Preliminary Marketing Statement

Having mastered the ABCs of the job search, you are now ready to draft your preliminary markeking statement. Write out exactly how you want to present yourself. Be sure to include:

- The type of position you are seeking
- The geographic areas you are considering
- The special knowledges, abilities and skills you have to offer
- Your short and long term goals

Once you have the basic information assembled, massage the sentence structure and syntax until you create a 10-15 second self-introduction that sounds natural and rolls easily off your tongue.

Write out your marketing statement in the space below.

CHAPTER FOUR

DESIGN YOUR MARKETING MATERIALS: Create a Winning Resume

G OALS HAVE BEEN WRITTEN; SELF-ASSESSMENT HAS BEGUN AND research is underway. NOW it is time to focus on your marketing materials. Your self-marketing kit should contain a resume, cover letter, writing sample/portfolio, transcripts, references, recommendations and any ancillary documentation relevant to your applications.

Let's start with the resume. Think of it as a sales document. To design an effective sales document, you must have a clear idea of the job you are seeking so that you can skew your resume to your target audience. An effective resume provides not only a clear understanding of what you have done, but also how that experience is relevant to the potential employers. That is why we have spent so much time concentrating on self-assessment and preliminary market research. (We will cover market research to a great extent in Chapters Five and Six.) Ideally, you created a resume file early in your career, adding experiences and accomplishments as they occurred. You should update this document throughout your career. But even if you have not created one, now is as good a time as any to begin. First, decide which information to include; pay close attention to the words you use to describe your experiences. Many employers use computer algorithms to scan resumes, searching for specific words or phrases. You want to use industry specific jargon to describe your experience. Then, concentrate on the format and style you want to use to best display your content.

Your resume is an opportunity to create a positive impression with an employer. Because this document is a self portrait, it is difficult to give generic advice on the preparation of a resume. There are no absolute rules to follow. Anyone who gives you resume advice that starts with *"you should always"* or you *"should never"* is wrong. Your resume is as individual as you are. There are many good websites that offer industry specific samples you will want to review to get some ideas (Google "sample resumes for *insert job title*"). Check out the website www.bestsampleresume.com for some ideas.

While there are no absolute rules, there are key concepts and general rules of thumb to follow concerning format and content no matter what industry you are interested in.

A resume should be brief. Conventional wisdom suggests resumes should be one page long. However, if you have had an extensive career, you do yourself a disservice by eliminating relevant information or cramming your content into one page. Expand to a second page. Make sure the second page is at least half full, with your name, address, telephone number and e-mail at the top.

Simple, descriptive language is key. Typically, computers read your resume first and software is designed to search for specific words, so format your electronic resume to work for you by investing the time to tailor it to specific positions. Try to incorporate the language used in the job postings to describe your experiences.

Name, address, phone number and e-mail should appear at the top of the resume. Phone numbers are essential and your voicemail message should be clear, professional and preferably in your voice. Also, be sure to have a professional e-mail address. Partygirl@gmail.com does not suggest a professional persona.

A JOB OBJECTIVE is not necessary. Your objective is to get the job for which you are applying. However, you might want to consider a **CAREER SUMMARY**, which highlights your professional background as it relates to the position you are seeking. It should consist of several statements that demonstrate your abilities, skills and credentials. Describe what you <u>can</u> do, not what you <u>want</u> to do. Avoid the overuse of adjectives. You can modify this section as needed to appeal to specific employers without needing to revamp your entire resume.

EXPERIENCE section can be formatted either Chronologically or Functionally. Chronological resumes are oriented by date, with the most recent position first and proceeding backward. This is the most popularly used and accepted format because it is logical and easy to follow. This is the format to use if you have a steady work history with no gaps and if your most recent job is related to your job target. If you have a substantial work history, consider adding Accomplishments under each entry to focus the reader on your successes. If you are switching directions, a functional resume may be more effective. Here accomplishments and experience are organized under broad areas of expertise or skills headings with the most important category (to the potential employer) at the top, followed by two or three other functions. This format allows you to organize your experience according to your talents. It also allows you to de-emphasize employment dates, company names and titles, which should be included under the heading **Employment**. Check out www.best-sampleresume.com for free examples of resumes in a variety of industries.

EDUCATION section should contain all pertinent information from your college/graduate school experience, including the official name of the schools, years of graduation, and a list of any appropriate academic and/or extracurricular activities. If you have attended an Ivy League school, consider leading with the Education section. If you had stellar grades in school, you may also want to keep your education section first for your first year or two after graduation. Otherwise your education should go after experience.

Consider including a section that draws attention to unique skills such as foreign languages or personal interests. The section may be titled **PERSONAL** or **INTERESTS**. Its purpose is to facilitate conversation or "break the ice" during an interview and to give the employer a more well rounded appreciation of your background. Make sure that your personal interests are descriptive— e.g., *"travel to the Far East, Mexican cooking and nineteenth century literature"* are much more effective than *"travel, reading and cooking."*

Also consider adding a section for PROFES-SIONAL AFFILIATIONS and/or COMMUNITY ACTIVITIES. This will enable you to list church or synagogue activities, board memberships, volunteer work, and any other extracurricular or leadership positions on your resume.

No Personal Information (height, weight, age, marital status, health) need appear on your resume.

Prepare a list of References that is separate from your resume. Prepare a separate sheet of paper listing references (three is usually an adequate number) to have available when you go in for an interview. Include your references' affiliations, titles and contact information. Ask people if they would be willing to serve as a reference before you give out their names and contact information. Even if someone has agreed in the past, it is important to check in with them again if some time has lapsed. The more your references understand about the job for which you are applying, the better able they will be to tailor their remarks in a favorable way. Be prepared to provide them with a copy of your resume and a "cheat sheet" that underscores your abilities, skills and talents.

Other tips and techniques to keep in mind:

- Use strong action verbs to describe experience and accomplishments. Be specific.

- Use "bullets" if your descriptions are longer than 5 lines. Start each with an action verb.

- Use CAPITALIZATION, **bold print**, *italics*, <u>underlining</u>, indentation and outline format to present information. Make it easy for the reader to scan. Research suggests that employers spend about six seconds with your resume before deciding whether to put it in the "yes" or "no" pile. Make sure the overall look is neat and clean.

- Use generous margins (but not so generous as to look skimpy). Balance the text on the page.

- Put dates on the right hand margin instead of the left so they do not stand out to the point that the employer will be distracted from the more important aspects of your resume.

- Proofread to eliminate errors and typos.

Once you have created your resume, you need to ensure it translates properly via e-mail. Send it to a few friends to make sure it opens properly and that there are no formatting issues. (For example, you may need to eliminate headers/footers.) When emailing your resume, it is best to send as a PDF file. You should also use the *Save As* function on your computer to create a second version of your resume in ASCII text or Rich Text Format. These are easier to use when posting resumes in on-line databases. (We will discuss this in greater detail in Chapter Seven.) Proofread the new document to be sure information translated properly during the reformatting process. Finally, recognize that some employers, fearful of computer viruses, may not accept e-mails with attachments. In those instances send your resume as the text of an e-mail message.

EXERCISE #11: Complete Resume Worksheets

Use this format to compile all the information for each category. Include EVERYTHING. You may ultimately decide not to include certain information on the resume, but do not edit at this stage. It may be worth including a college internship or long since past experience if it is relevant or uniquely interesting.

EDUCATION
(Include the official names of the schools, years of graduation, and a list of any appropriate academic and/or extracurricular activities.)

_____

_____

_____

_____

_____

EXPERIENCE
(Include full time and part time positions. Compile the information chronologically. You can decide later how to format the information on the resume.)

_____

_____

_____

_____

EXPERIENCE CONTINUED

_____

_____

_____

_____

_____

ACCOMPLISHMENTS
(Include significant projects you have worked on)

_____

_____

_____

_____

PROFESSIONAL AFFILIATIONS
(List Association Committees, Board Memberships, industry groups, etc.

_____

_____

_____

_____

COMMUNITY ACTIVITIES
(List pro bono activities, community groups, volunteer work, etc.)

_____

_____

_____

_____

PERSONAL
(List unique abilities, skills or interests.)

_____

_____

_____

_____

_____

For sample resumes in every industry, check out www.bestsampleresume.com

Typically when asked "what do you do?" people respond with a title. "I'm a student/ doctor/ teacher/ lawyer/plumber, etc." That rarely gives people enough information about you and it presents a unique challenge to job seekers who do not have a title. Instead, answer the question what do you _do?_ by focusing on verbs. Be sure to use powerful language to describe your capabilities.

**EXERCISE #12: Select Action Verbs to
Describe What You Do**

Consider the list of action verbs below. Highlight the verbs that best describe what you do. Be sure to incorporate them into your draft resume and in your self-marketing statement in Chapter Three.

ADMINISTRATIVE:
I....

accelerate

accomplish

arrange

classify

collect

compile

compute

coordinate

delegate

develop

direct

establish

examine

execute

file

handle

led

manage

organize

overhaul

oversee

plan

prioritize

produce

recommend

record

reorganize

review

schedule

streamline

supervise

word processing

COMMUNICATION (ORAL)
I...

address	interview
advocate	joke
arbitrate	judge
argue	lecture
articulate	listen
collaborate	mediate
consult	moderate
convince	observe
debate	participate
elicit	present
explain	recruit
express	resolve
influence	solicit
interact	speak
interpret	suggest

COMMUNICATION (WRITTEN)
I....

advertise	explain
author	express
draft	influence
edit	market

outline

persuade

present

promote

report

speech writting

summarize

synthesize

translate

write (technical)

write (speeches)

CREATIVE
I...

act

conceptualize

create

compose

design

develop

direct

entertain

establish

formulate

illustrate

imagine

improvise

invent

model

perform

photograph

revitalize

shape

simplify

sing

stage

visualize

FINANCIAL
I....

account

administer

allocate

audit

balance

budget

calculate

forecast

formulate

invest

monitor

negotiate

project

purchase

quantify

rate

record

report

research

review

save

scrutinize

simplify

solve

theorize

track

translate

uncover

value

HUMAN RELATIONS
I...

adapt

advocate

advise

aid

answer

arrange

assess

assist

clarify

coach

collaborate

counsel

educate

empathize

encourage

ensure

facilitate

guide

help

intervene

listen

mentor

motivate

prevent

refer

rehabilitate

represent

rescue

resolve

serve

simplify

supply

support

volunteer

MANAGEMENT/LEADERSHIP

I...

accomplish

achieve

administer

advise

analyze

appoint

approve

assign

chair

communicate

consider

consolidate

control

coordinate

counsel

decide

delegate

direct

emphasize

enforce

enhance

generate

hire

improve

increase

institute

lead

mentor

motivate

navigate

negotiate

organize

persuade

plan

preside

PROBLEM SOLVING
I...

analyze

decide

diagnose

examine

execute

PUBLIC RELATIONS
I...

conduct

consult

inform

plan

present

RESEARCH
I....

analyze

assess

calculate

clarify

review

streamline

supervise

train

plan

prove

reason

recognize

validate

promote

represent

research

respond

write

collect

compare

detect

diagnose

explore	locate
extract	measure
evaluate	organize
examine	search
extrapolate	solve
formulate	summarize
gather	survey
inspect	synthesize
interview	test
investigate	

SELLING
I....

build relationships	persuade
communicate	plan
contact	present
educate	promote
inform	schedule
organize	

TECHNICAL
I...

adjust	install
align	observe
assemble	operate
draft	program
engineer	repair

TEACH/TRAIN

I...

adapt	facilitate
advise	focus
clarify	guide
coach	inform
communicate	instill
critique	instruct
develop	motivate
demonstrate	persuade
enable	plan
encourage	stimulate
evaluate	teach
explain	

The purpose of your resume is to present your abilities, skills and credentials in an appealing way that inspires the reader to want to meet you. Make sure the overall appearance is attractive. It should be interesting and compelling, with a layout that looks professional and is visually appealing. Make sure you have emphasized your accomplishments and problem solving abilities and skills and provided specific information about projects, products and quantities with numbers/percentages when possible. Remember all sentences and paragraphs must start with strong action verbs in the present tense for your current job and past tense for all others.

Video resumes are just one of the new emerging technologies impacting job hunting. Some employers are beginning to accept them, but the trend has not quite caught on yet. There are companies offering to produce professional video resumes. Before you invest in this, consider whether or not your target industry accepts them. If you opt to make one yourself, keep in mind things like lighting and background noise along with powerful presentation skills (more about that in Chapter Six) will all work in tandem to create a perception of you. Be sure to "test drive" your video resume with those in the workplace (not just fellow job seekers) before you submit it to employers. Ask them, *"would you hire the person in the video?"* Remember, you never get a second chance to make a first impression.

The same is true for social media. It also plays a role in how potential employers see you so you want to consider your electronic reputation at the early stage of your job search. It is important that your profiles on various sites adequately convey the image you want people to have of you.

Most people use Facebook to maintain social relationships and LinkedIn to foster professional relationships, yet they are not exclusive. Potential employers look at both. Many job seekers have been disqualified based on sparse Linked In profiles or posts ranging from silly to inappropriate on Facebook. Claims of *"I'm not like that at work"* or *"I was just goofing around with some friends"* fall flat as your judgment is called into question. Every joke, tweet or picture creates an impression of you that can never be undone. The good news is you can control the impression. Be smart about it.

Your profiles and posts are similar to your resume in that they create an impression of you before people meet you. If you feel the need to share information about drinking and drug use or your sexual escapades use the setting options to limit who can see those posts. Any information shared publicly should be carefully considered. On LinkedIn, list interesting and relevant jobs, internships or volunteer work. List the schools you have attended and awards you have won. The more complete and detailed your LinkedIn profile is, the more points of connection you will find. However, there is no need to list everything you've ever done. Again, consider the image you are trying to create. Consider creating a Linked In Vanity URL to include on your resume. Simply click on your name in the upper right corner and select *Settings, Edit your Public Profile, Your Public Profile URL*.

Post updates periodically about your activities to keep people up to date. Remember, this is the place to highlight a success or an expertise. It is NOT appropriate to post comments about any job search angst. Always maintain a business like tone and consider what impression you are creating with your posts.

You are now ready to continue with more in-depth market assessment.

CHAPTER FIVE

LEARN THE RULES:
Conduct Market Research,
Part One

ARMED WITH INFORMATION ABOUT YOURSELF, A DRAFT RESUME and your marketing pitch, as well as preliminary internet market research, it is now time to test the waters by talking to people, otherwise known as networking.

Countless books and articles have been written outlining networking techniques and gimmicks to coach readers. However, you will NOT be effective with empty techniques and gimmicks. Networking rests on the basic principle that business, jobs and careers are built on personal relationships; therefore, **it must be genuine and sincere to be successful.**

Many people hate the thought of networking and are hesitant about "using" people or asking for help. Try to reframe how you think about it. Most people <u>like</u> to help others and those people in a position to help you might be insulted that they were not asked for assistance. It makes them feel good, powerful and important. If you are doubtful, consider whether you would be willing to share your knowledge or give names to friends or business associates in order to be helpful. When you establish a specific and relevant basis for a conversation—to ask for ideas, opinions, a reaction to your own thoughts—there is no reason for you to be turned down. Ask for something specific, something your contact can easily do.

The true purpose of networking is to get AIR: advice, information and referrals. It occurs naturally in all areas of life. For example, when moving into a new neighborhood, you probably would not hesitate to ask your new neighbors for recommendations about dry cleaners, grocery stores, dentists, etc. Or when planning a vacation you would not think twice about asking friends or family to recommend hotels and restaurants. In business it is common to ask colleagues to suggest accountants, bankers or computer systems. But for some reason, we hesitate to ask people we know about job opportunities. College friends, professors, family members, former employers, colleagues, neighbors, etc., are most likely in the best position to connect you to others in a position to hire you.

The first step is to identify <u>WHO</u> can help. Prepare a list of people with whom to network. Think about family members, friends, classmates, co-workers, professors, managers (past/present), service industry professionals (doctors, lawyers, accountants), professionals in the field. Consider <u>all</u> the people you know: commuter buddies, your parents' friends, people from your gym or religious institution. Then consider all the people they know. Add to the list every day. Keep track of who referred you and how people are connected to each other.

LinkedIn is a great resource for that. Launched in 2003, LinkedIn is the largest and most powerful business focused social media network, linking over 135 million people.

Anyone can sign up for free. Members can upgrade to a premium account but the free service is all the average job seeker needs.

LinkedIn is optimized to perform well in search engines so it is easy to find people (and BE found!) Adding contacts is the driving force behind LinkedIn but be selective about people you connect to. Focus on quality not quantity. Initially, limit it to people you know well enough to phone or email. Send them a personalized email invitation to link. Generic invitations are cold and impersonal and do little to foster the relationship. Eventually you can add new people you meet through your contacts or at conferences and other professional events.

Next, decide <u>WHAT</u> you want from each contact. You need to have a clear objective about what you are trying to accomplish before you contact anyone on your list. **Think through your strategy first.** Why have you selected this person to contact? What information do you hope to learn? To whom can they introduce you? There should be no mystery or hidden agenda as to the purpose of the conversation. Consider the following sample approaches to potential contacts:

To a geographic contact: *"You have lived in this city for so long and know almost everyone..."*

To a socially active friend: *"You have so many friends, you probably hear about things before anyone..."*

To someone who works in your field: *"You've been working in the same type of job I am looking for, I am sure you have some idea how my abilities and skills might be viewed..."*

To a professor: *"You know better than anyone what kinds of jobs are open in this field..."*

To anyone you admire: *"You always seem to have good ideas..."*

To someone you have helped: *"We have helped each other in the past, so I am hoping you can help me now..."*

To a LinkedIn connection: *"I saw that you are connected to Joe Smith at ABC corporation. I am interested to learn more about that organization. Could you introduce me?"*

It is important to understand what you can reasonably expect from professional relationships and what is outside those bounds. It is reasonable to expect:

- information
- referrals to others who can help you
- reactions to your ideas and theories
- assistance in formulating plans
- feedback about resumes, cover letters and approach
- moral support

It is NOT reasonable to expect A JOB will be handed to you.

Most people do not know of many current job openings. If the first and only question posed to your contacts is *"Do you know of any openings?"* you will more often than not receive a NO and an opportunity may be lost. By asking questions like *"What do you do and what alternatives are out there?"* or *"Where do you see someone with my abilities and skills fitting in?"* or *"Do you know anyone who works at X?"* you will uncover information that will eventually generate opportunities, preserve your relationships and enable you to reconnect with your contact throughout the job search process.

It is important not to limit your efforts to only those with influential positions and the power to hire you. Remember, networking should only be used as a communication process to acquire information, NOT as a manipulation used to acquire power and influence over others. If you are playing the "advice and information game" when you really believe networking is nothing more than the back door route to a new position, you are being insincere, misleading and you will not be effective. People who are close to your level of experience and even those junior to you or in support positions can be great sources of information. Be nice to everyone along the way.

EXERCISE #13: Categorize Your Contacts

List 30 people you believe might be able to assist you in your job hunt.

1.	16.
2.	17.
3.	18.
4.	19.
5.	20.
6.	21.
7.	22.
8.	23.
9.	24.
10.	25.
11.	26.
12.	27.
13.	28.
14.	29.
15.	30.

Divide the list into three categories:

A—those in a position to hire (this category may be very small);

B—those in a position to introduce you to others in a position to hire;

C – those with information or ideas

It is one thing to understand the concept of networking. It is quite another to know <u>HOW</u> to do it. The good news is networking is a learnable skill. Start with the easy ones, those friends and colleagues you feel comfortable calling. Invite them to lunch and say, *"I'm looking for a job and wanted to bounce some ideas off you."* During these initial meetings you will begin to become more comfortable talking about yourself, and, because these are your friends, they will be more forgiving if you stumble slightly as you refine your marketing message.

For people you do not know as well, use this four step process: (1) an e-mail, (2) follow-up phone call, (3) informational interview and (4) follow-up thank you note.

Send an **e-mail** to ask for <u>15</u> minutes of their time for <u>advice</u>. Do not put pressure on the individual to find you a job or to interview you. That may be a long term result, but at this point, an informative conversation should be your objective.

Dear :

Jack O'Neill suggested that I contact you about my interest in career opportunities in marketing (in New Jersey, etc). I am a graduate of XYZ School with experience in ...

(Your next paragraph should tell something about your background. Include your prior work experience, abilities, skills, interests, academic history, connection to the geographic region, etc. Your goal is to pique the reader's interest.)

I hope to benefit from the experience and knowledge of others in the field (in New Jersey) who might advise me on opportunities for someone with my qualifications. To help familiarize you with my background, I have taken the liberty of attaching my resume for your review. I would appreciate the opportunity to meet with you for 15 minutes for your guidance. I will call your office next week to see if we can schedule a meeting.

I look forward to discussing my plans with you.

Sincerely,

Your Name

Keep in mind that an e-mail is still a business correspondence. You should use a salutation. Grammar, spelling and proper punctuation are important. Create a secure e-mail address separate from your current work address or your school address. Yahoo, Google and your cable provider offer free e-mail accounts. Remember to select a professional name. Partygirl12@gmail.com does not create the impression a job seeker needs to create. All job search–related inquiries should come from this address and it should be checked frequently.

Nothing is more effective than a well written **email followed by a telephone** call 3-5 days later. The telephone is the most underutilized tool available to the job seeker. Prepare a script so you can clearly and succinctly introduce yourself and articulate your request. Your ability to present yourself and explain what you hope to gain from meeting with your contacts will determine their response to you. Why have you chosen this particular organization and, more importantly, this particular person to contact over all of the other possibilities? What specifically do you want to find out? These types of questions will help you to clarify your objectives in networking before you call or write contacts and will increase your chances of piquing their interest in meeting you. You must be prepared to say more than *"I am*

looking for a job and I was wondering if you know of any openings."
Consider instead:

> *"Hello, Mr./Ms. . This is Sally Smith. I am calling at the suggestion of Jack O'Neill. I sent you a letter last week explaining... (restate the first paragraph of your letter) and I was wondering if you might have 15 minutes next Tuesday or Thursday to meet with me?"*

Remember, you do not want to exert pressure on people to find you a job. You only want to explain the purpose of the meeting and articulate how you believe your contacts can be helpful. The objective is to unearth information about them and their job experience.

Choose a private, comfortable setting for making calls. Do not call while you are driving or from a public place with background noise. Starbucks is a great place to do job related research but not to make job related phone calls! Besides your script, keep a pen, pad and copy of your resume and letter at hand. Being prepared will help to ameliorate an attack of phone fright and will prevent you from omitting important information. Your script should include:

- whom you are calling (address the person by name)
- who referred you
- why you are calling (to determine the status of your letter)
- how you believe the person could be helpful

Your introduction should be brief, listener directed and upbeat. As the example suggests, consider giving the listener a choice between something and something, not a choice between something and nothing. For example: *"I was wondering if we might meet Tuesday afternoon or Thursday morning"* is more effective than *"I was wondering if we might meet next week."* Even if both Tuesday and Thursday are not convenient, offering a choice avoids complete rejection and steers your contact into discussing timing. Remember to confirm time and exact address, including floor and room number.

If people seem hesitant to grant your request to meet, clearly state that you are not looking for a job with them and that you are only looking for advice and information. For example:

Reluctant Contact: *"I really don't know of any openings. I'm not sure I can help you."*

Your Response: *"I appreciate your candor. At this point in my job search, I'm just trying to talk to as many people in the field as possible to get some feedback on my approach and brainstorm where possibilities may exist. I would appreciate it if you could spare 10 minutes for me. Does next Tuesday or Thursday work for you?"*

Suspicious Contact: *"If you are looking for a job you should contact HR."*

Your Response: *"Actually, I am not looking for a job at the moment, although I'd be happy to contact HR at a later day. Right now I am eager to meet as many people in the field as possible to get some feedback on my approach and brainstorm where possibilities* *may exist. I would be grateful if you could spare 10 minutes for me. Does next Tuesday or Thursday work for you?"*

Negative Contact: *"I can't help you. I'm not the person you should talk to."*

OR

"I don't have time to meet with you."

Your response: *Thanks for your candor. Could you suggest someone else I should talk to? Would it be ok if I used your name?*

If you are still met with resistance, politely bring the conversation to a close and than write a nice thank-you email, again stating your intended purpose. Mention your disappointment in not being able to learn from the person's experience and ask to be remembered for future reference. Attach your resume with this email.

Perhaps the greatest challenge when using the telephone is reaching your target. Voice mail has frustrated many job seekers. Be prepared to leave a detailed but short message of why you are calling and state a time when you will call back to alert your contact. **Do not simply leave a name and a phone number and expect a person to return your call.**

"Hello, Mr./Ms. . This is Sally Smith. I am calling at the suggestion of Jack O'Neill. I sent you a letter last week explaining... (restate the first paragraph of your letter) and I was hoping to arrange a time to meet with you. I'll call back this afternoon at 3 pm. If that time is not good for you and you would prefer to call me back, I can be reached at 212-555-2222. Thank you and I look forward to speaking with you."

Be sure to speak slowly and clearly, especially when leaving your phone number.

Reaching receptionists or secretaries can provide a unique set of problems. Keep in mind that it is part of their job to screen phone calls. Secretaries are trained to keep the unwanted world away from a busy boss.

Try to take control of the conversation from the beginning, following your script. Sound confident. If requested to give a reason for the call, offer, *"She is expecting my call. We have corresponded,"* or *"I am calling at the suggestion of Mr. O'Neill."* If your voice conveys uncertainty, you may be giving the secretary just cause to screen you out. NEVER try to deceive the secretary by saying, *"I am a friend,"* or *"it is a personal call."* You will only alienate your prospect.

Secretaries can be your best allies or among your biggest stumbling blocks. Be sure to get their name and establish friendly relationships. Remember, they have access to your target and are likely to share their impressions of you with the boss.

If you doubt that your target will return your call, indicate that you are going out and ask when might be a good time to call again. If after several calls, none have been returned, do not signal exasperation. This will make the secretary defensive. Instead, apologize for calling so often. Ask if you could schedule a phone appointment to break the cycle of telephone tag. The secretary may be moved by your respect for her time and either schedule a phone appointment or provide you with information about a better time to call, or, at least, place your message at the top of the pile.

If you cannot get the cooperation of the secretary, try calling before 9 a.m., after 5 p.m. or during lunch when your target person is more likely to answer his/her own phone.

Understand that it may take several attempts over a period of weeks—even months—to get someone's attention. Keep in mind that the way to get a response to any kind of marketing communication is to create multiple, <u>positive</u> impressions.

The Informational Interview
Once you are in your contact's office, it is your responsibility to lead the conversation. You should be prepared to:

- explain the purpose of the meeting
- show how your contact can be helpful
- present your background and abilities and skills to put the meeting in context
- ask questions to elicit the information you need
- present a pleasant, positive demeanor
- get the names of others who could be helpful
- be considerate of their time

The purpose of the meeting is to determine how your abilities, skills and talents could be used in different settings, so it is important to do a good job presenting them. The ability to communicate your qualifications to potential employers entails more than just informing them of your technical competence. You must be able to illustrate that you have the requisite personal attributes—things like problem solving abilities, analytical skills, assessment and planning capabilities—to perform the job. The examples you use to talk about your accomplishments should elucidate your thinking and problem solving style. The more concrete and specific you are, the better able your contact will be to think of possibilities for you and suggest additional people you should meet.

Go back to Chapter Three and review your examples from the Exercise #7: *Discover Your Abilities and Skills*. Again, you see why it is critical to engage in the self-assessment process <u>before</u> launching into the job search process. A common mistake people make when networking is to use the meeting as a therapy session. You do not want to inspire guilt, pity or dread. Your goal should be to make your contacts feel good about their ability to help you. It is important that you present yourself as positive, confident and self assured, not negative, needy and desperate. Never make your contacts feel sorry for you or responsible for your situation. Do not scoff at their suggestions by saying "I've tried that and it does not work"; otherwise your contacts will doubt their ability to help and begin to avoid you. If you need to express anger, bitterness, anxiety, etc., talk to a career coach or seek out a member of the clergy or a sympathetic friend before meeting with your contacts.

During your appointments you may want to address:

The careers of the people you are visiting:

- their background
- how their interest developed in this area
- what they like best/least about their work
- their "career steps" (what former jobs they held, what they learned from each, how they progressed from one job to the next)

Advantages and disadvantages of working with that:

- type of firm, agency or corporation
- geographical area

The structure of their organization and how it operates:

- whom they supervise, and to whom they report
- performance expectations
- advancement opportunities
- future growth potential

Characteristics the organization values in an employee.

Advice regarding how to make yourself an attractive candidate, including suggestions on:

- upgrading your resume
- interviewing techniques
- further educational and experiential qualifications you might pursue
- additional sources of information
- others in the field with whom you could speak

Information about any specific job openings you should consider

Once contacts get to know you, and you have asked questions about their career (showing genuine interest), it is their prerogative to offer further assistance. Towards the conclusion of your talk, their thoughts might naturally turn to what action they might take on your behalf.

You should express gratitude for offers of assistance and take notes if individuals suggest that you contact colleagues. You might add, *"Would it be OK if I use your name when contacting this person?"* If your contacts offer to send out your resumes for you or make calls on your behalf, make sure you arrange to get a list of those contacted so that you can take control of the follow-up process. Assuming responsibility for the follow-up process will allow your contacts to experience you as efficient and conscientious.

If your contacts do not offer assistance or additional names of people to call, you might gently ask if they could suggest names of individuals to speak to who could give you more information.

You may find that the 15 minutes you asked for stretched to a conversation lasting an hour or more. This usually occurs because people are flattered that you came to them for advice, and are asking about things of importance to them. However, it's up to <u>you</u> to stick to your preset time limit, and let your contacts take the initiative to extend the meeting, if desired.

People love to talk about themselves. This type of conversation tends to be very warm and animated, filled with good will. Even though they may not know of a specific job opening, your contacts are likely to keep you in mind when they do have one, or when colleagues are trying to fill a position, they may recommend you to them.

When you meet with people on your network list, take notes about the meeting. It would be helpful to start a file for each contact. Be sure to include:

- the contact's name (be sure you have the correct spelling)
- the date of the contact
- the results of the meeting
- follow-up that is required and the timeframe
- the person who referred you
- any personal information that may be helpful

- your impressions of the person and the organization

The job search process requires that you continually make phone calls, schedule appointments, write follow-up notes, contact new people, etc. It is important to record the dates and times for each activity to remind you what needs to be done. This will help to organize your days, which in turn will allow you to get more accomplished. Use the weekly action plan agenda you created in Chapter Two.

Follow-up Correspondence

When someone has taken the time to meet with you to provide information, advice and support, it is necessary and appropriate to send a thank-you note shortly after the meeting. While an e-mail is ok, a handwritten note—in the form of a note card or on your personal stationery—is better. It shows extra effort. Your message should convey gratitude for the time, attention and guidance shared.

People who help you should be kept apprised of your job search. Remember, the way to get a response to any kind of marketing communication is to create multiple, positive impressions. YOUR job search may not be the most important thing on your contact's mind. If you occasionally can remind people that you are still in the job search, other opportunities may present themselves down the line.

It is appropriate to reconnect with people to:

Update and inform. Reconnect with contacts periodically to update them on your job search activities or when new information arises. For example, if your contacts connect you to someone in their network, let them know how the meeting went. Keeping people up to speed is helpful, but don't overdo it. Only contact people if there is truly something of significance to report. If you find yourself calling or e-mailing more than once a week, you have wandered into the "pest" zone. Also, don't worry if your contact does not respond to your e-mail or if you do not speak with the person directly. Leave a **brief** voicemail message with the pertinent information. Don't ask them to return your call. Your goal is to minimize the amount of time and attention you ask of people. Your objective is simply to stay on their radar screen. If you haven't had a reason to connect, touch base every 4-6 weeks to check in. "Wanted to see if you've heard anything."

Solicit information and advice. Call contacts with simple questions. "I just scheduled an interview with "X" and was wondering if you might have 5 minutes to share any insights you might have." These types of solicitation should definitely not be made too often and the questions/guidance should be specific and in instances when their opinion would definitely make a difference. If you are considering asking them which tie to wear to the interview, you are wasting their time.

Share information of interest to THEM. Your job search activities may uncover information that may be of interest to your contacts. Perhaps you will learn information about emergent trends, client development opportunities or something of a personal nature. Make those connections whenever possible.

Finally, remember you want your contacts to always have a pleasant, positive experience during their interactions with you so that they will be inspired to refer you to people. It is NEVER appropriate to call your contacts to whine or complain. While the job search can be frustrating, use your friends and family or hire a career coach to help you through the rough patches, NOT your contacts. Most importantly, remember to let your contacts know when you have landed a position. Thank them again for their support and guidance and offer your willingness to return the favor.

After each informational interview, review your performance. Did you present your abilities and skills as effectively as possible? Did you craft your questions to elicit the information you needed? What could you have done better?

Organize the information you have received. Are there new books to read, new resources to consider, additional organizations to explore, new people to meet? Develop your plan of action based on this new information. Remember, the job search process is circuitous. Information you uncover while networking may suggest a need to revamp your resume or open up a new avenue of employers to research.

Informational interviewing requires a long term view, strategic planning and a commitment to working at it. It takes patience and perseverance to use this process to uncover job opportunities, but it is the most effective method to find a professional job.

CHAPTER SIX

BUILD YOUR NETWORK: Conduct Market Research, Part Two

BECAUSE THE INTERNET MAKES IT EASY TO "CONNECT" WITH people, many job hunters over use it and ignore the importance of face to face interactions. Being "linked to" or "friends with" someone is only the first step. You must take actions to nurture those relationships throughout your career, not just when you need something from them. And while relationships can be maintained or fostered easily enough online, human interaction is critical to making a positive connection last. You must be fearless about meeting people live.

In Chapter Five, the focus was on networking with people you know. Now we must focus on who you *need* to know. Anxiety often causes people to talk themselves out of participating in worthwhile networking activities that will enable them to meet new people and increase their visibility. The fear of walking into the office of someone they don't know or into a room filled with senior managers or total strangers is pervasive, cutting across boundaries of age, sex, race, socioeconomic level, professional and personal experience. But do whatever it takes to silence those discouraging voices in your head and motivate yourself to go anyway. Reassure yourself that once you are at the meeting or event, you will be fine. And, in the worst case scenario, if you <u>are</u> truly as miserable as those little voices in your head said you would be, you can always leave.

Challenge the myths you accepted as a child which may impede your ability to network effectively.

<u>MYTH 1</u>: **It is impolite to talk about yourself.**

We have grown up believing that it is tacky to use people for personal gain. Being polite means being unobtrusive, not asking direct questions, not talking about our personal lives and drawing as little attention to ourselves as possible.

<u>Reality</u>: You have many things to *offer* as well as to gain. By freely acknowledging that attending an event is good for you because it will provide you with the opportunity to mingle with senior executives, or to develop business, or to meet potential employers or simply because it feels good to support a cause, you will eliminate the feeling of "dishonesty" and "tackiness" and be able to enjoy the event and participate fully. The networking opportunities will develop naturally.

<u>MYTH 2</u>: **Don't talk to strangers.**

Ever since childhood parents instilled a fear about talking to people we did not know.

<u>Reality</u>: Consider the old saying, "Strangers are friends we haven't met yet." Think about what you have in common with others in the room. Are they members of the same industry or alumni or parents or church members or supporters of a political candidate, etc.? Determining the common bond makes it easier to approach people because they are no longer "strangers." You can then begin a conversation based on the common bond.

<u>MYTH 3</u>: **Wait until you are properly introduced.**

<u>Reality</u>: Because it is not always feasible to be introduced by a mutual acquaintance, you may need to "properly introduce" yourself. Design a two- to three-sentence self introduction that is clear, interesting and well delivered. (See your marketing statement in Chapter Three). Your goal is to tell people who you are in a pleasant, positive manner. Naturally, what you say will depend on the nature of the event. For example:

- <u>At a company function</u>: *"I recognize you from the elevator. I'm Katie McShane from the real estate group."*

- <u>At an industry convention</u>: *"Hello, my name is Katie McShane. I am a real estate lawyer from NYC."*

- <u>At a wedding</u>: *"Hello. I don't believe we've met. I'm Katie McShane, former college roommate of the bride."*

Fear of rejection often stands in the way of approaching new people. This particular obstacle is more imagined than real. Very few people will be openly hostile or rude, if for no other reason than that it is bad manners. To help overcome this fear, try adopting a "host mentality." Hosts are concerned with the comfort of others and actively contribute to that comfort. By focusing on making others feel welcomed and included, you will become more comfortable. Find the person standing alone and introduce yourself. That person will likely be grateful. But, even if you **are** met with rudeness, do not take it personally. There may be a hundred reasons why that person is not receptive. Simply move on.

The best networkers put people at ease from the outset, and that makes conversations flow naturally. People who are most successful at it are those who genuinely like people. There is nothing calculated or manipulative about attending events to meet people. Remind yourself what has brought this particular group of people together and why it is important for you to be there.

Mastering the art of small talk will ease any prevailing networking anxieties and is simple to do. If you read a newspaper or watch CNN or FoxNews you are ready for small talk. Use your observational skills to spark a lively, personal exchange. Consider one of the following three methods to get a conversation started.

- <u>Share an observation</u>. Comment on a current, relevant news event or the situation at hand. Remark on the facility, food, organization, traffic, parking dilemma, etc. Remember, the comment ought to be positive and upbeat. Look for those bridges that have led the two of you to be in the same room.

- <u>Ask an open ended question</u>. (EXAMPLES: *"How long have you been a member of this organization?" "How do you fit into this picture?" "How do you know the bride or groom?"*) Be careful not to fire off too many questions; you want to engage people in a conversation, not make them feel like they are being interrogated.

- Reveal something about yourself. Disclosing something about you helps to establish vulnerability and approachability. (EXAMPLE: *"I have worked here for 3 months and have never been to the 48th floor."*) Volunteering information about you will make the other person feel safe about doing the same. Be careful not to reveal anything too personal that may burden the listener. (EXAMPLE: *"My spouse just asked me for a divorce."*)

There is a natural rhythm to small talk. It should be interactive. After the initial introduction, the flow is probe, response, comment.

EXAMPLE: (at an industry event)

Introduce: "I don't believe we've met. I'm Mary Reilly."

Probe: "Which organization are you with?"

Response: *"I'm Jack DeMario, with ABC Corporation."*

Comment: "I've heard great things about ABC."

Probe: "What is your role there?"

Response: *"I am with the marketing group."*

Comment: "I just graduated with a degree in marketing."

Probe: "Does your company use social media to reach clients?"

Even if the other person does not ask you any probing questions, you will be able to move the conversation forward. Naturally, the comment and follow-up probe should be based on what was said.

In any networking situation, it is wise to ask great questions and get others to do most of the talking. This way you will learn valuable information about the other person and their jobs. Assuming Mary Reilly is looking for a job in marketing, the conversation is likely to flow based on their mutual interests. If Jack DeMario was with a group Mary had little interest in, it would still be wise to continue the conversation with a few probing questions.

> Introduce: "I don't believe we've met. I'm Mary Reilly."
>
> Probe: "Which organization are you with?"
>
> Response: *"I'm Jack DeMario, with ABC Corporation."*
>
> Comment: "I've heard great things about ABC."
>
> Probe: "What is your role there?"
>
> Response: *"I am the head of risk management."*
>
> Comment: "I have heard the term "risk management" a lot throughout college, but I have to admit, I am not really sure what it entails."
>
> Probe: "What kinds of things is your department responsible for?"

Not every conversation will lead to a new connection or a job opportunity. However, genuine curiosity is enough to keep the conversation flowing. At some point Jack is likely to ask Mary, *"Where do you work?"* or *"What do you do?"* and she can respond, *"I just graduated XYZ University with a degree in Marketing and I am looking to join a company interested in growing its social media presence. Does your company use social media?"* Jack may offer to introduce Mary to the head of marketing at his company or he may simply say, *"I have no idea."* Allow the conversation to come to a natural close and move on.

The objective of attending an event is to meet a number of people, so it is not rude to move on. It is important to circulate. Do not monopolize any one person's time, and do not allow your time to be monopolized by any one person. If someone has latched on to you, choose whether or not you want to make it your responsibility to take care of him/ her throughout the event, thereby missing other opportunities present in the room. To make an exit, offer a connecting gesture like a handshake or a pat on the arm or shoulder and simply say:

- *"I am sure there are other people you need to talk to. I do not want to monopolize your time. It has been interesting speaking with you."*

- *"Excuse me, it was nice meeting you."*

- *"Excuse me; there is someone I need to say hello to."*
  (Make sure you move to another part of the room.)

- To join the next group, simply say: *"Excuse me for interrupting, but I wanted to say hello."*

Another option would be to position yourself close to a group already engaged in conversation. Avoid groups that appear to be engaged in private, intimate conversations. Give facial feedback to comments. When you feel included (usually after you have established eye contact with someone in the group), feel free to join the conversation.

Remember to be open to others who may want to join a group you are already a part of. If you are doing the introductions, remember to "introduce up". Bluntly put, that means introduce the person with the lesser title to the person with the higher title.

If there IS something you want from someone you meet, decide whether it is appropriate to ask at that moment or if it would be sufficient to exchange information and follow-up at a later date. Often times, the latter is the better option. Say, *"I would love to learn more about how you use social media, but I don't want to monopolize your time here. Would it be ok if I contact you next week to set up a time to meet?"*

Jot notes on the back of business cards to ensure you remember what was discussed. Send an invitation via LinkedIn to build the relationship. Keep in mind, the person who collects the most business cards is NOT the winner. If you are simply collecting cards, you probably haven't established an impression and it is likely the person will not remember you after the event.

Business cards are a must in order to facilitate the exchange of information with people you meet. Place your business cards in an easy to reach place. You may want to invest in an attractive card carrying case. Once you have established rapport and decided you are interested in exchanging cards, offer yours first. People will typically return in kind. If they do not, you could also ask if they are on LinkedIn and send them a personalized invitation the next day.

Finally, you are completely responsible for what you bring into a room/meeting and for what you project onto other people. Think about how other people see you. Inferences about your abilities are based on the image you project. People are judged not only by the words they choose to articulate a thought, but also by the tone and body language used during the delivery. Competence is inferred by the way we speak about what we know. It is important to be mindful of the images you project, not so as to live up to the images of others, but to ensure that any inferences made about you accurately reflect who you are. To do so, you must develop effective communication skills. This is not to suggest that form is more important than substance. However, you do not want your "form" to impede your ability to project competency.

Perception IS reality. If you look and act like a loser, or someone who does not belong, that is exactly how people will respond to you. Your facial expression, posture and willingness to launch conversations matter. Your body language plays an important role in how people receive your message. To ensure your body always supports your message, consider the following tips.

Dress for success. Business casual has created distinct challenges in today's workplace. It is more difficult to define what dressing for success looks like. To state the obvious, your look should always be neat, ironed and professional. Pay attention to the details: hair, nails, shoe shine, etc. The packaging is important.

Make eye contact. Look people directly in the eye when you are speaking. This serves three purposes. 1) It demonstrates confidence. You appear in control. 2) It engages people. Your eyes are like magnets; people cannot look away. They will feel acknowledged and drawn in to the conversation. 3) It provides instant feedback to determine how your message is being received. You will be able to see if people are confused, doubtful, bored, etc., and adjust your message accordingly.

Use your body to project confidence. Your stance should convey power and authority. Stand tall with your shoulders back and your feet firmly planted about hip width apart. This will allow you to balance your weight and minimize distracting shifts from leg to leg as well as rocking backing and forth or swaying, which makes you look nervous and uncomfortable.

The same principle applies when seated. Your feet should be flat on the ground and your forearms should be placed on the table. Sit on the front two thirds of the chair to ensure you are sitting straight. While this is not the most comfortable way to sit, it is the most commanding. When you are in the listener role, you can assume a more comfortable position.

Understand the power of your voice. Your voice is a very powerful, seldom thought about, tool. Notice effective speakers. There is a pace and a rhythm to their speech patterns. They project their voices, use pauses for dramatic effect and always manage to have a conversational tone to better connect with the people with whom they are speaking. Speak slowly, enunciate clearly and smile when appropriate to let your enthusiasm and energy come through.

Be mindful of word choice. Some words don't belong in business. There is never a need for expletives, racial epithets or sexually charged language. Also be mindful of how you use words such as "like," "you know" and other colloquialisms. They signal a lack of polish and professionalism. And whatever you do, avoid calling anyone "dude" or "bro."

Remember to breathe. If your speech pattern is peppered with "ums," "uhs," "ers," "you knows" and "likes," it is probably because you are nervous and aren't breathing properly. At the end of each sentence, take a breath, focus your eyes and deliver the next sentence or thought. Power is never rushed.

Remember, communication involves the intentions and actions of the speaker as well as the interpretations of the listener. While the person delivering the message knows exactly what is meant to be conveyed, the words chosen and the manner used to present the information may support or completely negate the intent. And sometimes, no matter how clearly the intended message was presented, listeners receive information through their own set of filters, which may distort the intended message and result in miscommunication.

You cannot control how other people share or process information. But you can consider their style and adapt your own style to improve communication. The purpose of adjusting your style to others is not simply to be nice. It is more self serving than that. By giving your listeners what THEY need, you are more likely to get what YOU need from the exchange. For example, is your listener a fast moving, action oriented extrovert or a quiet, thoughtful introvert? Is this someone who likes lots of details and information or only bottom line information? Is this someone with whom you can think out loud or someone who only wants to hear the end decision? Answers to these questions can help you adjust your approach.

Dress and behave like a professional; be positive and upbeat; project a proud, confident image. Radiate confidence and people will be naturally drawn to you in every situation throughout your career. That will help to ensure that you have limitless resources in place when you need them.

EXERCISE #14: Attend an Event

Challenge yourself to attend a relevant professional event. Consider an alumni function, association meeting or community event; any place where you do not know many attendees. Practice your networking skills by making it a goal to meet 3 new people and strategize how to build the relationship after the event.

CHAPTER SEVEN

ON YOUR MARK, GET SET, GO!: Apply for Jobs

THE INTERNET IS A GREAT TOOL WHICH HAS MADE JOB HUNTING both easier and more difficult. It is easier to find opportunities and apply more quickly to a wider audience without the cost of expensive resume paper, matching envelopes and postage. However, because it is easier to apply, job seekers often apply to everything with little thought about finding the right match. They join "talent' communities, set up search agents, link to or friend everyone they can and spend the majority of their job search hours on the computer. Then, after applying to thousands of positions and receiving no interviews, job seekers get discouraged and ultimately quit trying.

To mitigate these difficulties, you must use on-line applications in conjunction with every other resource available to you in order to be effective. Sitting home in your pajamas applying to jobs on-line without doing any follow up is not likely to yield the results you want. Applying on line is just the first step.

To find jobs on-line, start with the broad search engines such as www.careerbuilders.com or www.monster.com. Their drop down menus and search tools will typically lead you to niche websites or company websites. (Revisit Exercise 4 in Chapter Two).

If you can apply directly through a company website, you should. Studies show they have a higher rate of return than applying to job boards. If you are having a difficult time locating the career section of a particular company, google "jobs at Company name" and scan the results to find the page that has the company name in the url. (It is usually not at the top of the search.)

Some career pages are easier to navigate than others. The easier ones allow you to download a resume and cover letter, answer a few EEOC questions and you are done. Others will allow you to download your resume but they also want you to fill out a form which covers the very information found on your resume. You must fill in those forms to increase your chances of having your attached resume reviewed. It is time consuming and annoying but necessary.

Some websites will allow you to download your resume and automatically fills in the form for you. However, make sure you review all the information to ensure it translated properly. (It does not always!)

Finally, there are those websites that require you to answer prescreening questions. These present a unique challenge because the questions are often written for a wide range of positions within the company and don't always make sense in the context of the position for which you are applying. Again, it is time consuming and annoying to answer these questions, but necessary if you want to be considered for the position.

The most challenging websites require you to answer a laundry list of questions in order to apply for a position. The Government refers to this section as SKA (Skills, Knowledge and Abilitites) but the questions come in a wide variety of shapes and forms. Some want you to write paragraphs to answer questions while others offer you limited drop down options. The questions with the * require responses while the others do not. Be as truthful and as thorough as possible when answering the questions; however, when the question is vague, always give yourself the benefit of the doubt in interpreting the question and crafting your response.

The hardest question to address is the salary question. If they ask "what is your current salary" there is no way to reframe the question so, if the question has an asterisk, you must give them the information in order to proceed. If it allows you to leave it blank, do that and deal with the question during the interview. If they ask "what salary range are you seeking" you should visit www.payscale.com and complete the "what if" scenario to come up with a realistic range. Again, if you can proceed without supplying a number, that is the best option.

Whichever type of website you encounter, be prepared to invest at least 30-45 minutes to complete the application. If you are in a rush, bookmark the page and do it when you have time. Many websites will not allow you to save an incomplete application and return later.

According to the Society of Human Resource Managers (SHRM), computers read your resume first, not a human being. Software is designed to search for specific words, so format your electronic resume to work for you by investing the time to tailor it to specific positions. At least 75% of on-line resumes are discarded for using the wrong words.

Incorporate the language used in the job postings to describe your experiences.

SHRM also indicates that more than 20% of resumes are screened out due to formatting issues. To avoid this issue, use the *Save As* function on your computer to create a second version of your resume in ASCII text or Rich Text Format to eliminate all the underlining, italics and graphics on your resume. These are easier to use when posting resumes in on-line databases. You will only need to proofread the new document once to ensure information translated properly during the reformatting process. Then you can cut and paste the document into the on-line database.

Even if a cover letter is optional, include one anyway. Its purpose is to support your candidacy by supplementing the information set forth in your resume and offer the employer a glimpse of your personality. A cover letter should:

- convince the reader that you are worth getting to know better.

- draw attention away from liabilities by addressing potential questions the resume may raise.

- emphasize salient achievements and accomplishments in greater depth than the resume does.

- introduce new sales material that is not included on your resume.

- demonstrate enthusiasm and knowledge of the industry.

A cover letter is the ideal place to focus on the specific abilities and skills you want to emphasize for a particular employer. Some general guidelines for writing good cover letters include:

- Use correct grammar, good sentence structure and standard business letter format.

- State the purpose of your letter. If you are responding to an ad, indicate the source. If you are writing at the suggestion of a mutual acquaintance, indicate that immediately. Cover letters should be slanted as individually as possible.

- Pinpoint how your abilities, skills and experience relate to the particular needs of the employer to whom you are writing. Focus your letter on the needs of the reader. Focus on what <u>you</u> can do for the employer. What credentials, abilities, skills and experience do you have that would help the employer? No one cares what the job would do for you.

- Always be objective when describing yourself to an employer. For example, instead of writing *"I am a hard worker," "I would be a great asset to your firm"* or *"I have many leadership qualities,"* show them by means of examples from your past: *"The experience I gained as director of the office is indicative of my leadership abilities."*

- Address your letter to a specific person by name and title whenever possible. You may need to do some research to identify the proper person.

- Limit your cover letter to three or four paragraphs. It should rarely be more than one page.

- Present unique or distinctive attributes, without using superlatives, in an attractive, professional and well written manner.

- Close your cover letter with a request for an interview indicating what action you will take—i.e., that

you will call them (within 7-10 days) to arrange a
meeting. Then follow through.

- Keep careful records of the positions for which you
  have applied. Maintain copies of your correspondence with dates indicating when you will follow-up.
  FOLLOW-UP is crucial.

EXERCISE #15: Craft a Cover Letter

<u>First paragraph</u>: Mention the name of any person who referred you to this employer <u>first</u>, if this information is available to include. Otherwise, start your letter with a powerful statement that will grab the reader's attention. Identify yourself and the type of position you are seeking. State how you heard about this job opening. *("As a summa cum laude graduate at Princeton with a B.S. in Economics, I am writing in response to your posting on Careerbuilders for X job.")*

<u>Second paragraph</u>: Explain why you are qualified for or interested in this particular position. Stress how <u>you</u> can benefit the employer and what <u>you</u> have to offer to them. Don't repeat word for word the text of your resume. Rather, highlight and embellish upon the most significant aspects of your background with regard to the particular employer. Consider using bullets to draw attention to your accomplishments. If you are responding to an ad, try to use the language used in the ad to describe your experience.

<u>Third paragraph</u> *(optional)*: If you are applying for a position in a different geographic location, explain your ties to or interest in that locale.

<u>Fourth paragraph</u>: Restate your interest in the particular organization, and express your desire for an interview. State how the employer may contact you <u>if</u> your address and phone number are <u>different</u> from the information on your resume. You may also state that you will call to set up an

appointment. If you are truly interested in this job, feel free to take the initiative.

If you choose to post your resume in a searchable database, make sure there is a confidentiality feature so that your contact information will not be distributed until you agree to release it to a specific employer. Also, make sure those resumes are dated so you can confirm a resume is the most current version.

After you have submitted your application, you still have work to do. Review the list of contacts you developed in Chapters Five and Six. Does anyone work at the organization to which you have just applied? Do not assume that because you discussed your career goals with them earlier they will automatically think of you. Reach out to the person.

"Mary, I wanted to let you know that I applied to the X position your company advertised on its webpage this morning. I would appreciate any tips you might have on how I can secure an interview."

Even if no one on your list works at the target company, consider the possibility that someone on your contact list knows someone who works at the organization to which you have applied. Use this as an opportunity to reconnect with your contact and remind them you are actively looking. Contact that person and say something like:

To a contact with a known connection to the employer: *"I wanted to let you know that I applied for a position at XYZ corporation advertised on hotjobs. I remembered that they were a client of yours. Could I ask* *you to mention my name to your contact?"* **Or** *"Do you know anyone in the sales department that I could follow up with?"*

To other contacts: *"I applied to a position at XYZ corporation and wanted to see if you knew anyone there."*

To a LinkedIn connection: *"I saw that you are connected to Joe Smith at ABC corporation. I just applied to a position there and would appreciate it if you would introduce me so that I can follow up on my application."*

Let's assume you do not know anyone with a connection to the employer. Get creative. Look at the investor relations page on the company website to see who is on the Board of Directors that you or one of your contacts might know. Check out LinkedIn's search by company feature to see if you can find the name of someone to follow up with. Even if you do not know the person or anyone who can introduce you, send that person an email or letter introducing yourself and express an interest in the role.

You could also Google *"Human Resources Director at XYZ Company"* to see if you can uncover a name or call the organization's general number and ask for the proper spelling of the head of human resources department or the department in which you have an interest. Do not ask to *speak* with that person. It will be obvious that it is a solicitation of some sort. Make two phone calls. That way, when you call back later in the day and ask for Mary Jones, your call will be less suspect and you will have a greater chance of getting through. Follow up directly with that person to ensure that your resume has been received and ask if there is any additional information you can supply. Always take the *"how can*

I be helpful to you" approach rather than the *"why haven't you called me in for an interview yet?"* approach.

Finally, when it comes to on-line resumes, think before you submit. Wait a day, rereview the job posting and decide if it is a good fit before you apply. Don't wait several days or weeks or the job might disappear, but do allow yourself a short amount of time to consider your qualifications for the position and your strategy for applying and following-up. It is the quality of the applications that makes the difference, not the quantity.

Keep in mind, ads are written for the *"perfect"* candidate and the *"perfect"* candidate rarely exists. If you possess 60% of the stated qualifications, consider applying.

Like job hunting on line, working with recruiters can be both a positive and a negative. Candidates who come through a recruiter come with a huge price tag, usually about a third of the candidate's first year salary. By using your contacts to stay in the information loop and uncovering openings, you can approach employers directly, thereby eliminating the fee and making yourself a more attractive candidate. However, with that said, it is still important for job seekers to learn how to incorporate headhunters into their job search activities.

Because it is the headhunters' business to know what is happening in the marketplace, they can provide valuable information about things like which academic and professional credentials are hot and which geographic regions have increasing opportunities. They generally do not work with entry level candidates, but if a recruiter calls you, take the call. Keep an open mind at least long enough to hear the pitch and see what you can learn.

Before you decide to proceed with a headhunter, ask what procedures will be followed as well as what precautions will be taken to ensure your privacy and maintain the confidentiality of all transactions. Generally, the process follows a similar pattern. First, you will be interviewed by the headhunter to determine what you are looking for and if any suitable positions currently exist. If so, you will be asked for your permission to send your resume to the employer. Do not give blanket approval to distribute your resume everywhere, particularly if you are working with several recruiters. That could create a fee dispute and cause problems for the employer. If you learn of an opening independently, do not let the headhunter send your resume. Send it yourself to avoid the price tag.

The headhunter's task is to present your credentials in such a way as to entice the employer to want to meet you. Provide the headhunter with as much relevant information as possible to make that step easy. Once that is accomplished, you can expect multiple interviews with the employer. If the employer determines that you are the candidate he wants to hire, you will begin salary negotiations through the headhunter.

It is important to remember that the fee paying employer is the headhunter's "client" while you are merely the "candidate." The role of the headhunter is NOT to help you find a job; it is to help his or her client successfully fill a position. The headhunter always works for the employer and is paid to tend to the client's interest. The headhunter is not your pal, nor your therapist. This is a business relationship, so the information you choose to share is critical to how you will be presented to her client.

The bottom line is once you have applied for a position—whether on line or through a recruiter--you want to talk to as many people as possible to make sure your resume gets noticed and you land the interview.

CHAPTER EIGHT

Get the Offer: Interview Strategies that Work

THE BASIC QUESTION IN EVERY INTERVIEW IS *"WHY SHOULD I hire you?"* Your objective is to translate your abilities, skills and attributes into benefits for the *employer*. It is now time to fully implement the winning formula: **Self Assessment + Market Assessment = Career Success!** You must be able to verbalize *why* your strengths are of *value* to this specific employer. Do not expect your past experience to speak for itself; be prepared to state the obvious.

The interviewer's objective is to assess your credentials, form an impression about your personality and determine the degree to which your interests and background correspond with the employer's hiring needs. Your background and record of accomplishments are amplified or diminished in the eyes of the recruiter by the general impression you create. Again, this is not to suggest that form is more important than substance; however, you want to ensure that the form you present does not create any barriers that prevent the employer from experiencing your substance.

The first few minutes of the interview are crucial. Employers make up their mind about candidates very early. Your handshake must be firm and confident, your gaze steady, your appearance impeccable and your confidence apparent.

Throughout the interview, decision makers are searching for clues that address the following questions:

- Can you do the job?
- Do you interact with people easily?
- Are you easy to interview, confident and clear in your answers?
- Do you listen?
- Do you ask sensible questions?
- Are you likeable?
- Will you complement or disrupt the department?
- Do you demonstrate good judgment?

Interviewers typically use one of five interviewing methods to learn about candidates. Understanding the differences among these interviewing styles and preparing a strategy to effectively deal with each of them will improve your chances for success.

1. Behavioral Interview. Precise questions designed to elicit specific information about how your accomplishments demonstrate the behaviors that have proven successful at their organization are asked. The questions are formulated from the contents of your resume. Strategy: Answers should be brief and should objectively emphasize *how* you achieved concrete accomplishments. Be concise but do not fall into the trap of responding with

monosyllabic yes or no answers. Review the company website to get a sense of the behaviors important to the organization and select stories that demonstrate success in those areas.

2. Nondirective Interview. The interviewer's intent is to get the candidate to do all the talking. This usually does not work to your advantage. Your goal should be to get the interviewer to do at least 50% of the talking. Strategy: Construct a narrative history of yourself in advance to enable you to make a clear, concise statement explaining your purpose at the interview. Attempt to draw the interviewer into the conversation by asking questions.

3. Stress Interview. This is perhaps the most difficult interview of all. Its purpose is to measure your poise and emotional stability. The interviewer tries to appear curt, argumentative and/or impatient, firing questions in rapid succession. The questions may be designed to bait you into a topical argument. Strategy: Remain patient and calm. Indicating annoyance, tension or nervousness serves no purpose. To avoid a debate, try to change the topic by asking a question. Remember, this type of interview is designed to rattle you.

4. Free Wheeling Interview. This type of interview lacks any semblance of structure or direction. Since many managers have limited interviewing experience, they have no tactical plan. Strategy: Control the flow of the conversation by opening the interview with highlights of your accomplishments and then move directly into your own questions. This helps put the interviewer at ease and helps to focus him/her on your assets.

5. <u>Hypothetical/Problem Solving Interview</u>. During this type of interview the employer will pose an industry specific problem to solve. They are trying to determine your technical knowledge. Oftentimes they are less concerned about you having the "right" answer and more concerned about your problem solving process. <u>Strategy</u>: Take a moment to consider the question. Do not be afraid of silence. It demonstrates thoughtfulness. Demonstrate that you can spot the issues and indicate where/how you would approach the problem.

While it is natural to be nervous in interviews, your goal is to focus on your message, not on your nerves. Remember, you would not be approaching this meeting at all if you were not qualified for the position. Your thorough preparation has made you aware of both your strengths and your weaknesses. But remember, the interviewer is there to see what you <u>have</u> to offer, not to hear explanations about what you don't have. When you practice answering interview questions, eliminate all "nos", "nots", "didn'ts", "althoughs", "buts" and "howevers" from your speech. Rephrase your answers using positive speech forms. This will prepare you to speak about yourself in a positive light.

Think of at least three main points you want to make. Use concrete and clear examples that demonstrate these strengths. Focus on these identified strengths during the interview and present them with conviction and enthusiasm. Remember that the interviewer must be able to see and hear the enthusiasm that you wish to portray.

Try to anticipate the types of questions you will be asked and prepare multi level responses. Write out your answers. Review and edit them. First, give a <u>brief</u> summary, akin to a verbal outline, covering all salient points. Second, pause to gauge the interest of the interviewer and give a more detailed description if the interviewer seems interested or asks you to go on. Be certain that your responses highlight your abilities and skills, demonstrate your knowledge and expertise and reflect your motivation and personality. Even if you believe it is obvious that you are highly qualified for the position, take time to collect your thoughts and think about your answers.

EXERCISE #16: Plan the Interview

Write out the answers to the following questions.

1. What are the three points I must make at some time during our conversation?

2. What are my most marketable abilities and skills?

3. What are the abilities and skills I most want to use in my next job?

4. What is the question I am most afraid of being asked? How will I respond?

5. What are the aspects (tendencies, interview abilities, comfort level, specific questions I am nervous about being asked) of the interview situation on which I most need to work?

EXERCISE #17: Craft Responses to
Interview Prep Questions

Rehearse your answers to the following questions.

1. Tell me about yourself. (What they're really asking here is, "What in your background makes you a good candidate for this job?")

2. What are your long range and short range goals and objectives? (Be sure to make the connection between your goals and this job for which you're interviewing.)

3. What do you see yourself doing five years from now? (Again, tie your answer into the position available. Never, ever say you want to be doing something unrelated.)

4. What two or three accomplishments have given you the most satisfaction? Why? (Talk about specific projects, especially if they are relevant to the position.)

5. In what ways do you think you can make a contribution to our firm/company?

6. In what sort of environment are you most comfortable? (Your favorite environment should be similar to that of the employer with whom you are interviewing.)

7. Why do you want to work with our company/firm? (Be specific. Show you've done your research. Make sure the interviewer knows that you understand their business).

8. What do you consider to be the strongest qualities in your personality and character? (List about 3 and relate them to the job opening.)

9. I see from your resume that you (play basketball <u>or</u> speak French <u>or</u> are interested in real estate, etc. This is <u>not</u> a statement where you answer "yes" or "no." Hear this as: <u>tell me more about</u> ....).

10. What else do you think I should know about you? (From your preparation beforehand you will have an additional strength or accomplishment that you'll want to highlight here. Don't say there isn't anything else. You're more exciting than that.)

Identify every question you dread being asked. Prepare a succinct answer for each. Practice saying the answer aloud. Go over each question and response repeatedly until you are desensitized to the stress each causes.

If you believe negative assumptions are being made about you (e.g., that you are too young to be taken seriously or too old to take supervision from someone junior, or lack a specific skill set, etc.,) address the elephant in the room by offering evidence to assuage their fears and prove their assumptions are not true. But proceed with caution. You do not want to highlight a "problem" the employer doesn't have with your candidacy.

Before you walk in the door, obtain information about the employer from as many sources as possible. You do not want to waste valuable time asking questions that can easily be answered by reading the employer's website or doing a Google search. The more information you have before the interview the better you will be able to make a convincing connection between your abilities and skills and the employer's needs.

Assemble your interview kit. It should contain:

- Contact information/directions to interview
- Extra copies of your resume
- Transcripts
- Reference list or letters

Expect the unexpected so that you will not get rattled if things do not go according to plan. Interviewers may change, you may meet more people than expected or client demands may affect the appointment time. And remember, every question counts. Something as innocent as, "Did you have any trouble finding us?" could start the interview off on a bad note if you carry on about traffic, bad directions, etc.

During the interview, you must:

Establish rapport—In addition to tangible things such as a good, firm handshake and appropriate eye contact, there are additional items that develop rapport between people. These include friendliness and sincere interest in the interviewer, as well as warmth and responsiveness to the interviewer. You must become aware of body language. Be sensitive to cues of boredom. If the interviewer keeps looking down at your resume or out the window, bring the statement you are making to a close.

Listen carefully—Try to hear the question behind the question and respond to the interviewer's concerns. Get the interviewer to talk about the position to uncover exactly what is being sought. This will enable you to illustrate how you can fill these needs.

Ask questions—Remember, this is a conversation; there should be interaction. Ask technical questions to demonstrate your knowledge of the field and to show that you are already looking for solutions to the employer's problems. Do NOT ask about benefits, vacations, pensions and hours until you know you have an offer. However, be prepared to answer questions about salary and benefits if posed by the interviewer. (Refer back to Chapter Two for tips on how to handle the salary question).

Get feedback—Before the end of the interview, ask if you have the qualifications they are seeking. If not, now is the best time to find out so you can adjust your approach.

Take control of the follow-up process—When interviewers indicate they will "let you know," ask if you can call on a specific day in the future. This may help to accelerate the decision making process. Also, let them know if you have other offers.

Maintain a positive attitude—Adopt a "have done—can do—will do" attitude. It is not always what you say that counts but how you say it. View anything negative as a challenge, an opportunity, and something exciting. Do not be apologetic about anything; handle your "Achilles' heel" factually and nondefensively.

You can help an inexperienced interviewer feel more comfortable by asking questions. Your prepared questions can demonstrate your knowledge of the field and your interest in the employer and provide the interviewer with an opportunity to relax by talking about something with which he/she is familiar. You can ask things like:

- *"What do you see as the growth areas of the company?"*
- *"What products are likely to do well in the next few years?"*
- *"What criteria are used to evaluate performance?"*
- *"What role does the position play in helping the company achieve its mission?"*
- *"What are the five most important duties?"*
- *"From a management perspective, what skills/attributes do you think are most important?"*

If you believe negative assumptions are being made about you, confidently address the issue in order to eliminate the perceptions.

- *"During other interviews, I have been asked about (my ability to accept supervision from someone younger than I am, or limited experience in X or my commitment to this geographic area), and we haven't talked about that yet."*

By offering questions that allow the interviewer to relax and think about the answers, the interview becomes a freer exchange of information, which benefits all the parties involved. You will appear more confident and the interviewer will feel more comfortable in your presence and will be more likely to recommend you. Your questions should not convey an undue concern over salary or time off or any of the more mundane aspects of the job. Stay interested in important aspects such as challenge, responsibility and those that show a mature and forward thinking mentality. The dollars and cents concerns can be ironed out after an offer has been made.

Hiring decisions tend to be based on somewhat subjective material. Unfortunately, trying to determine if someone "fits in" to a particular environment can lead to subtle forms of discrimination. While interviewers usually try to avoid asking personal questions, most want to know all they can about the applicants. Help them by providing information that you are comfortable with discussing and would like the interviewer to know. The information you volunteer about yourself will be different from what every other applicant offers and will help you stand out in the crowd. A word of caution: do not allow yourself to be lured into intimate chit-chat. Regardless of the kindness of the interviewer, <u>nothing</u>

is "off the record." Keep your comments job related and, if you can complement your resume in any way by adding something, do it.

Applicants who are not aware of what questions should and should not be asked are more likely to be victims of discrimination. The general rule of thumb is, if the information is not specifically job related, it should not be asked.

Examples of potentially *sensitive*—though not necessarily *unlawful*—subjects include:

- name origin
- residence
- age
- birthplace
- military service
- national origin
- sex
- marital status
- family size
- race
- color
- physical description (i.e., the "tall one," "the blonde one" etc.)
- physical condition
- photograph
- religion
- arrest record
- criminal record
- fraternal membership

HOW the question is posed can determine its lawfulness. For example, asking *"Are you a U.S. Citizen?"* or *"Where were you born?"* is different from asking you *"Are you autho-*

rized to work in the U.S.?" Similarly, while it is acceptable for an employer to inquire *"Are you willing to relocate?"* it is not acceptable for him/her to attempt to infer the answer to that by asking *"Are you married?"*

In most states there are laws that render some questions illegal, the general results being that an employer should not ask:

- if the applicant has worked under another name;
- the maiden name of the wife or mother of the applicant;
- an applicant to take a pre-employment physical examination or to inquire about the nature and severity of physical or mental handicaps;
- about marital plans, arrangements for child care, current or anticipated pregnancy status;
- about the occupations of spouses, parents or siblings;
- for information relating to family background that may reveal race, ethnicity, religion, citizenship and/ or national origin;
- about holidays observed or membership in clubs, churches and fraternities;
- about languages written, spoken or read unless the employer is specifically seeking to hire someone with that particular skill;
- for proof of age;
- for a photograph <u>prior</u> to the interview;

When you suspect an interviewer has lured you into a dangerous area, you have three response options.

<u>Answer the question</u>. Realize, however, that you are providing information that is not job related and you risk harming your candidacy by responding "incorrectly."

<u>Refuse to answer the question</u>. While you are in your rights to do so, you will probably alienate the employer and come across as uncooperative, confrontational and hostile. Not exactly the ideal description of a desirable applicant.

<u>Reframe the question</u>. Consider the intent of the question. In other words, try to hear the question behind the question. For example, is the employer asking about your birthplace because there is a concern about your social status or is it because the interviewer grew up in the same place and is simply trying to make small talk?

Avoid becoming angry, hostile or argumentative. Calmly examine the clumsily expressed question to uncover the underlying concerns of the interviewer. For example, an employer who questions a woman if she is married or about her plans to have children is not really interested in the candidate's personal life but rather is probably attempting to learn how committed the candidate is to the job. You may answer such a question effectively by saying, *"I am assuming by your question that you are concerned with whether or not I will be able to spend the long hours at the office required to get the work done. I'd like to reassure you by mentioning that throughout school, I held a full time job, did well in my classes, studied long hours in the library and was not held back in any way by outside responsibilities."*

It is appropriate to send a thank-you email shortly after an interview. It should be crafted not only to thank people for the time they spent with you and the information they provided, but also to restate your interest and clarify any pertinent information you want the employer to remember. Your email should be structured to affirm that you:

- paid attention to what was said;
- understood the interviewer's concerns;
- are excited about the job; that you can and want to do it;
- can contribute to the organization immediately.

Some general guidelines for writing strong thank-you emails include:

- Use a salutation.
- Use correct grammar, good sentence structure and standard business letter format.
- Pinpoint how your abilities, skills and experience relate to the particular needs of the employer as described during the interview. Focus on what <u>you</u> can do for the employer (what credentials, abilities, skills and experience you have that would help the employer), not what the job would do for you.
- Limit your thank-you email to two or three paragraphs.
- Close by affirming your interest/enthusiasm for the position.

If you interviewed with more than one person, you have two options. You could send a thank-you email to each person; however, do not send three or four people the exact same email. You ought to vary them to reflect a specific aspect of the conversation you had with each individual person.

The second option would be to send one to either the most senior person or the person with whom you established the greatest rapport and cc the others.

Try to avoid the temptation of interpreting what the employer is thinking. Just because you do not hear from the employer the next day or even the next week, do not assume a rejection will follow. Selecting candidates is a slow, time consuming process. While two weeks on your end of the telephone seems like an eternity, that same timeframe flies by in a flash for an employer. If three or four weeks go past and you have not heard from the employer, call to "check on the status" of your application and reaffirm your interest and enthusiasm for the position.

*"I wanted to follow up to see if there is any additional infor-
mation I can provide to help you make your decision."*

OR

*"I wanted to see if you have any sense of your timeline for
making a decision so I can adjust my search accordingly.
I am very interested in this opportunity."*

NEVER bluff and say you have an offer!

Do yourself—and the employer—a favor: Interview as if everything depended on you. Walk in with a clear idea of two or three selling points you would like to express. Use the interviewer's questions to introduce those points and back them up with real life examples. At the end of the interview, summarize your qualifications and articulate your interest and enthusiasm for the job. If you leave the interview having convinced the employer you have something to offer, nothing—not your color, sex, age, handicap, sexual preference, nationality, etc.—will stand in your way of landing the job that you want. Take as much control of the follow-up process as you can. Be sure to act in a professional manner; project an image of confidence and dependability and you can't go wrong.

CHAPTER NINE

CHOOSE THE BEST OPTION: Evaluate and Negotiate Offers

THE INTERVIEWING PROCESS STARTS WITH THE EMPLOYER buying and you selling. But, as you get further along in the process, the balance begins to shift. Once an employer has decided to make an offer to you, that employer is then in a position of selling the job to you. The tone subtly shifts from interviewing to recruiting as the employer is now invested in your candidacy. This creates a more advantageous negotiating position for you. Therefore, the longer you can postpone the salary discussions, the better off you will be.

Some people have unrealistic salary expectations and exaggerated notions of their worth to prospective employers. At the other end of the spectrum are those anxious job seekers who assume that by putting a low price on their abilities and skills they will stand a better chance of getting a job offer. If you don't think you are worth much, neither will an employer. Grounded in your knowledge of the market value of the position and your ultimate knowledge of your quality, you should develop a preliminary plan. Don't forget to check out www.payscale.com or www.salary.com so that you can have a realistic understanding of what these types of positions pay. You need to be able to articulate what you want **specifically**. Break down your financial and nonpecuniary needs into three categories:

It would be GREAT to have . . .

I would LIKE to have . . .

I MUST have . . .

To help you focus, review the section on your budget in Chapter Two and Values in Chapter Three. Work through "what if" scenarios. Anticipate compromises and plan exactly how far you are willing to scale back on your needs. When a definite salary offer is made, consider it for several moments before you respond. It is now time to negotiate.

The prospective employer wants to pay a minimum salary to hire a quality employee, which appears to be at odds with your goal of wanting to earn as much as possible. Avoid the trap of viewing negotiating as an adversarial process with winners and losers. Think of it instead as individuals working together to arrive at a mutually beneficial agreement. It is more than trading with others for the things you want: it is discovering ways you can work together to produce positive results for everyone involved. By using sound business principles such as preparing and rehearsing, emphasizing accomplishments rather than personal needs, learning and addressing the needs of the employer, asking intelligent questions and listening carefully, your stature is bound to grow, along with your negotiating leverage. Your approach should always be employer-centered, not self-centered. You must be able to describe your worth in relation to the position that has already been defined. Employers do not care that you have been unemployed for seven months; they do not care that you have $80,000 in school loans, or that you have a mortgage and two children in college. Those facts do not increase your **worth**. What *value* do you bring to the employer?

Most people hate the thought of negotiating. But the reality is that if you do not negotiate up front, you may be underpaid by many thousands of dollars over the years. The compensation package you draw at one organization can set the pattern for the level of income you can command when negotiating with another employer. Thus, the terms you agree on will have a far reaching impact on your entire career. It is not unusual for the difference between the earnings of two individuals to have far less to do with abilities, skills and talents than with each person's ability to negotiate.

A general rule of thumb regarding the discussion of compensation is **never to bring up the subject until an offer of employment has been made**. The goal is to give yourself and the interviewer a chance to get to know one another. That way both of you will have a better idea of how flexible you are willing to be with compensation negotiations. You want to ensure that you acquire enough information about the job so that you will be able to effectively communicate that you possess the necessary qualifications for the position. Your goal is to get the employer to invest enough time in you so that you can illustrate that you:

- have done your research on the firm or organization;

- expect to receive compensation appropriate for your level of qualifications and experience;

- want to be compensated on the basis of performance, not on past salary history.

Understand that before interviewing candidates employers have established a *predetermined budget* in their minds for the salary that they would like to pay. This figure, of course, is most financially beneficial for the employer. Most employers have some flexibility to negotiate salary, particularly for higher level positions, but, contrary to popular belief, everything is **not** negotiable. Many employers have rigid pay systems—particularly government agencies and corporations but also law firms that use the lockstep model of compensation. These firms try to keep salaries equitable within the organization by not paying anyone much above the norm. As the interview process progresses, the employer **may** consider altering the budget if impressed by the special skills or background of a particular candidate.

It may be at this point that you are asked what your salary expectations are, but be prepared because the salary question can crop up at any time during the job hunt, and it can come in many forms:

- *"What is your current salary?"*
- *"How much were you paid at your previous employer?"*
- *"What are your salary requirements?"*
- *"What is the lowest figure you would accept?"*
- *"How much do you think you are worth?"*
- *"Why should we pay you more than other managers?"*

You must be prepared to discuss the salary question whenever the **employer** raises the issue. (But remember, **YOU** should never ask about the salary until you are offered the job.) Be careful. If you state a figure outside of the range the employer has in mind—either too high or too low—you risk having salary used against you as an easy, objective screening device. That is why research during the early stages of your job hunt is so crucial.

Should the salary question arise early in the interview process and you feel you do not have enough information about the position, try to deflect the question:

- *"I am unclear about the responsibilities of the position. Could you tell me a little more about...?"*

- *"I'm looking for a fair market value for the responsibilities involved. I'd like to discuss that when I know a little more about what will be required and you know a little more about what I have to offer you."*

- *"My interest is in a complete picture. Salary is just one piece of the puzzle. Professional challenge, growth opportunities, benefits, work environment, and relocation are others that will influence my choice. For the right position and company I'm confident we can come to terms. What about xxxxx?"* (Redirect the discussion.)

- Or, if said with good natured humor, you might be effective by asking, *"Are we starting negotiations? Do you have an offer in mind?"*

Be careful when using humor. If you use the wrong tone or body language, intended humor could come across as obnoxious.

Another technique you could try is to turn the table:

- *"Do you have a range in mind, and, if so, would you mind telling me what that is?"*

- *"What is the normal range in your organization for a position such as this?"*

- *"What would the range be for someone with my qualifications?"*

By getting the employer to state a range first, you can then place the top of this range into the bottom of yours. For example, if the employer's range is $45,000-$65,000, your range should be $60,000-$80,000. Be prepared to articulate why you are worth the salary you are seeking.

If you cannot get the employer to reveal a figure first, try saying:

- *"From my research I learned that the range for marketing directors in this city is __. Does this fit your expectation?"* (Or, *"Is this the range you were considering?"*)

Notice this has nothing to do with what you are making now. Rather, it focuses the employers on the requirements of the position and on what a fair market value is for equivalent work. If there is an obvious gap between the ranges and your salary expectations, don't simply end the conversation. Go back to criteria and get off of the subject of salary. Try something like:

- *"Maybe I didn't understand the requirements of the job.* (Restate your understanding of the position.) *Is that a fair description of this position, and are there other requirements? From what you have told me about your needs, I was thinking my skills and background in xxxx and yyyy* (pick something that emphasizes the unique contributions you would bring to the job) *would be an asset, do you agree? Also, based on my research I learned that the range for such a position with your competitors would be…"*

Emphasize the level of skill and talent you bring to the table by citing achievements and using statistics, comparisons, and even testimonials to support your case. In other words, **state your value.** You need to explain why the employer will benefit by paying you more money than the predetermined budget.

Work *with* the employer—not *against*—to arrive at mutually beneficial solutions. Discovering what the other side wants is crucial to arriving at satisfactory agreements. Build a strategy that focuses on working out the best agreement for everyone. Seek to understand all dimensions of an issue. Focusing only on your own immediate payoff can have dire consequences, so learn to consider negotiations from everyone's perspective. Remember, the value of what you have to offer depends on the perceptions of the person or people you are negotiating with. To strengthen your negotiating stance, determine what the employer values and respond accordingly. It is your responsibility to calmly educate the employer on the value added component acquired by hiring you.

You can affect—positively or negatively—the way you are positioned in the minds of those with whom you negotiate by the attitude you project. Confidence is an extremely important asset at this phase of the job hunt. Organize your thoughts. Make sure you can get your main point across in the most concise and compelling way. Process an idea through to its logical conclusion by evaluating the possible responses you may get from the other side. Choose your words carefully. Focus on clarity and precision in your speech. State your position firmly. Carry yourself with confidence, and position yourself as a person with negotiating power.

Be open and honest about what you want, but remember to be careful about how much information you reveal.

Think about what information you don't necessarily want employers to have. Keep in mind that an interview is not a therapy session. Tell employers what they need to know or what they ask about. Remember, the more you talk, the more likely you are to sabotage your own efforts—so think through your presentation.

Don't be reticent to ask questions. Skillfully asked questions can transform negotiations from an adversarial conflict into a partnership. By asking questions, you make sure that the employer will talk more and you will talk less. Be careful about the types of questions you ask, and phrase inquiries in positive, neutral terms. Start with open ended questions and move on to narrower, more direct questions. Once you have asked a question, be quiet and *listen* to the response.

Throughout the negotiating process remember to constantly reinforce the perception that you are excited about the offer and that you want to take this position, even if you are disappointed with the figure. You do not want the negotiation to be an argument but rather a way that you can get to the place where you want to be in order to accept the offer. Remember, your strategy is to get to your top figure in a way the employer thinks is fair.

If you are unhappy with what has been offered, it is appropriate to come back with a counteroffer. The key is to emphasize the benefit to the employer of paying you more. Perhaps if the employer cannot meet your salary expectations, you may be able to convince the employer to give you "credit" for additional degrees, superior academic performance, past careers or skill sets. Perhaps you can convince the employer to create a new position that would better accommodate your skills, interests, and abilities as well as meeting the employer's needs. If moving to a different specialty or industry, keep in mind the employer may want proof of performance **before** feeling justified in giving you the income you want. Request a review and increase in six months based on your ability to meet a preset goal. Demonstrate your confidence in your abilities by saying something like:

- *"Let me prove I am worth this. I would be happy to come in at this salary if you could agree to review my performance in six months."*

Even after you are clear about the offer and are pleased with it, it is in your best interest **not** to accept the job just yet. Take time to reflect on what has been agreed upon:

- *"This sounds terrific. I'd like to think it over to make sure we haven't missed anything,"* OR

- *"This sounds terrific. I'd like to think it over to make sure we have covered everything. What is your timeframe? When would you like my response?"* OR

- *"I am very excited about the offer. Can you tell me what your timeframe for a reply is?"*

It is common professional courtesy for employers to provide candidates with at least 48 hours to consider an offer.

If you are waiting to hear from other employers, contact them immediately and let them know you have an offer and would like to clarify your application status before you make any decisions. A second offer in hand could enhance your bargaining power. However, **never** lie about having another offer. While the lie might work, it could backfire and create ill will if the employer ever finds out. When you compromise your integrity, you demean your value to others and to yourself.

If you are currently employed, you may find your current employer is surprised when you announce that you are leaving and responds with a counteroffer. If you find yourself in this predicament, you may want to ask yourself:

- Why did I interview in the first place? Do I really want to move or am I happy in my current situation?

- Is this counteroffer an indication of my value to the organization or simply a stopgap measure to keep me around until they can find a replacement?

- Should I accept the new opportunity or stay where I have established relationships and a good track record?

Deciding between two offers is anxiety provoking. Review your long term goals and consider if either position will enable you to reach your goals more quickly or take you in an entirely different direction. What impact will each position have on other parts of your life?

EXERCISE #18: Compare and Contrast Offers

To help you make your decision, go back to Chapter Three and review the values you highlighted. List those values and give each one a grade of A to F for how well each position satisfies that value.

VALUES	GRADE (A-F)
_____	_____
_____	_____
_____	_____
_____	_____
_____	_____
_____	_____
_____	_____

By comparing the jobs side by side, point by point, it will become clear which is the better offer for you.

Be sure to finalize agreements. Don't leave details hanging. It is often amazing how two people sitting in the same room can have quite different perspectives concerning what was agreed upon. To ensure that everyone is clear, you may want to summarize by saying:

- *"So, as I understand it, I will be expected to* (restate your understanding of the position) *in exchange for* (restate the compensation package offered)."

It is important to know when to stop negotiating and start the job. Reaching common ground and setting the stage for mutual respect and cooperation may be more important than the few extra dollars you might be able to obtain by playing games. Having your priorities in place will help you decide which things you are willing to sacrifice in the negotiating process. Keep the following negotiating tips in mind:

- Find out everything you can before you start to negotiate.
- Design a strategy that focuses on working out the best agreement for everyone.
- Deal fairly and honestly with people.
- Identify one person within the organization to negotiate with.
- Simplify and repeat your message until it sinks in.
- Translate your abilities and skills into benefits for the listener.
- Talk about **value** not **cost.**
- State what you want in clear and concise terms and listen for a response.
- Explore all your options. The more options you can generate, the stronger your position.
- Be prepared to explain why something is unacceptable and offer a counter-solution.
- Finalize all details.
- Always be mindful about how this negotiation might affect future relations.

Once all the "i"s are dotted and "t"s are crossed, you are ready for your first day at work. Now the real work begins!

CHAPTER TEN

ADVANCE YOUR CAREER: Cultivate Your Brand

A S A NEW EMPLOYEE, IT IS IMPORTANT TO RECOGNIZE THAT YOU are joining an organization with its own set of rules—both written and unspoken—for acceptable behavior. You must learn to be adept at navigating your way through the quagmire of office politics from day one.

Playing office politics conjures up images of the brown nosing "yes man" willing to sell his soul to get ahead. That is certainly one example; however, that is office politics at its worst. At its best, office politics simply is a cultural assessment of the employer; it is acknowledging how to accomplish things within your organization. Understanding the politics can mean the difference between a mediocre career and a quick rise to stardom. So, whether your goal is to some day rule the office or simply to get the best assignments, training, experience and exposure, it is imperative to understand the political landscape.

First, pay attention to the rules. Knowing the rules will save you from potentially embarrassing, career-altering goofs from which it might be difficult to recover. The written rules will explain things like time off to which you are entitled, reimbursable expenses, perks and benefits as well as established procedures for photocopying, proofreading, requesting additional support services, etc. Review Employee Handbooks and other manuals you received to familiarize yourself with the written rules.

The unspoken/unwritten rules are even more important though sometimes less obvious to discern. However, simple observation can uncover the important things. For example, observation can reveal how management reacts to employees who take all the time off to which the written rules say they are entitled; it may reveal that department leaders begin work at 8:00 a.m. each day and NOT 9:00 a.m. as the written policy states. Armed with all this data, you can determine what you need to do to advance your career within the organization. Pay attention.

In addition to knowing the rules, you want to be in the information loop. Listen to rumors and gossip. Don't spread it, don't comment on it and don't believe it is 100% accurate, but know it. Listen to the gossip to uncover the reputations of your peers and colleagues. Who have been labeled "superstars," "losers" and "troublemakers?" What characteristics do they have in common? Do you share any of these characteristics? Can you emulate the positive characteristics? Can you shed the negative ones? Again, pay attention.

Knowing the reputations of organization leaders will help you uncover not only who the politically powerful players are but also what skill sets are rewarded in this culture. If your long term goal is to be a leader at this organization, note the common attributes the leaders posses and think about ways to begin to develop similar attributes.

Know as much about your organization as possible throughout your tenure there. Periodically review the website and monitor the Facebook page and other literature your organization distributes to clients and new recruits. These documents shed light on institutional values, departmental cultures and norms. Remember, information is power.

It is important to understand power. At every organization, there are two kinds: *Position Power* and *Personal Power*. *Position Power* is based on a person's role within the organization: department manager, committee chair, etc., while *Personal Power* is an individual's innate ability to accomplish tasks and goals no matter where you are on the food chain. Career advancement is based on your ability to master your personal power. To do so, you must understand the golden rule: People want to work with those they can rely on to do quality work in a timely fashion. By developing a reputation as the "go to" person who happily performs the less desirable assignments with the same level of enthusiasm and attention to detail as the "sexy" assignments, you will be sought after by the powers that be because you make their lives easier.

In Chapter Three you learned that self-knowledge is the most reliable tool to run an effective job search and ensure career success. The ABCs apply throughout your career. You must continually:

--catalogue your **A**BILITIES

--acknowledge your **B**ELIEFS

--**C**OMMUNICATE your message effectively.

Maintain your own personnel file that contains information about your long term and short term goals as well as significant assignments and accomplishments, seminars attended, professional and community activities, etc. Think of it as an unedited resume. Update this document quarterly. Use this information to prepare an "Annual Report" prior to your annual performance appraisal.

EXERCISE #19: Prepare Your Annual Self-Appraisal

Each year, BEFORE your formal evaluation, take stock of your own performance.

List:

1. Major projects worked on.

2. Significant accomplishments for the past year.

3. List any knowledge, skills or abilities not being fully utilized in my assignments. Describe how they might be used better.

4. List internal activities you participated in that contribute to the organization's mission (i.e., recruiting, committee assignments, etc).

5. List professional and community activities of the last twelve months. Include external activities (speaking engagements, articles written, conventions and seminars attended, community activities, etc.).

Ask:

1. Is my workload insufficient, satisfactory, or too much?

2. Am I receiving a sufficient variety of assignments to enable me to grow? If not, what can I do to address the issue?

3. Have I had regular opportunities to discuss my work with supervisors? If not, what could I have done differently to get needed feedback?

4. Have I received and acted on supervisors' suggestions for improving my work?

5. What are my goals for the next year? In what areas would I like to improve and what is my action plan to accomplish this?

Consider any difficulties (personal or professional) that may have impeded your performance, but do not put this information in writing. Think about whether or not it would be appropriate to verbally share that information during your review. For example, if tending to a family illness earlier in the year is responsible for lower than expected performance it might be helpful to point that out so your productivity can be viewed in perspective. Carefully consider the information you want to share. And, even if you choose not to share specific information, if there is something impacting your performance, make sure you design a strategy to deal with it before it becomes a bigger issue.

Benchmark your progress against your colleagues. If others appear to be getting more sophisticated work, ask yourself why. Is it because you have not proven yourself to be reliable? Is your substantive work not up to par? Answers to these questions can help you see yourself through the eyes of your superiors and enable you to address issues before they become monumental. And, before you assume there is some great conspiracy by the power structure to sabotage your career, determine how your behavior may be contributing to the situation and try to correct that first.

Remember, no one cares more about your career development then you do. Take the lead and avail yourself of every resource available to you, including professional relationships. You should be concerned with the process of building and using networks as a permanent aspect of your career to broaden your field of vision in order to make informed, smart decisions. It is imperative to establish strong mentor relationships from the start of your career. Who you know is important but who knows you is the key to solidifying your professional brand.

Participate in formalized mentor programs; however, do not rely solely on such programs or simply hope people will notice you and offer to take you under their wings. It isn't enough. Solid mentor relationships evolve naturally, not through administration. Certainly participate in formal programs, but do more. Create a support system or Board of Advisors. Establishing a network of mentors will allow you to learn from different styles, develop a range of skills and consider various perspectives of an issue. Think of these people as resources to help you develop your brand, plan and execute your career goals and help you navigate difficult situations. Network internally to increase the chances of making an impression on decision makers, monitor the rumor mill and learn about business groups beyond your own. Volunteer for committee assignments; attend corporate events; strive to be visible in the organization and build a reputation as a good corporate citizen.

Remember, **Self-Assessment + Market-Assessment = Career Success.** Like good drivers, career strategists drive defensively. They are mindful of road and weather conditions; they are alert to road signs indicating a needed lane shift; and they plan alternative routes in case of emergency. Be mindful of economic forces and world events which will impact your career journey. Today's business world is changing constantly and it is important to be up-to-date about changes impacting your industry. Pay attention to your environment and use your pre-established goals to map out a path to avoid any obstacles while at the same time developing strategies to cope with inevitable transitions.

Transitions typically fall into one of four categories:

Anticipated and voluntary. In a perfect world, all transitions would be the result of strategic decisions initiated by you.

Unanticipated and voluntary. Sometimes, through no direct action on your part, the perfect opportunity lands in your lap. You have the luxury of accepting or declining the opportunity based on your current needs and interests.

Anticipated, but involuntary. Many times people wait until others make a career decision for them. There may be warning signs that a transition is imminent, but rather than take action, you wait, allowing others to control your fate.

Unanticipated and involuntary. Perhaps the most unsettling transitions fall into this category, typically because they tend to be negative. Everything was going along as usual—or so you thought. You believed you were productive; you know you've been busy. Your last reviews were positive and you even received a year end bonus. You didn't see any warning signs until the transition was thrust upon you.

To avoid experiencing involuntary transitions at work, pay close attention and constantly assess and reassess your current situation. Look for clues like:

- having difficulty with a supervisor

- being assigned less important tasks/duties
- not receiving a bonus
- being avoided by supervisors, colleagues, subordinates
- receiving negative feedback/performance review
- not being personally productive or engaged in your job
- changes in the economy or business cycle that might impact your industry

If you see these signs, take action. Either fix the problem (if possible) or recognize you can't change the situation (and sometimes you can't through no fault of your own) and strategize your next move. Always try to avoid unanticipated and involuntary situations by actively anticipating and constructing self directed voluntary transition plans.

One of the greatest impediments to change in any undertaking is that people withdraw from a situation rather than explore what the alternatives might be. It **is** possible to find joy in your work. Successful alternative arrangements **are** possible—**if** you are willing to diverge from the norm. Trust yourself, others and the process to lead you to a better way. Once you have evidence of the possibilities, it will be easier to take action. As you learned in Chapter Two, you always have a choice.

Understand that the way you think about a transition can make it easy to handle or impossible to manage. It is not the event that is determinative; rather, it is the way you choose to experience the event. Your frame of mind affects your actions. For example:

BAD ATTITUDE

I screwed up. I'll never work again.

There is no more bankruptcy work. I don't know how to do anything else.

The real estate market has dried up here. I will be living in my car soon.

IMPROVED ATTITUDE

It was a hard lesson to learn but I will be better having learned it.

I will use what I know about bankruptcy to segue into debt financing work.

I'll relocate to where the real estate market is hot.

Attitude drives behavior and a positive attitude is critical to success.

This is especially true in the case of involuntary transitions. They are the most traumatic because they imply "failure." Even when you know it is time to leave your position, your ego takes a pounding when someone else tells you its time to move on. But consider the following failures:

- **Babe Ruth** struck out 1330 times en route to the Hall of Fame.

- **Elvis Presley** was banished from the Grand Ole Opry after only one performance and told, "You ain't going nowhere son."

- **Oprah Winfrey** was fired from her job as a TV reporter and advised, "You're not fit for TV."

- **Walt Disney**'s first cartoon production company went bankrupt.

- **John Grisham**'s first novel, *A Time to Kill*, was rejected by 15 agents and a dozen publishing houses.

- **Edgar Allan Poe** was expelled from West Point.

- **Abraham Lincoln** lost eight elections, failed at two businesses and had a nervous breakdown before becoming our 16th President.

Nothing succeeds like failure. Learning opportunities, which are necessary for growth and development, sometimes come in the form of what would traditionally be defined as "failure." The world is filled with examples of people who used failure as a springboard to success. This is not to suggest you should go out of your way to fail to achieve your career goals. Simply accept the fact that failures are going to happen. Readjust the prism through which you view such failures and you can use them to your advantage.

As you work on accepting change more readily, remember the important thing is that you take charge of your own career development. Identify the changes you need/want to make and then be proactive about making those changes happen. ASSUME RESPONSIBILITY. No one cares about your career development more than you do. Don't wait for others to lead you through the quagmire. Remember, planning your career is like solving a business problem. Define objectives, develop strategies, monitor progress and take corrective action when needed. The beauty of the career planning process is that YOU get to define the objectives based on your personal definition of success. Whatever option you choose, know that as long as you are able to demonstrate to employers that there is a well thought out, coherent plan aimed at building a portfolio of skills, the choice will be well received. It is scary to head into the unknown. But remember that basic principle you learned in high school physics: *Bodies in motion stay in motion; bodies at rest stay at rest.* Take action.

Think about the direction you'd like your life to take. Go back to Chapter One and review the the first exercise you completed, **Developing Your Dream Action Plan**. Determine what type of experience you need in order to progress along your chosen career path. Stretch yourself to acquire new skills/knowledge to remain in constant demand and at the same time invest in developing an expertise. Such a strategy will enable you to have a competitive advantage. Specializing in one area alone can be risky, market pressures may render you obsolete. But make sure you are not so much of a generalist that you have not developed proficiency in any particular skill. A balance of the two is a better strategy. Base your mix of expertise and flexibility on the overall development goal you set. Areas of new exposure are not limited to the development of technical expertise but include other more general skills as well. As you develop your technical skills, don't forget to focus on "soft" skills—things like working in teams, time management, negotiating, communicating, understanding diversity, delegating and adapting to change. Such intangibles are often "silent discriminators," indicating who is on the fast track and who is not. Soft skills enable you to apply your hard skills in a variety of situations, thereby increasing your value to the employer. By serving as an officer or director of community groups, on alumni boards, or in church and synagogue groups, you can build these skills. Experience gained in any situation counts.

You may determine that you are on the correct path. In that instance, your action plan would simply be to continue doing what you have been doing and reevaluate your progress annually to compare your achievements to your intended objectives. Each year, ask yourself:

- Am I satisfied with my current career/life situation?
- Has any new exposure sought been gained?
- Has my level of responsibility increased? Is that what I want?
- Does the current work environment continue to be receptive to my career objectives?

If the answer to these questions is no, you may determine that a change in employment, a redirection of your career path or an industry shift is in order. Think about the choices you have made. Can you make a different choice to realign your career with your goals? Revisit the reflections exercise you completed in Chapter Two.

As you travel towards your dream, you want to position yourself to always be in the proper mental and financial state to take advantage of opportunities as they arise. Any change at work will impact your life, AND any change in your life may very well impact your work too. For example, embarking on a new job/career when you are in the middle of an unsettling divorce, tending to a terminally ill family member or starting a family may not be a good idea. Do what you can to manage such events to limit their impact on your career choices, but accept that some things are simply beyond your control.

While you can't always control your emotional state, you can typically control your financial situation. Tend to your finances early in your career. Managing your finances from the beginning of your career will provide you with the freedom to pursue opportunities of interest throughout your career. Financial security creates an air of confidence and independence and allows you to follow your passions and live well. Refer back to the exercise in Chapter Two to revise your budget.

Do not hesitate to spend some of your own money to ensure your employability. Invest in training, career development and education. Enroll in seminars and workshops covering topics like public speaking, management or client development to enhance your portfolio of abilities and skills. Consider periodically consulting with a career coach to keep you focused and on track.

Make wise choices about which investments to make. Education and training alone don't ensure success, as many well educated, unemployed professionals can tell you. For example, while an advanced degree **may** increase your marketability in some of the more technical fields or help you transition from one specialty to another by providing intense training and knowledge quickly, an advanced degree could also **decrease** your marketability. Some employers have their own training programs and hesitate to hire candidates with advanced degrees who command higher salaries. Before you decide to invest in any educational program, make sure you are doing it because you have a genuine interest in the subject matter, not simply to add a credential to your resume. Find out if your employer (or target employer) values the extra schooling and do a cost/benefit analysis. Remember not only to factor in tuition and related school costs but also your lost wages during the time you are in graduate school.

Whether you find yourself in a transition voluntarily or involuntarily, you will no doubt ask yourself questions like:

- Is there some way to combine my work with my other, equally important interests?

- Are there jobs available at my level and salary expectations or will I have to settle for less?

- Do I give up on my chosen field and do something else and if so, what else can I do?

These questions can be overwhelming because there are no immediate answers. Don't get stymied and opt to stay stuck in an unhappy situation or simply avoid the questions altogether. Playing it safe and staying in a position you have outgrown will damage your career. Remember, choosing to do nothing is still a choice you are making. Most people end up happier after a transition. The hard part is living through the unavoidable discomfort and uncertainties.

How often you change positions, jobs or careers typically matters less than WHY. However, you must be able to articulate a logical progression down a coherent path. Do you have a good story line? Employers easily understand people moving on to develop new skills or industry knowledges or to broaden their portfolio of experiences. However, when the moves appear to be a chase for salary increases or fancy titles only, your loyalty and perhaps judgment may be questioned. The onus is on you to articulate the story line and illustrate the wisdom in the decisions you have made along the way. Again, refer back to the *Reflect* exercise completed in Chapter Two to help you create your story line.

As you can see, we end where we began. Career success is a circular and continuous process that requires you to continually assess and articulate the value you add to the marketplace based on your abilities and interests. That involves a dedication to continuous learning and regularly benchmarking your abilities and skills, nurturing your professional relationships and monitoring changes in the workplace.

Self-Assessment + Market-Assessment = Career Success!

It also requires maintaining a future focus to anticipate and plan for transitions. A focused, but flexible career development plan will serve you well throughout your work life.

YOU have the power to create the career—and life—you want, but you have to DO something to make it happen. Take action and enjoy the journey.

"Happiness is not something ready made.
It comes from your own actions."
--Dalai Lama

APPENDIX

Consider this a preliminary list of websites to launch your job search. To help you assess which websites are the best ones to use to meet your specific objectives, consider:

- the number and kinds of jobs posted on the site;
- the primary salary levels of the posted jobs;
- the cost of using the site;
- the availability of other job search information, such as interview preparation, negotiating tips, etc;
- how easy the site is to navigate, how well it is maintained and how often it is updated.

If you choose to post your resume in a searchable database, make sure there is a confidentiality feature so that your contact information will not be distributed until you agree to release it to a specific employer. Also, make sure those resumes are dated so you can confirm a resume is the most current version.

Finally, if you do not see what you are looking for here, google "jobs in (industry) or (geography)" to find additional useful sites. Remember to save the ones you like under favorites.

GENERAL JOB BOARDS (FREE)
http://www.careerbuilder.com/
http://www.monster.com/

http://www.glassdoor.com/index.htm
http://www.indeed.com

FEE BASED JOB BOARDS
https://www.theladders.com/
http://www.policyjobs.net
http://www.politicaljobs.net
http://www.hound.com/

ACADEMIC JOBS
http://jobs.chronicle.com/section/Jobs/61/
http://www.academickeys.com/all/choose_discipline.
php?go=find_a_job
http://careers.insidehighered.com/
http://www.academic360.com/

BLUE COLLAR JOBS
http://www.bluecollarjobs.com/
http://www.unionjobs.com

COMMUNICATIONS/MEDIA
http://www.mediajobs.net/
http://www.iwantmedia.com/jobs/

ENGINEERING JOBS
http://www.engineerjobs.com/
http://www.engcen.com/engineering.asp

ENVIRONMENTAL JOBS
www.ehscareers.com
www.Ecojobs.com
www.Environmentaljobs.com
www.ejobs.org
www.sustainablebusiness.com/jobs
www.ecoemploy.com/jobs

FINANCE JOBS
www.efinancialcareers.com
www.jobsearchdigest.com
http://www.careers-in-finance.com/re.htm

GOVERNMENT JOBS
http://www.justice.gov/careers/careers.html
http://www.usajobs.gov/
http://www.opm.gov/job_seekers/
http://plum.jobs.topusajobs.com/
http://thehill.com/employment/
http://hillzoo.com/jobs/
http://www.senate.gov/employment/po/positions.htm
http://www.uscourts.gov/uscjobvac/query/index.
cfm?task=uscourts

HOSPITALITY JOBS
http://www.hcareers.com/
http://www.hospitalityonline.com/
http://www.hospitalityjobsite.com/
http://wineandhospitalityjobs.com/

INTERNATIONAL JOBS
http://www.internationaljobs.org/
http://www.fpa.org

LEGAL JOBS
http://www.cable360.net/jobs.html
http://jobs.law360.com/JobSeeker/Jobs.aspx
www.lawcrossings.com
www.gobiglaw.com
www.goinhouse.com

MEDICAL JOBS
http://www.medicaljobs.org/
http://www.healthecareers.com/
http://www.allhealthcarejobs.com/

PHILANTHROPY/NON-PROFIT JOBS
http://philanthropy.com/section/Jobs/224/
http://www.humanrightsjobs.com/
http://www.idealist.org/
http://pslawnet.org
http://foundationcenter.org/getstarted/guides/job.html
http://www.rileyguide.com/nonprof.html#think
http://www.rileyguide.com/jobs.html#law
http://www.policyjobs.net/World_Think_Tanks/

PUBLIC RELATIONS JOBS
http://www.prsa.org/jobcenter/

SPORTS JOBS
www.jobsinsports.com (fee based)
http://www.teamworkonline.com/

TECHNOLOGY JOBS
http://technologyjobsadvice.com/
http://www.dice.com/

WRITING/PUBLISHING JOBS
http://www.writejobs.com/
http://www.bookjobs.com/
http://www.mediabistro.com/Magazine-Publishing-jobs.html

RESEARCH TOOLS
http://www.vault.com/wps/portal/usa
http://www.payscale.com/
http://www.salary.com/

Best Companies to Work at in Various Cities

http://money.cnn.com/magazines/fortune/
bestcompanies/2011/states/WA.html

ABOUT THE AUTHOR

KATHLEEN BRADY-CURRIE IS AN IPEC CERTIFIED CAREER COACH with 25 years of experience helping students, recent college graduates, lawyers and other professionals identify their career goals and design action plans to achieve them. She is a recognized expert on topics including job search strategies, resume writing, networking and interviewing techniques and recovering from a layoff. She also works with clients to improve workplace skills such as communication, leadership, client development, time management, delegating, delivering feedback and effective mentoring.

Brady-Currie started her career at **Columbia Law School** and went on to serve as Assistant Dean of Career Services at **Fordham University School of Law**, National Director of Staff Recruitment and Development at **Jackson Lewis** and Manager of Associate Professional Development at **Milbank Tweed Hadley & McCloy, LLP**. She is also a past president of the **National Association for Law Placement** and a founding member of the **NALP Foundation for Research and Education**. A frequently published author, she has published three books: Mastering The Art of Success (Insight Publishing, 2011); *Navigating Detours on the Road to Success* (Inkwater Press, 2005) and *Jobs for Lawyers, Effective Techniques for Getting Hired in Today's Legal Marketplace* (Impact Publications, 1996). She is a certified provider of the Highlands Ability Battery and a member of the International Coach Federation.

She can be reached at <u>KBrady@careerplanners.net</u>, 48 Wall Street, 11th Floor, New York, NY 10005. Find her on Facebook at <u>www.facebook.com/KBCareerPlanners</u>

CPSIA information can be obtained at www.ICGtesting.com
Printed in the USA
BVOW002114240413

319072BV00001B/1/P